Into the Backlands

a Peace Corps Memoir

Kenneth E. Dugan Fliés

Lost Lake Folk Art
SHIPWRECKT BOOKS PUBLISHING COMPANY

IN
DIE

Rushford, Minnesota

Front cover photo of the author by the author's
Peace Corps colleague, Dick Wittman.

Map of the São Francisco river drainage basin in Brazil
created using Natural Earth and USGS data. Map file is
licensed to "Shanon1" under the Creative Commons
Attribution-Share Alike 4.0 International, 3.0 Unported,
2.5 Generic, 2.0 Generic and 1.0 Generic license.

Cover, graphic & interior design by Shipwreckt Books.

For Millie Binder
my beloved wife and soulmate

Into the Backlands

Map of eastern Brazil *II project area*

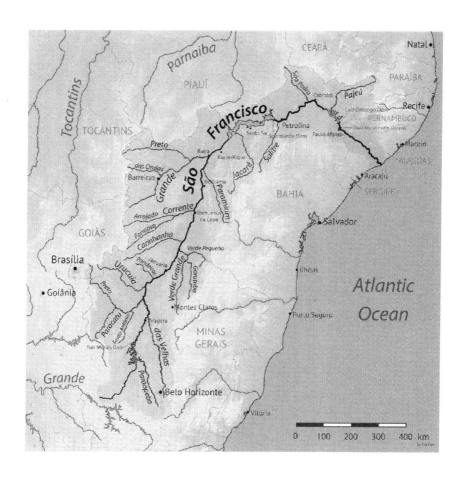

I was present at the creation when the bright flame of conviction took hold in the imagination of the country and the Peace Corps became a promise fulfilled.

—Bill Moyers

1. Backland terror

P luto didn't have much of a howl left in him, but one night, a little more than three months after completing Peace Corps training and arriving in Brazil, Pluto's determined howl was enough to get my attention. The torrential rains that pounded our roof each day during the tropical rainy season had finally abated for the evening, and I was about to slide off to sleep when Pluto summoned me back to consciousness.

The old Rottweiler was just about as out of place as I was, both of us left to fend for ourselves in the tropical hinterland. Years earlier, a group of German engineers had brought Pluto with them when they came to build the small hydro facility below the big falls. But when the builders left, Pluto stayed behind. Though storms usually sent him bolting for a dry place under the porch, something had triggered his guard dog instinct. I opened my eyes to notice that the yard outside was flooded with light—quite unusual since our normal source of lighting, the small hydro facility, was idle during the rainy season.

Heavy thumping on the front door snapped me to attention. My mental faculties slowly awoke wondering what the emergency might be. There was no imminent danger of flooding the high ground my house stood on, and tornadoes and wind storms were uncommon in my village of Correntina. Had there been a local calamity or some other reason requiring evacuation? Was there unexpected tragic news for me from home? I quickly slipped on some clothes, opened the door and found myself face-to-face with three state militia soldiers, their rifle barrels pointed at my head.

Instantly, the childhood I spent living a tranquil, sheltered farm life in Minnesota belonged to another existence, not mine. In six months since reporting to the Peace Corps, I had known various forms of fear. I had lived through race riots in the American South, participated in events of an international nuclear confrontation, witnessed still more riots in Brazil, crossed rivers infested with snakes and piranha, and survived serious illness. But all these fears were part of the great Peace Corps adventure. They withered in stature to this overwhelming moment, facing drawn weapons and an assault of harsh words. This was true fear.

Being relatively new to Brazil, my Portuguese was mediocre at best. Understanding what these men wanted with me, therefore, was out of my grasp. Clad in bandoliers crisscrossing their shoulders, they reminded me of characters in a cheap Western movie, bandits who shoot first and ask questions later.

The principal trooper blurted out questions so rapidly I had no idea what he wanted. Even if I had been fluent in Portuguese, any modicum of composure evaporated when my front door opened. A legion of panic-laced thoughts coursed through my mind. My heart pounded in my ears.

The soldiers appeared to understand that I was not cognitively impaired, although I am sure I gave every appearance of callowness, what with my stuttering, slurring and ineffable responses. I vaguely came to understand that something had gone missing or was stolen, however, I had no idea what it was or why they suspected me. Eventually frustrated that he could not get his point across, the trooper inquired about my project Jeep. "Jeep" was a universal word and a part of the local vernacular. I guess he thought using it would elicit at least some sort of response.

"*Onde é seu Jepe?*"—Where is your Jeep? The trooper repeated the phrase slowly, as if he were querying one of his children.

I responded with a simple phrase. "*Não tem Jepe!*"—I don't have a Jeep!

He looked at his compatriots with an air of resignation that seemed to convey that they would be doing the world a service if they put the gringo and his skinny old dog out of their misery right now.

The militia men must have decided that a person so ignorant of their language posed no legitimate threat. I heaved an inner sigh of relief when, one by one, they detached their gun belts, leaned their firearms against the wall, sat down on the veranda stoop, and lit cigarettes.

"I think you are smart enough to understand that we are looking for a Jeep," said the lead trooper. "As you can see, we came in our own Jeep." I did my best to follow his Portuguese as well as his reasoning. He continued with a statement I'd heard before that translates something like this: "We hope you don't think we fell off of a cabbage truck on the way into town." My vocabulary was limited, so he may have said "ox cart." The militia man explained, "This is a very isolated little town, at least eighty miles from Barreiras, where we came from, and close to the same distance to Lapa in the east. These are the two nearest places with a doctor, a hospital, and an airport. I am not sure who you work for, but I am certain they did not put you here without transportation. We know you have friends in our town of Barreiras, and they have a shiny new Jeep." He exhaled a long plume of smoke and narrowed his gaze. "So where is your Jeep?"

I knew my answer had better be good. Thankfully, my nerves had calmed allowing me to recover some facility with the language. I told my new "friends" that I had no Jeep, but I planned to go to Rio de Janeiro in the near future to meet up with one of my colleagues and drive back in a project Jeep.

This brought more raised eyebrows from the troops. They knew Rio was one thousand miles away, that in this rainy season the roads to the east were virtually impassable, and there were no fewer than three major rivers to cross—none with bridges.

The leader was not convinced. "Well, we know that either you or an associate of yours was in Barreiras two days ago driving a shiny new Jeep just like the one belonging to the two Americanos who live in Barreiras. We were told they are compatriots of yours."

I stood my ground. "You're welcome to have a look around, but I have no Jeep," I said. "In fact, there are only two Jeeps and a single truck in the whole seven-thousand-square-mile county."

The militia men wore resolute expressions that told me they were not buying my denial. They looked me up and down. One of them said, "You look barely old enough to shave, and yet you would have us believe you live in this remote place with no vehicle to get out if you became ill or injured? How do you get around?"

"I borrow a horse from the local Padre when I need to go somewhere."

Laughter erupted. One of them joked, "Oh, so you are one of those American cowboys from the Old West like we see in the movies—a Pony Express man!"

I said, "No, but you could say I was a cowboy. I grew up on a farm in Minnesota tending to dairy cows."

This sparked their curiosity and finally broke the ice. It looked like I was off the hook.

I went on to admit that I did not live by myself; I shared the house with two colleagues, both of whom were in Rio de Janeiro for training. One was an engineer who needed more knowledge about the principles of Brazilian hydro so we could get the electrical facility up and functioning. The second was a female health worker who went to Rio to learn more about Brazilian health programs.

The mention of an engineer passed without notice, but the news of an American female living on-site grabbed their attention and immediately transformed the tenor of the conversation. One of the militia asked if I knew an American girl living in Barreiras, also purportedly a member of our organization. I wasn't sure how to answer the question. Thinking more clearly, now that they weren't pointing rifles at me, I assumed this might be a trick question to establish that I had been in Barreiras. I decided, given the presence of guns and bullets, that honesty was the most prudent course to pursue.

"Yes," I said. "I am well acquainted with a girl named Ginger who is a member of our group. She was here over the Christmas holiday to celebrate with me and my American companions, Dick and Silvia."

Stereotypical Brazilian males, the militia men quickly forgot about their original mission and instead focused on women—one woman in particular, my friend and colleague, Silvia. If I had learned anything in my short time in-country, it was that Brazilian men were obsessed with beautiful women. Sensing the positive shift in their mood, I told them that my housemate Silvia was easily Ginger's equal when it came to beauty.

As the militia men well knew, Ginger was a long-legged, blond, blue-eyed Texan with a demure personality that could melt the heart of the worst desperado. If Silvia was her equal, they were eager to know when she planned to return. I confessed that Silvia wouldn't return for several weeks. An air of dejection descended upon the soldiers and they got back to the mission at hand.

They had come to Correntina tracking a plow thief. Someone with a Jeep very similar to that of my colleagues in Barreiras had surreptitiously taken a plow from the local *Comissão do Vale do São Francisco* depot. CVSF authorities suspected the thief was an American who had earlier made inquiries at the depot. Jim, one of the Americanos, and a fellow Volunteer, was stationed in Barreiras with Ginger working on an agriculture project. When the authorities questioned Jim about the plow he suggested that an American who lived somewhere south, toward Correntina, my little village, might know something.

It took me a while, but once I understood that their main concern was finding a missing plow, everything suddenly came into focus. There was no question who was behind this hostile action.

Two days earlier, I had received a visit from a Volunteer posted one hundred miles south of Correntina. During our training, he earned a reputation as highly talented but headstrong and unpredictable, always ready to tackle the most challenging situations.

Indeed, I'd talked to him when he passed through Correntina on a mission to find a plow, and again when he reappeared days later with a plow in the back of his Jeep. On that return visit, he seemed awfully anxious to be on his way. His Jeep, however, was low on gas and oil. He'd driven hard over terrible roads to put some distance between himself and Barreiras, where he had found the plow. He was so broke that I had to purchase gas and oil for him. At least this time he offered me collateral in the form of a half-empty bottle of rotgut cognac. By the look and smell of it, I thought it might better suffice as motor oil. I was a teetotaler, so I told him no thanks, that I would trust him to make good on my gas and oil loan. During all this time, he mentioned absolutely nothing to me about stealing the plow he carried.

In the not-too-distant future, this same buddy, the plow-thief from the south, would be profiled by a team of researchers retained by the Peace Corps. Being a blind study, the report referred to my illustrious colleague as XXX. They described his stubbornly contumacious nature as follows: "XXX placed in the lower quarter of his group by final selection and is doing some of the best work in the field. XXX is a bit of a maverick and a difficult fellow to predict. While willing to listen to others, he is highly opinionated and resists authority. As a PCV, he has shown some excellent qualities. Frustrated by his initial contacts with the CVSF, XXX did not sit back and wait, like many of his fellow Volunteers. He headed for the boondocks, reasoning that's 'where I could do something.'" \1

The militia men waited impatiently for me to finish putting two and two together. "Gee," I said, "I wish you would have mentioned the plow earlier."

All of them looked exasperated.

To ease the tension, I shared what I knew. "A colleague of mine did come through here a few days ago driving a shiny new Jeep with a plow in the back, but he said nothing about it being stolen."

At this news, the militia men jumped up from the stoop, stomped out their cigarettes and began to strap on their gun belts.

"So where might we find this colleague of yours?" The head trooper retrieved his rifle from its resting place along the wall.

"Montalvania," I said.

All four men froze. The leader cast a somber look at the others. All of a sudden, they didn't seem to be in a big hurry to leave.

Later, once I learned about "bandit country," I would understand their hesitation. Unlike my normally quiet little town, Montalvania was what was known as a "convict colony." There were several towns of this nature in Brazil where criminals, including murderers, could go to live undisturbed by any court of justice. These towns operated by their own system of law, and regular law enforcement personnel steered clear of them.

M ontalvania lies roughly one hundred miles from Correntina on a road that passes through several small towns. Knowing XXX, he surely would have stopped along the way to quench his thirst with a few beers. With any luck, the militia could detain him before he even got to Montalvania. Mum of course was my status relative to providing any detail to the militia about XXX's penchant for the amber nectar. I hoped the gas I bought that morning would get XXX to Montalvania.

I should have known XXX was a rogue from the moment we met in training. The militia men left me the impression that, what with the thief having a day's head start hauling a rusty old plow to Montalvania, it was best to just forget about investigating further. Besides, Montalvania was across the Bahia State line in the State of Minas

Gerias, outside the jurisdiction of the Bahia State Militia; not to mention all the red tape in the way of getting anything done. An old plow was surely not worth the trouble. The leader indicated that his boss would not be happy, nor would the CVSF folks, however, they would not want them going to Montalvania and starting a border war either. The militia men seemed relieved that the great plow chase was over.

No one was more pleased than me when I gave the soldiers directions to Dona Vivi's boarding house in Correntina. Sometime later I learned that the man who founded the lawless town of Montalvania originally came from Barreiras, headquarters of the militia. I think the leader knew more than he let on the night he rousted me and Pluto.

Although I sought adventure in leaving the realm of my youth, I did not envision it would include an episode like that evening. My life literally passed before me when I stared into militia rifles. I briefly feared that it might end before it really got started.

Sitting alone, in the dead silence of the dark night at my kitchen table, still unnerved and unable to sleep, I contemplated the evening's adventure as well as the many other bizarre events that had transpired on my journey to Brazil's remote interior. My youthful cunning and charm may have moderated the fear I experienced that night, may have helped to disarm the situation, but could I count on youthful cunning and charm in the future? As I thought back over how I had made it this far, I couldn't help but wonder what other life-changing adventures lay ahead. I wondered: maybe I should have accepted XXX's bottle of rotgut cognac after all.

2. Call to adventure

I n childhood, we are introduced to the enchantment of legends and fairytales, to heroes and villains, to treacherous journeys and untold perils, to strange and exotic lands promising treasures to be claimed, and to venerable sages and sacred kings who guide travelers in their harrowing quests. These tales often involve a *call to adventure* requiring the hero or heroine to take risks, face danger, and endure unimaginable challenges and sacrifices that ultimately lead to profound transformation. [2]

President John F. Kennedy, at the close of his 1961 inaugural speech, issued his own call to adventure with these words: "Ask not what your country can do for you—ask what you can do for your country."

The Peace Corps would become one of Kennedy's major initiatives to fulfill this call to action. Similar to quests in legends and fairy tales, the Peace Corps' mission conjured visions of distant lands filled with both treasure and danger, summoning youth to take their own hero's journey of transcendent personal enrichment and discovery while projecting the grand image and values of America. The Peace Corps required America's younger generation to accomplish what the President envisioned in his message. Along with the willingness to take risks, America's first Peace Corps Volunteers believed they had the character, skills, and fortitude necessary to complete their mission.

I was a farm boy, born in the idyllic hill country of southeast Minnesota, the second son in a family of ten boys and one girl, when I decided to answer Kennedy's call to adventure.

The toe of Minnesota in the southeast is known as the Driftless Area. Between 100,000 to 11,000 years ago, the last great glaciers flattened most of the state before receding to reveal vast prairies, boreal forests and Minnesota's famous 10,000 lakes. The Driftless

Area of the Upper Mississippi River, however, was spared by the glaciers. Natural erosion alone created rolling hills, tall limestone bluffs and broad valleys teeming with magnificent hardwood forests, pasturelands, navigable rivers, and trout streams. The Driftless Area is the only part of Minnesota with natural caves. For centuries, the land of tall bluffs and deep river valleys has been a sacred and mystical home for Native American tribes; for others, the first settlers and their descendants, it's been a fairy-tale place.

My family's farm sat high on hills overlooking the Mississippi and the blue bluffs of Wisconsin across the river to the east. My parents' ancestral home, the town where we attended church growing up, Kellogg, Minnesota, was located eight miles northeast of the farmstead along the Mississippi. We went to school in Plainview, however, where we also enjoyed most entertainment like movies, and conducted all of our commercial activities. Plainview—located eight miles southwest of the farm—was an agricultural center twice the size of Kellogg. Twenty miles to the northeast lay Rochester, home of the famous Mayo Clinic.

In this setting, I learned the values of family life, a love for the environment and all living things, and useful skills for future endeavors. By age sixteen, I left the farm to live and work with another farm family. A year later, I was employed by the large vegetable processing company in our small town. For the next two summers, I worked in their field operation using mechanical and agricultural skills learned on our farm. At age eighteen, I completed high school and headed off to college.

The collegiate atmosphere provided me with a greater exposure to questioning certain career paths that seemed simple enough during my parochial education, but now seemed feeble in addressing the self-enrichment part of the career equation. Studying philosophy and other world topics caused me to question what my life was all about and recognize in myself a growing yearning for adventure. The more I stared at the Peace Corps posters that had recently sprung up at the college, the more I felt the call to adventure. These thoughts eventually swelled to a point of no return for me. It was late winter in Minnesota, and I needed to get away, to discover something new, so I took the plunge and applied for the Peace Corps. Unbelievably to me, a little more than six weeks later, May of 1962, I was accepted as a Peace Corps trainee. Back home, I encountered a significant degree of resistance from my parents, particularly my mother. She implored me to wait until the Peace Corps became better established; wait until I was older and had completed college.

This was one of few intimate discussions I had with my parents over the course of my youth. A large dairy farm is a twenty-four-seven operation, all work and routine, with little time for social or emotional nurturing of eleven children. My mother's sudden concern therefore came as a bit of a shock. As much as I understood that it was natural for a mother to want to protect her sons, I also realized the necessity of pursuing an adventure to achieve manhood. When I attempted to convince my parents that the invitation pertained only to training, they countered with arguments of their own.

Then they asked what I planned to do if I was not selected to go to Brazil after my three months of training. I would not have sufficient funds from summer employment to return to college.

My mother asked, "Exactly how much are they paying you during training?"

"If I read the fine print correctly," I replied, "seventy-five dollars a month."

"Wow, that is a whopping two hundred and twenty-five dollars. I don't know of many colleges that will take you in over the next year for that amount!"

My parents made it clear that they were in no position to advance me the funds. Without a college deferment, I would stand a high probability of heading to the jungles of Vietnam. My parent's position was indeed sobering.

When I joined the Peace Corps in July of 1962, approximately 3,000 Volunteers participated in training, served overseas, or had been recruited for placement in project host countries around the world. Becoming an actual Volunteer after training was a risky proposition because by June of 1963, the Peace Corps had received some 58,000 formal applications. Of these, only twenty-five to thirty percent—14,000 to 17,000 recruits—were invited to training, and only half of those were ultimately accepted. In the end, one applicant out of eight or nine was accepted to go overseas. My parents thought this through in ways I had not contemplated. From their perspective, the odds were stacked against me.

My parents attempted to present a rational argument, realizing the old carrot-and-stick incentive system they employed when I was younger would no longer work. On a 640-acre dairy farm there was a lot of work to be done. It was an incredibly large undertaking in an area and era of principally 160-acre farms when farmers were just beginning to transition from plowing with horses to using tractors. Working a 640-acres farm with dairy cattle, beef cattle, hogs, sheep and chicken, as well as annual crops, might keep a small army busy. But we were ten boys, the eldest barely in his teens. In addition to my dad's list of daily chores, he believed we needed even more challenges to teach us to maintain order. For instance, we planted four acres of cabbage that we cultivated with hoes on rainy days when normal field work was not possible. If the cabbage patch was maintained in an orderly fashion, we got to go to the County Fair. We also grew a half acre of cucumbers to pick every other day after breakfast for pickling. Again, if everything was in order, we were rewarded with a Saturday night at the movies.

One of the biggest tasks on the farm was to get the three crops of summer hay put up into the barns for winter feed, which was an essential ingredient to maintaining healthy cattle during the long winter months. Making hay was one of the toughest, dirtiest jobs on the farm when I was young. But when we finished, we were rewarded with a trip to Whitewater State Park for a picnic and an evening of swimming. After each of the three hay crops were in the barn, we went to Whitewater.

The only remaining carrot in the equation that might have changed my mind about joining the Peace Corps had its genesis in putting the hay up and being rewarded with a trip to Whitewater State Park. A gem of the Minnesota State Park System, Whitewater had one of the few real swimming beaches in the Driftless Area, other than the Mississippi River banks. There are no lakes in most of Southeast Minnesota.

I remember it was late on this particular evening after making hay. Most people had left for the day. The swimming hole in fact seemed to be deserted. I gazed at the pool for a few moments before a young blond girl wearing a bright red swimsuit emerged into the twilight from the water. She proceeded to climb up onto the diving platform and perform all sorts of athletic flips and dives.

The girl, only ten to twelve years of age, looked vaguely familiar although I could not recall who it was. My old brother Bill was watching too. I said to him, "That girl is very talented. She looks familiar. Any chance you know who she is?"

Bill said, "Of course I do, she's a girl from my class. Her dad owns a Dodge Chrysler dealership in town, plus a farm implement business, plus he installs most of the new televisions in the area, and he operates the school bus lines. I wouldn't mind getting to know her better so in two or three more years when I am old enough to drive maybe I can get a good deal on a car from her dad."

Bill, who loved sporty cars added, "She's probably practicing by herself. I did see her older brother's hotrod in the parking lot. He's most likely off in the woods making out with his girlfriend. I heard this young gal is already a certified lifeguard. See that little cross and emblem on her red swimsuit? That's for lifeguards. I heard tell, the final swimming test to get certified, you have to swim a couple of miles down the Mississippi River nonstop, snakes and all. Obviously, she is quite the swimmer."

It all sounded quite intriguing. But it wasn't so much the allure of cars and television as the mystique of this girl who emerged from the pool that day that interested me most. A magical mermaid or mythological nymph, she settled in my soul and seemed to form a unique spiritual bond that I never forgot.

While my parents' arguments did little to persuade me to defer my Peace Corps ambitions, a chance encounter at the Whitewater beach years earlier, that they had inadvertently created by taking me there as a reward for making hay, might possibly change my mind.

Although two years earlier I was a shy rural farm boy, a very popular girl who was also a great athlete and the junior class president asked me to the junior-senior prom. This was the same beautiful mermaid I had watched perform acrobatics off the diving platform at Whitewater State Park a few years earlier.

A high school athlete myself, I came to know Millie casually, admiring her many talents as a student, cheerleader, majorette and athlete. She seemed to bring joyfulness to everything she did. Being a year older than me, Millie typically dated upper classmen. I considered her out of reach and out of my league. All that changed of course when she invited me to the prom in the spring of 1959. It seems the upper classman she was dating at the time was a minister's son whose denomination did not permit their youth to dance. I suspected most of the other upper classman she might have asked already had dates to the prom. It was to be a one-night stand-in affair.

In her youth Millie's family spent time in Hollywood, California, visiting Millie's great uncle George. She was in her early teens when she met singing idol and movie star, Ricky Nelson; the famous Nelson family lived next door to George. Both she and Ricky played the drums in bands. Millie also played the accordion, while Ricky had an affection for the guitar. They would become friends, and Ricky took Millie on dates to the movies. Just a teenager himself at the time, Ricky was making over $100,000 a year. Ricky would remain her idol. Millie often mentioned she would like to live in California. I'm sure Ricky was a part of that dream.

Nevertheless, Millie and I remained sweethearts for three years before I left for the Peace Corps. From the first time I saw her on the diving platform at Whitewater, something told me that she was a unique soulmate, sought after and coveted by romantics like me throughout history. While it was exotic lands and the promise of reward that I sought on my call to adventure, I also had some trepidation about possibly losing the treasure I had already gained, namely Millie. The local doctor called her "Million Dollar Millie." In her later years, Millie's convertible had vanity license plates that read SLVRFOX.

In small town rural America when I was growing up, many young people who dated for the length of time Millie and I had got married. It was almost customary for couples to marry before a young man headed off to military service. This was not an option for me when I joined the Peace Corps. Millie and I agreed it was an adventure not to be passed up. We believed our love would endure, although we knew there was a great possibility we might not see or speak to each other for almost two years.

Eventually my youthful idealism prevailed. I left for training in July 1962 at nineteen years of age, one of the youngest Volunteers to serve in my project, or in the entire Peace Corps for that matter. A teenager who led a relatively isolated life on a Minnesota dairy farm would relocate to the remote interior of Brazil, one of the largest underdeveloped countries in the world, to serve its inhabitants during one of the most turbulent decades in American history. This was my call to an adventure I believed I needed to fulfill.

During the twenty-one months I served in Brazil, I would never hear Millie's voice, or the voice of any family member or friend. Communication by mail was exceedingly slow. It could take months to hear of death or tragic circumstances involving people I knew and loved. Stationed in a very remote location with no medical facilities or communications other than a telegraph, I was not visited by Peace Corps country management or medical personnel for periods of up to six months.

Assigned to the Brazil II project in the São Francisco River valley in northeast Brazil, I was posted in Correntina. Technically the second Peace Corps project to be implemented, Brazil II was preceded by the Brazil I project that had started up six months before my group arrived. Comprised of a 4-H group trained by its national foundation, 4-H volunteers were posted with host country associates mainly in the developed southern regions of Brazil. It was a common practice in the early days of the Peace Corps to launch projects quickly with established international organizations.

The Brazil II project would be a bold transition away from projects managed by existing U.S. or international organizations. It was the largest Peace Corps project ever in terms of Volunteer numbers: 180 applied to serve on the project; 120 selected for training; and 90 eventually deployed, more than any single project in any country anywhere in the world. Only fifty-four Volunteers would complete the full two years of service in the São Francisco River Valley.

The project was conceived and developed by the Peace Corps in collaboration with CVSF, a Brazilian regional development organization formed in 1946. *Comissão do Vale do São Francisco*, the organization in fact that XXX stole a plow from, aided in the development of the impoverished northeastern region in Brazil, an area surrounding the São Francisco River. Approximately 1,800 miles in length, the São Francisco is the longest river located entirely in Brazilian territory, and it's the fourth longest in South America. The Brazilian term for this region is the *Sertão*, interpreted to mean hinterlands, backlands, or even the outback. For the most part, its elevation is less than 500 meters and the area typically receives between twenty and thirty inches of rainfall a year compared to sixty inches in many other parts of Brazil, most of this from January to April. Rainfall, however, was erratic. Some years, only a minimal amount fell, leading to droughts. Other years, rain fell in torrents, leading to severe floods.

The CVSF was established to emulate many of the accomplishments of the Tennessee Valley Authority in the United States regarding hydro power, industrial development and agricultural development. In addition, developments in healthcare, education and other sectors were expected to move the region from essentially nineteenth century subsistence into the production-oriented twentieth century. To accomplish these goals in support of the commission, the Peace Corps provided human resources: the engineers of varying disciplines, the geologists, agronomists, veterinarians, agriculturalists, mechanics, fisheries experts, nurses, social workers, and others with specialized skill sets, such as radio operators.

When the CVSF was established, one percent of Brazil's annual budget was earmarked to support project implementation. In the late 1940s and 1950s, this was a relatively significant amount of money and led to many developments undertaken by the commission. By the 1960s, however, uncontrolled spending by the national government combined with heavy foreign borrowing, and subsequent inflation led to a national budget deficit and a huge foreign debt that was strangling the government. To meet these challenges, the government had to make serious budget adjustments in their spending. Consequently, the CVSF budget was severely curtailed.

Fulfilling the lofty goals envisioned by the commission and the Peace Corps for the Brazil II project, with little or none of the expected counterpart funding, proved to be quite elusive. Brazil II was also affected by no fewer than four major national and international events that occurred during the project lifetime. Two of these would take place before my group even reached Brazil.

In October of 1962, the Peace Corps trained recruits for the Brazil II project at the Tennessee Valley Authority facility in Muscle Shoals, Alabama. While trainees were there, James Meredith attempted to enter the University of Mississippi as the first African American at an all-white southern university. This ignited race riots across the region, causing the President—for the first time since the Civil War—to send armed National Guard troops into the South.

Because the Brazil II project had several African American men and women as trainees, activities had to be conducted under armed guard. Strict curfews were enforced.

Then, on October 22, 1962, the United States faced one of its greatest tests of the Cold War, the Cuban Missile Crisis. Coincidentally, this was the same day my newly sworn-in Brazil II group began its journey to South America. While in service in Brazil, the group would suffer the loss of its inspirational leader and founder, President Kennedy. Peace Corps Volunteers would live through a revolution and witness the overthrow of the Brazilian government by the military.

As it played out on the international stage, the inauspicious prelude to my Peace Corps service served as a portent to the real adventure lying ahead of me. I would be sent to Correntina with no resources or support for the agricultural work I had been recruited and trained to perform. In spite of my youth and these challenges, the life lessons from my upbringing—flexibility, versatility and adaptability—combined with the support of the many wise men I would meet on my journey, favored my success. It would indeed be a journey filled with danger, but treasure as well, in the form of personal enrichment and the discovery of unforgettable people, places, and experiences. Adventure is what I sought. And adventure is what I discovered in Brazil.

3. Training in cowboy county

P reparation for my great adventure in the backlands of Brazil commenced on Sunday July 22, 1962. I took my first ever airplane flight to Oklahoma City. We passed through a Midwestern thunderstorm so violent that I quickly became familiar with a barf bag. The shine of my adventure dimmed in my psyche. Not a particularly stellar day in aviation, that same Sunday a Canadian Pacific flight crashed in Honolulu killing twenty-seven people, and the Mariner-1 spacecraft, one of America's early forays into space, was destroyed after takeoff. I was beginning to comprehend more clearly my mother's angst concerning the unknowns of this adventure.

My second great awakening was stepping onto the tarmac at Will Roger's Field. Summers can be hot and humid in Minnesota but nothing like summer in Oklahoma. I had an instant sensation that someone had set a hot, five hundred-pound anvil on my head. Another portent, I suspected, of things to come. With my feet finally firmly on the ground, however, I headed off for three months of training for the Brazil II Peace Corps project at the University of Oklahoma in Norman. I was joined by an assortment of individuals more diverse than any I had met in my life. Fourteen of the trainees, thirteen of them women, were destined for the Brazil I 4-H group already in Brazil. A few of the women were engaged to be married to men in this group and became affectionately known as the Mob—the Mail Order Brides.

Upon arrival, we received a training manual that stated the program goal was to provide Volunteers "with the best training possible to insure the most successful performance of this specific assignment within the limitations of individual ability and time permitted for training ... therefore, the curriculum has been designed to satisfy these personal needs as well as to fulfill the purposes and objectives of the project." \3

Our instruction immersed us in all things Brazilian: Portuguese language, local culture, and distinct geography. Significant focus was placed on understanding our partner organization, our identity as Americans, and America's *noble* goals around the world, specifically in Latin America. Beyond linguistic and cultural knowledge, our training was also meant to prepare us "psychologically, socially, intellectually, physically, and technically" for our assignments. \4

Although we received no direct political training, fully half of our training hours—seventeen lectures in all—were devoted to significant foreign affairs issues. The subtle message that Latin America, and Brazil in particular, were not bastions of stability, gave us reason to think we had plenty to be concerned about. The U.S. State Department and the Peace Corps focused a lot of resources on Brazil in the early 1960s principally because of the leftist direction of the Brazilian government, the Bay of Pigs debacle, and the ongoing Cold War with the Soviet Union.

Part of the impetus for creating the Peace Corps came from the bestselling 1958 political novel, *The Ugly American*, by William Lederer and Eugene Burdick. The authors painted a less-than-rosy picture of American foreign policy in southeast Asia, and the fallout spread around the world. *The Ugly American* exposed questionable U.S. government dealings, as well as the practices of private American enterprises abroad. Such was the case in Latin America where many underdeveloped countries were known disparagingly as Banana Republics.

Author Elizabeth Cobbs Hoffman described the Foreign Service personnel depicted in *The Ugly American* as "so-called representatives of America who transplanted the abundance they knew back home into 'golden ghettos' in foreign lands where they could live without experiencing even the smallest privations." \5

As Volunteers, we received a not-so-subtle message that the Peace Corps, with its lofty goals, would attempt to eradicate this unfavorable image abroad. Our personal brush with the golden ghetto would come in 1963 when we were denied passage into the U.S. Embassy in Rio de Janeiro. Embassy access is supposedly a right afforded to all U.S. citizens abroad, including individuals actively working for the U.S. government.

Nowhere in Latin America was the image of America of greater concern to the United States than in Brazil. The people of Brazil comprised half the total population of Latin America; the vast majority of them lived in subsistence poverty. \6

In 1962 the Brazilian economy was plagued by extreme inflation and a critical deficit of foreign investment. Communist factions, especially in labor unions and among rural peasants in the northeast part of the country where our project was to be implemented, were fast becoming entrenched in the failing political system.

While we got the big picture, little was mentioned of the clandestine approach the United States used to confront this situation, undertaken at that time by the U.S. Central Intelligence Agency. An article in *Counterspy* stated that "Brazil's democratic system at the start of the 1960s proved unequal to the difficult challenges posed by its foreign exchange constraint. Since President Goulart was elected by a 'populist' coalition of voters spanning class lines, the party system itself discouraged strategies that might put a significant group at a disadvantage. In this atmosphere, the coup of 1964 became a *sine qua non* for new U.S. credit." \7 This explosive scenario underpinned the political atmosphere our group was sent into like lambs to the slaughter.

One of the first big social functions of training took place soon after our arrival in Oklahoma. I knew it was going to be an interesting evening based on one of the very first interactions I observed. We gathered in a large hall for a meet-and-greet event. One young man quickly established himself as the doyen of the group by his genteel manners, eloquent speech, and fine apparel—with a pedigree to match. He came from a wealthy family that resided on Fifth Avenue in New York City, and he was a recent graduate of Princeton University.

He made the circuit around the room, introducing himself in a pleasant, humble manner, "Hello, I am John. Geologist, Princeton."

People were duly impressed. Except for one person.

There was a husky guy silently slouched against the wall, staying to himself, his clothes tattered in places, with Buddy Holly style thick glasses and shaggy hair. His appearance reminded all of us of a giant sloth reminiscent of those in photos in the jungles of our ultimate destiny.

John from Princeton approached him with an outstretched hand and repeated his greeting. "Hello, I am John. Geologist, Princeton."

"Dave. Asshole." Not what John was expecting.

Utter silence instantly cloaked the room. Dave broke it with a big chuckle.

Over time, I would come to understand this was Dave just being Dave. Ironically, he was an Ivy Leaguer himself. Cornell. Even more ironic, Dave became one of my best friends. We both were former college football players and loved athletics. We were similar in age and in agricultural interests. Beyond this, however, we were a bit like oil and water. Dave was a New Yorker from Long Island who proudly pointed out that his mother was the chairperson of the Bird Watchers Society of Long Island. I was a Midwesterner. The only birds my mother was interested in were chickens and ducks to feed her hungry farmhands. While family was dear to me, Dave rarely spoke about his. In the two years that I knew him, I never determined whether he had siblings or who his father was. Dave did not take to religion. I was a practicing Catholic and a teetotaler. Dave, although only twenty years old, almost failed to make it through selection because of a perceived or actual problem with what he termed "laughing water" and "old red eye."

Despite his mannerisms, Dave was easily the most brilliant person in our group. For example, at the outset of language instruction, we took aptitude tests to determine our proficiency levels. Dave placed in the top tier of students, all of whom already spoke Portuguese or were totally fluent in Spanish. Dave's fluency was believable except for the fact that he had never spoken or studied any language other than English. Instructors would later confide to some folks in the group that they felt his I.Q. landed him in the genius range.

Serendipitously, with project Volunteers eventually scattered over 15,000 square miles in the São Francisco Valley, Dave would be stationed in my relative vicinity. I would come to count on him to relieve the inevitable tedium, as in the case of the Bahia State Militia. I would also come to know him by his alternate identity: XXX.

While Dave would be one of the central figures in this new epoch of my life, there were many others. Trainees hailed from thirty-four different states and ranged in age from eighteen to seventy-three. Our project had the distinction of having the oldest female and male recruits of any project in the field or in training at this early juncture in the Peace Corps. During training, both would be flown to Washington, D.C., to meet with President Kennedy. Naturally, I mainly gravitated toward those of like age, interest, and abilities. Athletics appeared at the top of the list, and physical education became a natural outlet.

The physical education component of training consisted of a lot of running. For me, a skilled high school and college athlete, sports became a defining measure of my position and status within the group. Typically, I placed in the top handful of competitors during our mile-long morning runs. Life on a farm helped since I had to do a lot of running through pastures and fields chasing cattle and sheep. I greatly valued being one of the top runners in this set of peers, some of whom were collegiate distance runners.

One of the best of these was an eighteen-year-old African American from North Carolina named Jimmy Peace. I can still hear him saying, "Hi! I'm Jimmy Peace of the Peace Corps!" Jimmy had the distinction of being a state champion miler. He was one of those guys with a runner's physique—all legs. It was no surprise that he placed first every morning. No one was particularly offended by this, except for the fact that he loved to rub it in and constantly reminded everyone that no one could outrun him or ever would.

Jimmy's boastful ribbing began to grate on some of the guys, including four other African Americans. But it especially bothered a couple of the white Southern boys, Georgia Buck, Alabama Steve, John the Virginian, Sweet Sammy from Mississippi, and a farm boy from North Carolina. Of these, Steve, John and Sammy were dignified southern gentlemen of the first order, whereas Buck was a bit more righteous about protecting the image of the South, and the Carolina farm boy was feisty as hell and always looking for a fight.

The Southern boys finally hatched a plan to beat Jimmy at running the mile. Unfortunately, the plan included us Yankees because we had the better athletes and runners. The Southerners said they would overlook lingering hard feelings about the War of Northern Aggression—known to us as the Civil War, of course—if we would see fit to go along with their scheme. It all seemed like good fun to us given our mutual boredom with studies.

There was one hitch in the plan: Jimmy. He always had to lead the pack right from the beginning all the way to the finish. No one could keep up with him the whole way. But what if we used our strongest specialty runners to set the pace? Sprinter Charlie was an excellent collegiate quarter-miler. Dave and I were solid half-milers. Two more guys had been college milers. The basic idea was for Charlie to run a strong quarter-mile pace and force Jimmy to strive to maintain the lead. Dave and I would run a brisk half mile, and the milers would hold a strong pace for the mile.

Finally, the Defeat Jimmy Plan was put into action. The instructors were a bit surprised to see what unfolded, but I think they caught on quickly as Charlie took off at an unusually quick pace, with Jimmy glued to him. Finally, Charlie dropped back and after a few hundred more yards, Dave and I started closing in. At about the three-quarter mile mark Jimmy's fate was sealed. He could barely put one rubbery leg in front of the other and looked like a beached seal flapping about trying to make it into the ocean. Jimmy was finished. He slowed to a walk as the milers moved on past him along with a group of casual runners, who were oblivious to what was happening.

From then on, Jimmy decided to run with the pack at a normal mile pace. He still could have won, but he rarely took the opportunity to do so. Many of the Southerners thought it was all quite fitting and referred to it as a "race for racial equality." The irony was that they had it all backwards—whites had to keep up to the African American. I believe Jimmy knew there was a bigger message. He grew up in the Southern culture of the day. One had to know one's place. For at least one of the Southerners in the group, Jimmy's place was not at the front of the pack.

But Jimmy would reap a bit of revenge weeks later.

A group of us traveled north to Kansas State University in Manhattan for two weeks of intense training in advanced agricultural agronomy and agricultural engineering. Because soccer was the national sport of Brazil, we also started daily soccer practice. Jimmy didn't have much experience with soccer so Sprinter Charlie, Dave, and I worked with him to hone his skills. With his long legs and speed, he seemed to be an ideal winger to move the ball rapidly up field.

When we got back to Oklahoma, a friendly soccer rivalry developed between two groups that eventually formed teams: the Engineers and the Aggies. The Engineers, mostly Ivy Leaguers from the East Coast, prided themselves on their experience with sophisticated sports such as lacrosse, cricket, and soccer. They felt it was time to demonstrate to us farm boys, the Aggies, the true art of soccer. In their estimation after all, we were just a bunch of sodbusters whose only skills were handling pitchforks and horses. A match was scheduled. We knew that with three former collegiate football players on our team that our style would be one of more brawn, less finesse.

Brawn was indeed the operative word to describe the match. The Aggies won 2 to 1. The Engineers sustained two injuries while we Aggies remained unscathed. I had the honor of setting up both goals with my good friend Sprinter Charlie punching them in. After that match, we heard a lot less about pitchforks and horses.

Unfortunately, in a later game there was another casualty for the Engineers, Sweet Sammy from Mississippi. Why they had Sammy, with his diminutive physique, playing defense is hard to understand but in his valiant effort to stop one of the goals we scored, Sammy suffered a broken leg. It happened in a scrum near the goal so no one admitted to delivering the critical blow. But Jimmy did have a suspicious presence in the mix.

Soccer would become an avenue of acceptance in the group. It would serve a similar function once I reached my final destination in Brazil.

O ther than the excitement of running and soccer, training at Oklahoma settled into the dullness of repetitive studies and the absorption of material a bit over the heads of most trainees. Though physical fitness, reasonable proficiency with the Portuguese language, adequate knowledge of the people and culture, national identity and mission were important, the main emphasis was on technical training. After all, the basic recruiting goal of the project was to supply sophisticated technical assistance to the Brazilian CVSF. It was certainly what the University of Oklahoma training stressed.

Our project training manual stated: "All students will receive basic information in the multi-purpose facets of water resource development; municipal water, industrial water, water resource economics, flood control, navigation, irrigation, and recreation." \8

Imagine the dilemma of the university instructors aiming to provide sophisticated technical refresher training to a group of over a hundred students who, for the most part, lacked rudimentary knowledge of hydrology. These basic learners included nurses, public health people, individuals with agricultural degrees, teachers of home economics or arts and crafts, geologists, a few engineers, and a couple fisheries experts. Of the degreed professionals, only a half dozen had actually worked in their discipline beyond college. Approximately thirty of us had practical farm or mechanical experience, fifteen were health assistants or technologists, and ten were technicians in radio, electronics, or some form of trade. At least fifteen trainees admitted to having no specific skill set whatsoever.

In retrospect, this part of our training seemed too academic given the profile of our group and our destination—an impoverished area with few municipal water systems, little industry, and periodic droughts that sometimes lasted up to four years. But ours was not to question why. Despite some serious issues with personnel selection and training right from the start, everyone plodded on and hoped for the best. We dutifully sat through the water sessions, spent two weeks at Kansas State University in technical agricultural classes, and spent three weeks at the Tennessee Valley Authority in Alabama, learning practical applications of theories that we little understood. Most of us felt intimidated by this part of our training, assuming that our inability to master the material might eliminate us from the project since surely the CVSF had high expectations. In the months ahead these complexities would have dire consequences for the project.

One highlight of our training occurred when we received a visit from representatives of the commission, led by the effervescent Dr. José Pacheco Pimenta, whom we dubbed Dr. Pepper. Ever the optimist, he repeatedly rebuffed our concerns about our lack of experience, seemingly convinced that Americans could do anything. His constant mantra was, "Come anyway, you can learn!" This optimism, however, resulted in overselling our capabilities and potential project results to the actual commission managers in the field. This would lead to significant animosity and diminished opportunity between various managers and Volunteers.

While technical training presented tough mental challenges, the constant pressure of psychological testing and evaluations was nerve-wracking. Several psychologists administered all the standard tests known to the government in an attempt to discover who you really were, what motivated you, and how you might handle stress. Testing included the Edwards Personal Preference Schedule, the Minnesota Multiphasic Personality Inventory, the Holtzman Inkblot Technique, and the Peace Corps Attitude Inventory. Weekly interviews left us uncertain of our selection status, which seemed to be part of the strategy to determine tolerance for stress. My mother's prophetic words about Vietnam began to play over and over unrelentingly in my mind.

Shortly before we left for further training at the Tennessee Valley Authority in Alabama, the Peace Corps staged a big party at the Locket Hotel in Norman with a live band, snacks, and beverages, including beer. You could even bring your own hard alcohol for mixing if you were of age. After all the hard work, some entertainment seemed appropriate. Few suspected, however, that this was all part of the psychological program to see not only how we were handling the pressure of training but especially our reaction once the stress eased.

Some failed this test badly. Six trainees were carried off to bed, one trainee was found stoned on the sidewalk outside the hotel, and another was found sitting out in a pasture under a tree the next morning, completely disoriented. The cops also escorted one to the police station.

In all, seven individuals were immediately deselected from training. Rumors circulated that forty trainees were put on probation as a result of the party and behavioral limitations noted during training. It's worth mentioning that Dave—the infamous XXX—easily could have been dismissed for getting pretty hammered that night, but he was put on probation and thus survived the purge. I believe that had it not been for the fact that he was recognized by group leaders, the faculty, and most trainees as the reigning genius, he would have been history. Without Dave, my harrowing episode with the stolen plow, as well as many of my adventures in the Brazil, might never have happened.

In the end, only fifty percent of those who initially came to Oklahoma would complete two years in the Peace Corps. Perhaps Senators Strom Thurmond of Alabama, John Stennis of Mississippi, and some other senate hardliners may have been partially right when, in questioning Sargent Shriver during hearings for the establishment of the Peace Corps in 1961, they said, "The only people the Director would get to apply for this Peace business were a bunch of draft-evading, dope-smoking, hippie rejects." \9

Thank God I stuck to soft drinks that night. I was up the next morning and off to Sunday Mass. Thus ended the Oklahoma and Kansas phases of our training. We were off into the wild blue yonder once more, the deep woods of Alabama beckoning us to see and experience what the practical aspects our mission to Brazil was supposed to be all about.

4. Bedlam in Alabama

We flew next to Muscle Shoals, Alabama, for training at the Tennessee Valley Authority, or TVA, compound. My first night flight, seeing city lights below and the moon so brilliant above the clouds left a lasting impression. The flight had a very calm and serene feel to it and washed away much of the stress we had experienced. There was a general feeling of new beginnings, with everyone on board having survived the initial elimination process and the daily routine of superficial studies and testing. It was exciting to think we were now going to experience the type of work more specific to our mission. Even though this would be a short technical course, the training would turn out to be overshadowed by one of the most eye-opening experiences of my life and my first real taste of the eruption of the lingering national racial issues in the country.

We were housed in mobile trailers near beautiful Wilson Lake, formed by the Wilson Dam, situated on deeply wooded acreage of tall southern pines and trails along the Tennessee River. It was late September and the stifling heat we experienced previously in Oklahoma was more tolerable. The landscape was much more reminiscent of my home in southeast Minnesota, with its hills, great forests and rivers, versus the barren wastelands of Oklahoma that had little more than occasional oil derricks, rather than trees, to break up the dismal landscape. The rivers, occasional hills, and dense forestation of northern Alabama greatly lifted my spirits.

Our home in Alabama was a complex of twenty-four trailers located in the far southwest corner of the sprawling TVA compound composed of more than a dozen major buildings. The towns of Muscle Shoals, Florence, Sheffield, and Tuscumbia were nearby, but we would never be allowed to venture into any of them. Possibly this was meant to be the first taste of the isolation we would experience in Brazil. Four people were assigned to each trailer with one designated leader in our little village. This distinction fell to me, even though I was the youngest, which may have indicated I was in good stead at the moment with the evaluators. But that prospect didn't make me any more comfortable in the role, especially when my trailer mates pushed the limits.

Our campsite was two and a half miles from the main buildings in the compound, so we boarded buses every morning for meals and classes. Just as living in the isolation of our trailers appeared to be a transitional introduction to our future life in the hinterlands of Brazil, this also was the case with food. The main meals included novelties such as black-eyed peas, okra, rice, eggplant, and sorghum. Everything was fried, from bread, fried dough, to steak. The most noticeable difference of food culture was the Southern fondness for the full breakfast, known as a fry-up, a tradition handed down in their largely English-Scottish heritage. Of course, no matter what else you ordered for breakfast there was the ever-present hominy and grits.

At our first breakfast, I overheard my new buddy Dave jousting with John, his Ivy League nemesis, in the chow line. "Hey, John, there is no continental breakfast here. It's grits, biscuits and gravy, so don't be asking for quiche, crudité and croissants, or saying, 'Yes, I'll have cappuccino,' when they ask if you want coffee."

At night, we walked back to camp, usually in the dark, on a main road that ran through the complex. This road bisected the complex from northeast to southwest. On its northern end, the road crossed the Wilson Dam and the Tennessee River, and on its southern end, it connected to roads leading to Sheffield and Muscle Shoals. We were instructed to head directly to our trailers and avoid contact with the locals in automobiles, who did not regard mixed-race groups such as ours favorably. According to what we'd been told, miscegenation, or mixed-race marriage, was a fairly common practice in Brazil. There were laws, however, banning it at that time in the Deep South. Even interracial dating was taboo. Since there were already four or five mixed-race couples dating in our group, we had to be as discreet as possible.

Once we were back for the evening, guards were posted and we were not permitted off the grounds. Everyone seemed to adhere to the nighttime restrictions, although Dave snuck out of the camp on several occasions only to appear a short time later with some good old Southern moonshine called Red Eye. He would take a few swigs from the jug and then pump out a couple hundred push-ups. Or he would grab a massive sledge hammer and beat it against a tree. Sometimes he'd appear at my trailer door well after midnight and say, "Let's go run it out." I think all this activity was his way of calming his mind and relieving mental tension. I never took him up on his offer to go for a run at night, however, we did continue our morning-run tradition along the roads outside the camp.

After about a week in Alabama, we traveled around the Tennessee Valley to see several TVA reclamation projects. It turned out to be fortuitous timing. On one of these trips we spied a drive-in movie theater that had blown down. Across what remained of the screen someone had written, "gone with the wind." A few days later our training program as originally intended, was also "gone with the wind."

All hell broke loose in Dixie when a black student named James Meredith applied for entry into the all-white University of Mississippi. In light of this, it became dreadfully apparent that a mixture of whites and blacks living in the woods on the TVA premises did not bode well for our continued stay. Rumors began circulating that we would be evacuated and sent back north, terminating our training early, or that we would resume training at another location.

Immediately, security at our camp was doubled in the form of Alabama State Troopers. I'm not sure we felt that safe knowing that their law enforcement counterparts, Mississippi State Troopers, were blocking Mr. Meredith's entry into the university on orders from the governor. Other measures were taken as well. No longer would we walk to camp. Buses with armed guards on board transported us. Lectures and especially any evening social events now took place in an old ice plant a short distance from our trailer site. We still went on our morning runs outside the camp, but at our own peril. For safety sake, miler-phenom Jimmy Peace, and the rest of the African Americans, had to remain in camp. They settled instead for calisthenics with the girls, a huge embarrassment to Jimmy who believed he was destined for the Olympics one day and wanted to keep training.

Over the next few days the South would become a renewed battleground of states' rights. Alabama was home to the national headquarters of the Klu Klux Klan; home as well to the grand wizard Robert Sheldon. The standoff with James Meredith was the spark many had been waiting for. Carloads of Alabamans were on their way to Mississippi to take part in the uprising.

Our Peace Corps group, racially diverse and dominated by Northerners with liberal leanings, raised serious suspicion among Alabamans who stayed behind. We represented the possibility of a local uprising as well.

"What were those do-gooder peaceniks living on the Tennessee Valley Authority property (who were supposedly training for some foreign mission) really doing down here? No damn federal government was going to use the guise of a foreign peace mission to create a precedent for integrated education right in our midst!"

Raised in the Midwest, young and a bit naive, it was hard for me to understand why the Southerners were so upset. All public schools in the country had been ordered to adopt desegregation by the Brown v. Board of Education Supreme Court ruling in 1954. Mr. Meredith seemed like a good first step for Southern universities to solve a lingering, ugly problem. He was an Air Force veteran, the grandson of a slave, and the illegitimate great-grandson of a white Mississippi Supreme Court justice who had fought for white supremacy. He seemed like a perfect fit since he was a nine-year military man in a part of the country that esteemed military service. He had the educational credentials for admission, and he was of a mixed-race.

I knew racism existed elsewhere, but not to this degree. While we were training in Oklahoma, there had been an incident at a restaurant in Norman when they refused to serve the African Americans in our group. As a result, our group boycotted the restaurant. [10] This was my first real exposure to the prevalence of racial bigotry that existed in the United States. We would later learn that our training had been originally slated for the University of Texas, not Oklahoma. But because of the interracial nature of our group, Texas refused to host the training.

*T*hings remained tense for several days in Alabama with riots spinning out of control. Two white men were murdered, 166 U.S. Marshals and forty-eight American soldiers were injured. Thirty of the Marshals sustained gunshot wounds. [11]

I have read that many historians and scholars believe the conscious warrior and his American ideals ended with the last battle of the Civil War. Witnessing the furor of many Southerners during the Meredith crisis, I came to better understand those who say the Civil War never ended for many in the South. Eventually, after President Kennedy sent federal troops to quell the riots, James Meredith gained admission to the University of Mississippi; he would attend classes accompanied by armed guards, just like us Peace Corps trainees.

Our training became an unfortunate debacle due to the racial uprisings across the South. The capstone of our training called for visits to various locations in the Tennessee River Valley to get firsthand experience related to all the water resource training considered to be such an integral part of our curriculum back in Oklahoma. But that would not happen. We were kept in lockdown for the remainder of our time in Crimson Tide country, and the rest of our training would take place in the old warehouse previously used to store ice.

Training finally came to an end and most were glad for it. I made the final cut, unlike twenty-four out of the 108 Brazil II project trainees who started. (And Mom was so concerned I might not make the cut.) An additional twenty-four of the final selectees would go home soon after arriving in Brazil. Many of us found the highly secretive selection process perplexing because several of the dismissed trainees seemed to be just what the Peace Corps sought out in their advertising. And then there was the mystery of selection dates. Upon notification of attaining Volunteer status, I received a Peace Corps Volunteer identification card signed by Peace Corps Director Sargent Shriver with a photo I had submitted when I entered training. Strange indeed that the card was dated September 19, 1962, two days after we arrived in Alabama for our final training and three weeks before final selection. Had a decision been made by this time that some of the trainees were good to go?

In some ways, it seemed like we'd spent a lifetime in Alabama. I was ready to leave it all behind as I boarded a plane in Muscle Shoals and flew to Atlanta en route to my next destination, Rochester, Minnesota, for ten days of home-leave with friends and family.

5. Flight into the unknown

My short pre-service visit at home went by rapidly. There were so many friends and family members to say goodbye to. We had a wonderful time, but all the while my thoughts looked ahead to the adventure waiting for me. I said goodbye to my mother and father at the farm, then rode with Millie and her dad to the Rochester airport, where I said goodbye to my sweetheart. We kissed, I remember, her father pretending not to watch. We embraced for the last time and promised to write letters to each other.

From Minnesota, I flew to New York City. All I remember from that overnight in the Big Apple is car horns and other city noise. The next morning, I departed for the promised land of Brazil. Known for its beautiful beaches and rain forests, its citizens reverently called it a paradise on earth. To many of us new Volunteers, Brazil was a Third World nation.

Thoughts of paradise, a few weeks of training on sunny beaches in Rio de Janeiro, danced through our heads as the mammoth Pan Am jet lifted off from Idlewild Airport. I felt like Odysseus embarking on a mythic voyage of transition from the past into a future rebirth.

Billed as a ten-hour non-stop flight to Brazil, we landed early in Port of Spain, Trinidad, due to alleged minor engine problems. One look at the airport's bleak surroundings and I figured the pilots would have to fix the problem themselves. I didn't see a mechanic's hangar large enough to accommodate a McDonnell Douglas DC-8 jetliner.

Many hours passed before we learned the real reason for our unscheduled layover. It was October 22, 1962, the very day President Kennedy announced that the U.S. Navy would blockade the island of Cuba until the Soviet Union removed ballistic missiles capable of carrying nuclear warheads. The Cuban Missile Crisis, a tense, thirteen-day geopolitical standoff between two great Superpowers, led many

35

observers to call it the most dangerous thirteen days in history.[12] While the world stood at the brink of nuclear war, we Volunteers were grounded in Trinidad with nothing to do but wait and see how events played out.

Later information revealed that all civilian flights crossing the Caribbean to Latin America had been grounded. Our charter had not been notified. Pan Am officials called it an "oversight."

Trinidad served as headquarters for the U.S. Naval Command Center in the Caribbean, which conducted all naval operations concerned with the blockade. Any of the medium range ballistic missiles installed in Cuba could reach targets within a 1,200-mile radius, meaning they could strike as far north as Washington D.C. The entire old South that had given Kennedy trouble only weeks earlier would fall within the range of Soviet missiles as well. The northern shores of Latin America, including Trinidad, could become targets. Strategically, Trinidad might have been one of the prime targets to counter further U.S. naval action.

While government officials contemplated what to do, the Brazil II Volunteers remained in considerable danger in Trinidad. Apparently, an earlier plan had called for holding our group in New York City. If necessary, we could be sent to India as India had requested Volunteers with project skills similar to Brazil II. The point is, Washington knew a planeload of Volunteers were departing for Brazil, which begs the question, if alternative plans existed, why was our flight allowed to take off in the first place? High-level government officials from the President on down knew the blockade would be announced.

Cuban leader Fidel Castro seized power in 1959. Cuba and the Soviet Union became allies in 1960. In 1961, President Kennedy authorized an ill-fated invasion at the Bay of Pigs. None of these events were lost on Brazil, which had strong leftist leanings at the time. The State Department anticipated potential repercussions from the missile crisis might cause harm or even death for Americans, especially in Rio de Janeiro were riots erupted as soon as the blockade was announced. The Peace Corps was not interested in this type of publicity. Unfortunately, the alternative India plan was undermined the moment we left the United States.

Remaining oblivious in Trinidad definitely turned out to be a better option than being in the air over the Caribbean on a return flight to the United States or headed east toward India. In the bizarre uncertainty of geopolitics, or the plot of a page-turning thriller, Russians could have shot down our plane to test our young President's mettle; or the Americans might have downed the plane and blamed it on the Russians. The latter scenario would put the Russians on the defensive while creating a national furor at home, providing cover for the U.S. forces to invade Cuba and remove the missiles. Worse yet, it could set off a limited war of the sort favored by many in Kennedy's Defense Department.[13] With tensions high, anything could have happened.

The reality of these hypothetical scenarios was revealed years later through data acquired under the Freedom of Information Act. Early in the Kennedy administration a man named Edward Lansdale headed up Operation Northwoods, a clandestine project to consider ways to overthrow Castro. Possible actions that made the list included hijacking a U.S. aircraft and blaming it on the Cubans, and shooting down a civilian airliner—the passengers could be a group of college students off on a holiday—staged to look like the Cuban military had done it.[14] Loosely fitting the shoot-down category, my group qualified as an expendable unit if provocative gamesmanship were chosen as the avenue of conflict resolution. So, was it really a mistake that our lone plane was not notified about crossing Caribbean airspace, or were we being offered up as pawns in a Superpower chess game? This question will probably go unanswered for all time.

Planning for a blockade began after Kennedy was shown aerial photographs of missile sites under construction in Cuba. Two days before Brazil II was grounded in Trinidad, naval and air maneuvers were in motion behind the scenes, including assigning bombers, submarines, and other elements to implement the blockade. One hundred eighty naval ships were ordered to the Caribbean. One hundred fifty aircraft and tankers were relocated to Florida, and Strategic Air Command B-47s prepared to strike missile sites. By October 26, the U.S. implemented the Chrome Dome missions. NATO forces were put on full alert. Long-range B-52 bombers armed with nuclear weapons continuously circled the borders of Russia—something the Soviet Union was probably well aware of given the nature of military intelligence capabilities at the time.[15] It defies almost any form of logic to assume that the powers in Washington could perform this level of sophisticated planning and yet not be aware of our flight.

For us, ignorance was bliss. As this high-stakes game of international conflict swirled around us, we were being fed the ambrosia of youthful merriment: rum, dancing girls, ocean breezes, palm trees, and endless sunshine. However, we could not remain in Trinidad indefinitely, no matter what the precipitous state of the Cold War was right then.

War would eventually be averted; the missiles were removed from Cuba. Secretary of State at the time, Dean Rusk, claims he described the moment the crisis ended in simple terms: "We were eyeball to eyeball, and I think the other fellow just blinked." \16

Meanwhile, thirteen days before the other guy blinked, the issue remained: what to do with a plane full of Peace Corps Volunteers sitting in Trinidad? Sending us back to the United States made no sense and, given the blockade, few other countries would have been eager to grant permission to land. The only flight plan filed and valid was to Brazil. So, by late in the day on October 22, the purported mechanical problems were resolved and we said good-bye to the land of rum and sun. Taking off from Trinidad in the early darkness, it seemed that we were passing from one unknown into an even greater unknown, much like a mythological hero destined for adventure.

We arrived in Rio de Janeiro in the early morning hours. The only crisis we experienced was what we termed the "toilet paper caper," which occurred in the customs line with one of our own, a crafts artist named Bob. He took his turn and, when requested, dutifully opened his suitcase for inspection, only to reveal that it was filled with toilet paper. The customs official immediately wanted to know what this was all about. Bob had previously lived in Mexico where he discovered the toilet paper to be both thin and expensive. Because Brazil was also in Latin America, he didn't want to take any chances. The official didn't buy Bob's personal hygiene reasoning, however, believing instead that there was something more sinister at work. There had to be another reason. Everyone waited. Seconds ticked by. Then Bob proclaimed that, actually, the toilet paper was a special kind of tissue required for his artwork, used to properly clean his brushes. The official conferred with his colleagues for a while before finally accepting the explanation. After nearly an hour's delay, he waved us through customs. Crisis averted.

While sequestered in customs, we still had no idea what was going on in the world. It had been a long day and night and we were anxious to get to our hotel near the American Embassy, clean up, and settle in. We rode the bus along Rio's streets lulled by dreams of sandy beaches and the other fine sights of what many referred to as the most beautiful city in the world.

As we approached our hotel, we saw a throng of people massed outside. Our initial elation, thinking we had encountered an organized greeting party, turned sour when we realized many in the crowd were in a heighted state of hysteria. Many shouted slogans, others waved placards and newspapers, still others began beating on the sides of our buses. The mob pressed closer to the bus brandishing Brazil's leading newspaper, *O Journal,* with its frontpage banner headline that day, "*O Brasil Invadido Hojé por Centenas de Yankees!*" A few of our group's more accomplished Portuguese speakers quickly translated it for the rest of us: "Brazil Invaded Today by Several Hundred Yankees!" This was no welcoming committee. This was a riot over the news of our arrival conflated with the Cuban missile blockade.

The U.S. had notified Brazil that we were coming regardless of the international crisis and requested local police protection for us. Well, Brazil's strong leftist faction was led by Carlos Lacerda, governor of the State of Guanabara, which included Rio. Lacerda's response was to stage this well-organized reception. Just as the U.S. government seemed to forget that we were flying down to Rio, they also seemed to forget that Carlos, their biggest Communist adversary in Brazil, was the main man in charge of the city.

After Alabama and our delay in Trinidad, this was just another major crisis to weather. Plans dictated that we would check into the hotel before heading to our training location in Rio, where we would be housed by host families for a month of in-country acclimation, acculturation, and further language study. Eager to turn in for some long-awaited rest, we unloaded our baggage, hauled it into the lobby of the hotel, and commenced checking in as instructed, including Bob with his suitcase of toilet paper.

American Embassy officials had gathered to assess the situation. It was obvious that this was a dangerous environment because no one knew how long the missile crisis would last. If the barrage of phone calls from our families and friends to the Peace Corps office in Washington was giving them headaches, far greater repercussions would occur if any of us were killed or seriously harmed because of the decision to continue on to Brazil rather than to send us home or to another country. After intense discussion, somebody decided that sending us to the breathtaking in-country training location of Copacabana was not the most prudent plan. Our baggage never left the hotel lobby. By 6:00 a.m., after only a couple hours of rest, there were knocks on our doors along with curt instructions to get dressed and come to the lobby. Once assembled, we were told to find our luggage in the pile and get back on the buses.

Again, we were oblivious to what was going on. We were told only that a decision had been made to move us to a safer location. While loading bags aboard the buses, we were surrounded by a large crowd of mainly college students, possibly leftist sympathizers sent by the Brazilian government. Despite their hostility, they seemed confused by the blue flight bags we all carried, each with the Pan Am emblem on one side and a large PC encircled by stars on the other side. They didn't understand why they were sent to protest, believing that "PC" stood for *Partida Communista*—Communist Party. I was never certain, but that adroit linguistic ploy sure seemed to bear the mark of my clever buddy Dave. Dave to the rescue.

Although no one said anything, as we watched the bright lights of Rio recede in the distance, we got the feeling that we would not be training here. Some of the individuals in our group who were well into their forties and fifties had wearied of the constant shroud of secrecy and misinformation that persisted throughout the entire trip. They demanded that the Peace Corps director on the bus provide some answers. Unflappable as always, the director indicated that the immediate safety of the group was the number one priority. He explained that our destination was five hundred miles into the center of Brazil, a remote, and thus very safe, dormitory complex. A few years earlier the vacant dorm had housed workers for the construction of the Três Marias Hydro Dam on the São Francisco River. Possibly the remote location sounded exciting to the director, whose previous diplomatic assignment had been Paris. He had enjoyed two of the most coveted diplomatic assignments in the world, Paris and Rio. For him, it was an adventure, but he would soon return to Rio.

Sensing our unrest, he contended that the international situation made it unrealistic for us to return to the United States and that we were in some respects safer than our families and friends back home.

He reasoned, therefore, that we should focus our thoughts and prayers on the folks at home since in the worst-case scenario of nuclear war we were more likely to survive. The group received these sentiments with no particular revelry.

Several weeks later I received a letter from home, the first from Millie, she expressed that she, like most other Americans, was in a state of near panic due to the threat of imminent nuclear war. Many Minnesotans wondered whether they would see another sunset or sunrise, though in fact, given the range of Soviet ballistic missiles, my home state would at worst have been subjected to limited nuclear fallout, that is unless one of the Superpowers launched a full-scale attack. Millie said that immediately after hearing President Kennedy's announcement my mother called her to find out if she knew anything of my whereabouts. Millie, like my mom, and the parents and friends of all my fellow Volunteers, were incredulous and panicked that our flight was sent into this potential war zone. In the event of a nuclear disaster, our flight might have never returned.

The previous year, still in high school, I won first place in the local science fair. For my project, I designed a fully equipped bomb shelter and constructed a scaled-down model, along with instructions on what to do in the event of a nuclear disaster. In a later letter, Millie indicated that my parents were besieged with panicked calls from people wondering if the plans still existed. "If you think the Brazilians see you as a hero," Millie wrote, "that sentiment is eclipsed by your stature here at home!"

On the drive home from taking me to the Rochester airport the day I left for New York, Millie's dad delivered a somber parental message. He cautioned her to not put all of her hopes and dreams in her deep love for me, as I was going on a journey that could be fraught with danger. Only one day after his prophetic message, that reality took its most dangerous turn. Yes, we may have been the lucky ones, but I felt a deep sense of panic and fear for the fate of my loved ones.

Our buses labored on through the drenching rains of Brazil's rainy season along curvy mountain roads, past mudslides, and into the foggy landscape of the highlands of south central Brazil. We arrived at three o'clock in the morning in the major inland city of Belo Horizonte—Blue Horizon. We had been traveling continuously for more than thirty-six hours by plane and bus. We definitely needed a little blue horizon.

Ominous as our arrival was, it contrasted starkly with that of the previous Peace Corps group. They experienced a smooth transition from training to installation at their project. This was one of many major differences between our group and virtually all other Brazilian projects that entered the country. While our tenuous arrival caused by the spiraling international crisis was enough to severely shake the confidence of some Volunteers, it was but one more in a series of significant challenges Brazil II project Volunteers would face.

6. Reality sets in

Finally, we spent a night in a real bed and got some much-needed sleep. The next morning, we left for Três Marias. One of the buses broke down, so we did not arrive at our destination until midnight. We would soon come to understand that breakdowns along deserted highways would be characteristic of travel in the interior.

Once we arrived at our location, we fully comprehended the secrecy cloaking our hasty departure from Rio. The barracks site had not been used since completing the hydro dam years earlier. The facilities were in disrepair, to say the least; and after seeing the living quarters, I thought "Mary Mother of Jesus" might have been a more appropriate name for the place. There were bunk beds, but in some cases no mattresses and in all cases, no bedding. What little they did scrounge up in Belo Horizonte went to the women in the group. Cockroaches ran rampant, windows had no screens, and some did not shut at all. Most of the cots were too short for the tall guys in the group. Clearly, this was not Copacabana.

Training began with pomp and circumstance. The Peace Corps flew in a contingent of high-level government officials to lend an air of importance to what had been chaos. Our illustrious guests included the Deputy Ambassador, a couple of officials from the Agency for International Development—USAID, and the director of The Alliance for Progress, all of whom painted a fairly bleak picture of Brazil. We also heard presentations from officials of the São Francisco Valley Commission.

The speakers pointed out the main actors in the political turmoil we'd witnessed upon arrival. Leftist Carlos Lacerda, Mayor of Rio, had welcomed us to Rio. Then there was Leonidas Brizola, governor of the State of Rio Grande do Sul, brother-in-law to President João

Goulart, and head of one of the largest Communist labor unions in the country. Brizola had taken to the airwaves prior to our arrival to claim that American capitalists sent to exploit the country would arrive in a military plane. He advised people not to cooperate with us, and not to accept us in their towns. Ironically, there were already two Peace Corps 4-H Volunteers working in Brizola's home state of Rio Grande do Sul.

We knew a lot more about Brazil at the moment than we did about events taking place in the rest of the world, including the Cuban Missile Crisis. We had no idea, for instance, that earlier on the day training started a U2 reconnaissance plane had been shot down over Cuba and the pilot killed. President Kennedy and his top advisors originally stated that such an act would justify a declaration of war; they would forgo meeting again and simply attack. But the President did not remain true to his word. It was disconcerting to imagine that had our Brazil II charter flight been shot down as many of us had feared, we might have become, like the U2 pilot, little more than a footnote in history. [17]

During our hiatus in Três Marias, we heard from numerous American and Brazilian officials. Most of the speeches were relatively dull and would have been more effective after we'd spent time in the field. However, the session with the unctuous Mr. Wolfe, Brazil director of the U.S. Food for Peace program, was the exception to dull. A former feed salesman and one-term Congressman from Iowa, Mr. Wolfe had somehow snagged a plum job in Rio, a long way from Elkader and the cornfields of Iowa's second district.

Mr. Wolfe's session became animated when someone asked what we should do if we discovered Food for Peace corruption in our project area. Rumors had proliferated throughout our training that the Food for Peace program was a money-making bonanza for local politicians. Mr. Wolfe told us to contact him if we found out that food was being sold illegally. He would personally see to it that law-breakers were prosecuted.

After Mr. Wolfe left, our Peace Corps director told us to ignore ninety-nine percent of what this international political lightweight had said, and that any problems should just be reported to him, the director.

"Sticking our noses into this would be the quickest way for us to wear out our welcome," the director said. He suggested we might even find ourselves in the hands of Brazil's de facto legal system, face down in a remote river. Politics was not to be our game.

Not everyone heeded this advice. In my project area, our future Volunteer leader would rat out a local politician for improper use of U.S. funds. It was not long before rumors surfaced locally of his impending demise. The whistle-blower was immediate transferred to Rio to complete his service in the company of the colorful Iowa Feed salesman, Mr. Wolfe.

A s training in Três Marias drew to a close, Volunteers met individually with the director to receive posting and coworker assignments. We'd been supplied with tentative placement information during our training in Alabama, tentative because some of the Volunteers did not survive the final selection process. I was assigned, along with two other Volunteers, to Correntina, a town located in the extreme western part of Bahia State, about seventy-five miles west of the São Francisco River.

Being posted in Correntina struck me personally as a linguistic coincidence. The Corrente River flows through the town on its way to the São Francisco River. *Corrente* is similar to my surname Fliés because they both refer to flowing rivers. My ancestors lived in eastern Luxembourg on the banks of the Moselle River, and I've been told my surname means "from down by the flowing river." Fliés would be a hard name for Brazilians to conquer, so over time many village folks translated it to Ken do Rio Corrente—Ken from the Flowing River. As for Kenneth, my given name, the Brazilians struggled with the *th* sound. Fortunately, they were very familiar with the name of the American President. Since Kenneth was close in spelling and pronunciation to Kennedy, I became Senhor Kennedy. However, *d* is pronounced as *g* in Portuguese, resulting in Kennegé. To add a further twist, my surname without an accent is the English word for fly, a much-despised insect prolific in Brazil. Fly in Portuguese is *moscas*. So, my other monikers became Kennegé Moscas or Senhor Moscas.

Our project team was headed to a town that had a flowing river with a series of falls and an ultra-modern, albeit small, hydro dam. Years earlier, the commission had hired Germans to build the dam but ran out of funds to make it reliably operational. Therefore, one of the Peace Corps Volunteers in Correntina, Merrill, was an electrical engineer, a recent graduate of the University of California Berkeley. Merrill went by his abbreviated middle name, Dick, a wise choice since Merrill was very problematic for Brazilians. But of course, with that tricky *d* he would be Gick to locals.

I came from a family of eleven children. Dick was his Mother's only child. He had an older step brother from his Dad's previous marriage. While my family struggled to meet day to day expenses of a large family and farm, Dick's parents were very successful subdivision developers in San Diego. His parents wished for him to take over the family business, but he was intent on forging his own identity and in his words, "Finding a way to make the world a better place."

Tall, blond, blue-eyed, Dick always wore a white shirt and Levi's. Hustling about at a maddening pace, he rarely appeared without a clipboard; always taking notes. In that respect, he fit the mold of what the locals understood to be an engineer based on the German engineers who originally built the hydro dam.

The third member of our team, Gail, opted to use her middle name Silvia to avoid the troubling *g*. Silvia graduated from Stanford University majoring in international relations. A summer spent working as a hospital nurse's assistant led Peace Corps to post Silvia as a health care specialist in Correntina. Silvia's family, like Dick's family, was well-to-do. Silvia's dad was a very successful real estate developer in the Chicago area. She had one sibling, a sister. Both Dick and Silvia were graduates of two of America's top universities, and cultured in many other aspects of life, while with one year of college I was barely off the farm.

If her family's position in Chicago were not status enough, prior to joining the Peace Corps, Silvia had been engaged to the son of one of the largest real estate developers in San Francisco. Also blond, blue-eyed and quite attractive, Silvia possessed an air of sophistication unmatched by most locals. She even smoked cigarettes, which she held elevated between two fingers, a favorite pose of Hollywood starlets seen in films and magazines of the day. Women smoking was unheard of, and contrary to local mores. I was a practicing Catholic. Dick was a professed agnostic. And Silvia was a Protestant, albeit a limited practitioner. Being a religious farm boy, I assumed that the transition to life in a small, remote rural community would be one slight advantage I might enjoy.

The Peace Corps mission statement defined our roles: "The PCV has been invited to do a specific job. The basic objective is to assure that the trainee has the required skills for his particular assignment and has the primary prerequisites, knowledge, and attitudes to accomplish satisfactorily his assignment abroad." [18] Accordingly, the placement of Dick and Silvia in Correntina made sense. There was the hydro dam for Dick and there was a rural health clinic for Silvia.

The Peace Corps trained me in agriculture, but I soon discovered there was no established agricultural presence or capabilities in Correntina. I would be starting from scratch, something I may have considered too formidable had I known it beforehand.

As for the rest of the Brazil II ag Volunteers, some two dozen in all, they were posted initially at established commission agricultural stations. Not only were there no commission agricultural capabilities in Correntina, but the nearest agricultural station lay forty miles away, across two rivers with no bridges. And of course when I started, I had no form of transportation to get there. It would be six months before I had a Jeep, the last of the Volunteers in our group to receive one, although this was understandable given that I was stationed in the most remote location.

At times I had to scratch my head regarding the logic of placing me in Correntina. There were nine Volunteers under the age of twenty in the project. All except me were placed in the São Francisco valley in larger communities with hospitals and other major support facilities. Out of the other eight, all but the Plow Thief Dave, Sprinter Chuck and I were located in towns, each where a married Volunteer-couple lived onsite, possibly to provide a parental presence.

Adding insult to injury, two months after arriving in Correntina I would be left by myself for six weeks with no transportation and no medical facilities other than a clinical doctor who only diagnosed illnesses and dispensed medicine. Ultimately, I was left in a state of confusion as to how the Peace Corps administration determined our final location placements or team assignments. No analysis or reasoning was ever shared with us. I was left to wonder, and to hope, that there was some intelligent ulterior motive for my assignment in Correntina.

It seemed fitting that we departed from Três Marias for our duty stations in the São Francisco Valley on Halloween, the liturgical day to remember the dead, since it marked the end of another strange phase of our Volunteer experience. Over the next few months, two dozen of the project members who had weathered the trials of our unique adventure would leave the project. Still others would journey to locations hundreds of miles from me. I would not see them again for eighteen months. Many changes would take place in the interim, and we would truly be different souls when we gathered together again.

7. End of the World

The ultimate day of reckoning arrived. We left the deprivations of Três Marias behind and returned to Belo Horizonte for a flight to the north and the much-heralded São Francisco River valley. I would be posted in the Northeast Region with a dozen other Volunteers. Our headquarters, the very poor town of Bom Jesus da Lapa—literally Good Jesus of the Grotto—would be the gateway to everything we did in the months ahead. If we needed supplies, money, medical attention, or hospitalization of any serious nature, we would go to Lapa, which was also the regional headquarters of the commission and the nearest town with commercial bi-weekly air transportation.

Situated along the banks of the São Francisco, Lapa is memorable for a large limestone formation rising up alongside the river that flows through otherwise flat terrain. The natural grotto carved out inside the imposing bluff has been a pilgrimage site since the seventeenth century.

In the 1902 Brazilian war epic, *Os Sertões—Rebellion in the Backlands*, the journalist and sociologist, Euclides da Cunha, who has been compared to Tolstoy, provides moving descriptions of Lapa. The grotto there is known as the Mecca of the *sertanejos*—backwoodsmen—who from 1895-1898 battled Brazil's republican army until the army crushed them.

Lapa's high, bell-shaped bluffs enclose a capricious, echoing grotto where the nave of a dimly-lighted church was built. Stalactites hang like candelabra from the roof, diluvial corridors run off to the sides filled with ancient ossuaries. Combined with the thrilling legend of a monk who supposedly lived in the grotto with a jaguar, the stunning geology of Lapa rendered it the most favored destination of pious pilgrims who came there from the most distant places. \[19]

49

There'd been a gold rush in the 1650s, just to the south in the State of Minas Gerais. During this gold rush, hordes of poor people from the northeast stopped in Lapa to be blessed for good luck. Since then, the poor and the wretched have continued to come and pray in the cave in hopes of salvation. Many remained permanently. Today Lapa is a major religious center, a poor man's version of Lourdes in France, Fatima in Portugal, or Guadalupe in Mexico.

The penurious state of this community, great poverty everywhere, stuck me like a thunderbolt. Along the river, people lived in hovels, bleak beyond description; streets filled with beggars, naked children, and people with all sorts of disabilities. Only the surreal local cemetery topped it. Poorly kept, the cemetery had a burial box sitting right by the entry gate awaiting its next customer. The local priest who gave us a walking tour of the city explained that infant mortality was a major problem, represented by the numerous small wooden crosses in the far distance.

Although depressing at first, Lapa seemed like a much better place on subsequent visits. With a commercial airport, a hospital, and other features of a larger town, it would serve as a respite from the isolation of Correntina. In addition, the only other Americans that I would have any regular contact with besides Dick lived here. Six of my fellow Volunteers resided full time in Lapa, as well as five others who were stationed there intermittently. Four of these men were six-feet-three or taller so to see them walking down the street together was a real spectacle, especially since most Brazilians averaged five-feet-six.

After spending my first day in the São Francisco Valley in this depressing place, I boarded the commission's four-seater Cessna with Dr. Torres, the regional commission director, for my first glimpse of Correntina, my new home. The Cessna was our primary link for basic necessities, mail, or visitors during the rainy season when roads became virtually impassable pools of mud. The only alternative to Lapa from Correntina was a day-long boat ride. During my eighteen months in Correntina, only two of my fellow project Volunteers would ever come to Correntina by any method other than small aircraft.

As we neared Correntina I could see the landscape change from flat alluvial plains along the muddy São Francisco to a series of valleys and rolling green hills carved out by a dozen beautiful rivers on the eastern end of a vast upland prairie. From the air, the rivers were as blue as the sky from which they appeared to descend. My heart leapt at the sight of the hills and valleys, so reminiscent of my homeland in southeastern Minnesota. After my brief time spent in the shocking deprivation of Lapa, it seemed that I had suddenly transitioned from the portal of hell to the gates of Eden.

The town of Correntina was originally named Nossa Senhora da Glória do Rio das Equás, or Our Glorious Lady of the River of the Mares. Tradition has it that in the late eighteenth century a large rancher to the south lost several prized mares only to find them near my village, hence the name. For a time, the names of both the town and river flowing through it changed from this mouthful of words to something more manageable, Rio Rico, or Rich River, after gold was discovered in the late 1800s. In 1866, the village became the county seat, and by the start of the twentieth century, acquired its current name based on the river's name change to Corrente.

The city of Correntina has an elevation of close to 2000 feet with the surrounding hills reaching up to 2500 feet. Normal altitude range in the São Francisco Valley area is 500–1500 feet. Fifty miles west of Correntina, the terrain transitioned from river valleys to a broad plateau that extended another hundred miles to a great escarpment— *Serra Geral do Goiás*—on the border of the neighboring State of Goiás. More than 20,000 square miles in area, the State of Bahia formed the eastern edge of the vast central savanna plateau of Brazil known as the *Cerrado*. In 1962 this was essentially a no-man's-land with few inhabitants and no towns. [20] One young Brazilian friend once took out a map of South America and drew a straight line through the west of Brazil all the way to the Andes Mountains in Bolivia and on to the Pacific Ocean. Along this line spanning thousands of miles, and bordered in either direction by hundreds of miles, there was not a single village or town. Beyond Correntina, the land was truly vast, and truly remote.

Before landing, I observed from the air Correntina's four major attractions: a series of three water falls, the towering church on the town square, a large school under construction across the river, and the hydro dam complex below the main falls. A quaint sight but access appeared to be limited and challenging, which became quite evident when I realized that the cleared area on the edge of town served as a landing strip that ran up and over a hill. Pilots had to buzz the airstrip before landing so the resident donkeys and cattle could be dispersed by either Jeep or hired boys. The donkeys proved remarkably stubborn. Sometimes the plane would almost touch the hairs on their backs and they wouldn't budge.

The pilot, whom we came to call Wild Bill for his flying antics, maneuvered the plane expertly and was obviously a skilled bush pilot. He reached heroic stature every time he delivered mail or took us somewhere of necessity. The arrival of an airplane was a major event for the community, so by the time we taxied to the edge of town a large crowd met us. Dick and Silvia were on hand, having flown up earlier, along with several local dignitaries such as the mayor and local priest.

After the official greeting, Dr. Torres, Dick, Silvia and I toured the town. Except for the hydro dam complex, where we were housed, I soon discovered that we had essentially entered a life akin to the latter decades of the nineteenth century in America. There were few if any modern appliances and the only medical facility was a walk-in clinic with a single general practitioner. In the entire county of Correntina, there were exactly three motorized vehicles; most travel took place on foot or horseback. Instead of tractors, oxen still hauled materials or worked the fields. The telegraph was the sole form of contact with the outside world, and mail arrived on a sporadic basis, sometimes up to three months after dispatch.

There was little law and order. Most justice had to wait for the arrival of a circuit judge. The local constable received a pittance for pay, compensated primarily through room and board instead. The nearest bank to procure funds sat in Caetité, 165 miles away across three major rivers, one of which was the width of the Mississippi, and the two widest had no bridges.

The commission airplane was the only regional aircraft at our disposal in the event of an emergency. A Presbyterian missionary who had a small plane and lived ten miles from Lapa could be summoned, if he was around. Correntina's airstrip could only be used during daylight hours, and the only form of communication to summon a plane or other type of assistance was the telegraph at the hydro complex, which functioned only during work hours.

This was my new world. A significant degree of culture shock soon set in, making even Três Marias look good. Being fond of euphemisms, our enthusiastic Peace Corps leader, Sargent Shriver, liked to say, "Peace Corps brings an idealist down to earth." [21] This was indeed that moment of epiphany as firm and permanent as the earth beneath my feet.

Undeniably, the gem of Correntina in both beauty and power was the Grande Cachoeira, or Big Falls. In the late 1950s, German engineers built the 11,400-horsepower hydro dam with a current-generating capacity of 4000 kilowatts, expandable to 8,000kW, one of only three such technological wonders within hundreds of miles. When fully operational it supplied electricity to a dozen towns and thousands of people. A canal, roughly fifteen feet deep by twenty feet wide by 660 feet long—more than two football fields—carried water from the flood gates above the falls to the turbine in the power plant. Occasionally, it doubled as a gigantic swimming pool, after snakes and lizards were removed at the end of a long pole, that is.

At the conclusion of our tour, I felt perplexed by the absence of any modern agricultural facility that would have confirmed the purpose of my assignment. The only building that came close, a cotton mill totally bereft of any ginning equipment, sat like a misplaced giant at the end of the airstrip. Its only function during my time in Correntina had to do with a Rockwell Aero Commander dual-engine, six-passenger airplane and a pilot named Ernesto, who flew-in officials from time to time. On takeoff, the Aero Commander would come barreling over the hill, its engines screaming at full throttle, sliding and swerving in the mud and rain, charging at the cotton gin like a giant grizzly bear closing on its prey. At the last possible moment, the airplane would lift off and pull up its wheels, barely clearing the top of the cotton gin. Ernesto told me it was the riskiest landing strip anywhere in Brazil, admitting that there was zero tolerance for error, and the thrill of navigating the sloped airstrip gave him a tremendous rush.

So, the cotton mill yielded no answer to the question of my purpose for being assigned to Correntina. George, our country director, and Dr. Torres, our regional leader, claimed that individual Volunteer placement was outside their areas of authority. As an engineer, Dick was obviously posted to get the hydro dam up and running, and Silvia's healthcare assignment made sense due to the existence of the local health clinic, whereas my presence was a mystery.

Dick, with his technical lingo and a slide rule tied to his belt, truly looked the part of an engineer, just as he claimed. The local male contingent surmised that Silvia—in their made-up fantasy, given her natural beauty and the discovery that she possessed minimal nursing qualifications—was really there as Dick's mistress; possibly the mistress for both Dick and me. The first thoughts of Brazilian men, those with a hedonistic outlook on life, always seemed to run to women and sex. They could not fathom that our government would send us here without accommodations for our sexual desires.

Cohabitation by unmarried male and female Volunteers required significant Peace Corps oversight. How Peace Corps administrators could have allowed it is mind-boggling, since it was something extremely countercultural to predominantly Catholic Brazilians, with their strict dating mores. This would create a serious social problem as well, especially with Brazilian women. Most of the female Volunteers, including Silvia, would eventually be transferred out of the valley.

Unlike both Dick and Silvia, with their blond hair and blue eyes, I did not resemble the Germans, nor did I speak complicated engineer lingo; therefore, I could not be an engineer. So, there must have been some other mysterious purpose for sending me to Correntina. When I explained to the locals that I was a farm boy and had some Peace Corps training in sophisticated aspects of agriculture, I was met with skeptical looks. They well knew that the commission had absolutely zero agricultural capability or presence in Correntina. They also began to wonder how much I really knew about agriculture, since the planting season for traditional crops had started the previous month with the coming of the rains, so there would be little or nothing to do with agriculture for at least a year.

Some concluded that my story was very suspicious, and it stood to reason that I was a CIA agent sent to protect the other two Volunteers. After all, I was young and physically very fit, perhaps even skilled in martial arts for all they knew. Considering Brazilian government propaganda at the time, my being a CIA operative made all the sense in the world. Views would change in time, but local rumors went a long way in influencing how we were approached those early days at Correntina.

I would later be told the CIA story got its roots from Ton Tonio, the Jeep driver for the commission. His real name was Antonio, but he stuttered, so it came out as "Ton Tonio." He was a smug little guy who could barely see over the steering wheel of the Jeep. He looked every bit the part of the cartoon character Speedy Gonzales, and his preferred apparel was a huge hat, shorts, and sandals. His old rickety Jeep was one of only two in town and was anything but speedy. Being the Jeepster in town gave Ton Tonio tremendous stature. Wherever he went, there were usually a dozen kids hanging on his Jeep. He also happened to have one of the only radios in town, so he raced around spreading the news like a local Paul Revere—good or bad, true or untrue. As such, the locals referred to him appropriately as *Boca Motorista*—Motor Mouth.

Maybe Dr. Torres was right after all and the real reason for my placement in Correntina was because I was more of an engineer than I thought. Dick was steeped in the theoretical aspects of engineering but less equipped with the mechanical skills essential to the hydro facility's operation, which is where my capabilities were strongest. Together we made a fine team.

Whether this was indeed the thinking of the Peace Corps brass I would never know. Dick's placement in Correntina was one of the rare location assignments, spot-on from a technical standpoint, that the Peace Corps got right from the get-go. My placement in Correntina would also eventually prove to be a good move, technically. With little definition of job responsibilities from the Peace Corps, and little support from the commission in the first months after our arrival, the hydro dam, with its mechanical workshop, provided an arena for us to create work opportunities early on, and to develop our own resourcefulness in managing exigencies.

8. Like home after all

One of the early directors of the Peace Corps programs in Latin America, Frank Mankiewicz, emphasized the theme of community development as a central focus of the Peace Corps. This premise was built on the experience and success of early programs like ours. According to Mr. Mankiewicz, a Volunteer goes into the indescribably poor slums of Latin cities, or the utterly cutoff villages and "must make immediate visible common cause with the people he is to work with." He went on to say that the Volunteer's "first job is to get to know the people and the setting of their lives; the Volunteer starts building a community." [22]

A community is built of like-minded people and, as with all Volunteers, that would be my challenge in the early days. But in some respects, that challenge was minimized due in large part to a few like-minded individuals who became great assets to my survival and success. These individuals facilitated my integration into this "cutoff village" to the point that I took part in every social, religious, and economic activity, including those of town dignitaries and leaders down to the lowly *sertanejos*—farmers and field hands. They existed as the community of people that in many respects made it seem as if I had never left the small town and rural setting of my youth. A few key figures stood at the heart of my odyssey.

Padre André Berénos was of African descent. He came to Correntina by way of Dutch Guiana. A commanding physical figure in any crowd, Padre stood more than six-foot tall and carried significant heft. While the Church permitted the wearing of white non-liturgical garments for clergy in the sweltering heat of the tropics, Padre always wore a long-sleeved ankle length black cassock and wide brim black pilgrim's hat, with an ever-present white handkerchief in the sleeve to wipe away the constant sweat. When he was not wearing his hat, with his short-cropped hair, he gave one the image of a Buddha lost in the backlands of Brazil.

At age twenty-nine, André Berénos entered the priesthood, and at age thirty-seven he came to pastor his first parishes in Correntina and the neighboring town of Santa Maria, located downriver. I was soon to discover that not only was he a towering figure physically, but also, that he was without peer intellectually, spiritually, and socially in the vast country west of the São Francisco River. From the moment I first stepped off the plane in Correntina until the day I left, he would be the central Brazilian figure in my life.

Padre André spoke excellent English, which helped us to become fast friends and collaborators on numerous projects. In the months ahead, traveling together through the countryside or sitting together by the flowing river, we were always in conversation. He continually impressed me with his quick intelligence, ebullient nature, and avuncular manner. Without his spiritual guidance, cultural insights, and undying support of all I attempted, my experience would have been exceedingly more difficult. It almost seemed as if the hand of God in some miraculous way had led me to this place and to Padre André.

To gloss over the fact that there were rough patches on this journey would be dishonest. I knew my share of loneliness, bad news from home, setbacks in attempts to establish meaningful work, and general struggles in adjusting to the privations of a new culture. It was Padre who helped me traverse these rocky sections along my path with his encouragement and inimitable sense of clerical humor. On my first Sunday in Correntina, I accompanied Padre to church and he had me kneel at the altar with several other community leaders during the service. In his ten-minute homily, he spoke of the Alliance for Progress, the Peace Corps, and President Kennedy, and offered encouragement regarding the wonderful things we were going to do during our time in Correntina.

Reflecting upon my time in the Peace Corps, I often marvel at how a nineteen-year-old youth, who lived a relatively sheltered life before going to Brazil, found the strength to survive emotionally for twenty-one months in a remote and limited setting deprived of physical contact with loved ones.

The answer I believe evolved from three great pillars of my life. The first pillar, my strong religious faith and practice, infused my youth. Finding a religious outlet in Correntina, especially my unique relationship with Padre André, proved crucial. The second pillar, comprised of my close colleagues and my ability to integrate into the community of Correntina through sports, family, and friendships, was also fundamental in my youth. The third pillar of course was my commitment to Millie, the love of my short life up to that point, and her commitment to me. We exchanged more than one hundred letters, and although they were only written words, letter-writing forged a bond strong enough to sustain us during the arduous journey of prolonged separation.

Brazilian society is said to be matrilineal in nature, driven by strong mother figures. This was definitely the case with the Coimbra family, whose members became part of my second pillar away from home. The mother, Dona Maria, was the family's driving force. Whereas my mother was a reserved, poised woman, Dona Maria was convivial and demonstrative, fluttering about like a happy stork whenever you came near. She took the lead in all things related to the family. Dona Maria became a surrogate mother to me and treated me as one of her own for the duration of my stay.

Their family of six boys and three girls fell slightly short of the eleven I was used to back home, but they made life every bit as interesting. Antonio and Adelson were my age and two others, João and Pedro, would become students of mine once I began teaching classes at Padre's school. The eldest daughter was a nun and another daughter was engaged to the mayor's son. But much like my mother, Dona Maria was disappointed that none of her boys had yet opted for the priesthood. In a large Catholic family, this burden was typically relegated to the second son. Dona Maria would badger Antonio—he became my best friend—about this on occasion. I don't think I ever let on to Dona Maria that I was also a second son.

Within weeks of our arrival, both of my Peace Corps colleagues would be summoned to Rio for six weeks of routine training, Dick in elements of Brazilian hydro engineering and Silvia in health care. Although this was the type of in-country training we were supposed to undergo upon arrival, I was not sent. Supposedly the Peace Corps did not deem it beneficial for all three of us to desert the town at once so soon after we'd arrived. In fact, I would receive no further formal training in anything at all.

When Dona Maria discovered I was living away from the city in a house by myself at the hydro complex, she would not stand for it. Most evenings I would go into town to visit and then walk a mile in the dark late at night to my house, encountering dogs and drunks along the way. The local dentist was the worst drunk of all. Whenever I passed by, his dogs awoke him from a drunken stupor, and I'd be obliged to stop for a nip of cheer with him. In time, I heard about his patients. His drill was operated by a foot pump, and his hypodermic needle used to administer analgesics looked like something we used to give shots to cattle back home on the farm. When you saw people around town or at the market wearing a large head bandage, you knew they'd been to the dentist.

Dona Maria remained insistent: either one of her sons would stay at my house during times I chose to remain in the countryside, or I would stay at her house in town. There was no refusing.

The two Coimbra boys, home on holiday, were studying English in Goiânia and had relative facility with the language. They were as keen on improving their English as I was on learning Portuguese, so we would spend many evenings together working on our language proficiency. In our struggles to learn our respective languages, we inevitably made blunders that resulted in bouts of laughter.

One particularly memorable gaffe involved horticulture. The brothers asked me what I'd been doing that particular day, and I quite proudly told them that I was planting bananas in my yard. This was the wrong thing to say. First of all, the trees are *bananeiras*—both the tree and plant—not bananas, the fruit. This prompted the first round of laughter. Second, in Portuguese slang, to say you were planting bananeiras meant to say that you were "standing on your head." I would learn that bananeiras sprout and grow quite naturally, almost anywhere, and that I had a lot to learn about Portuguese slang.

Fine guitarists, the Coimbra boys not only helped me learn how to play this instrument but also made sure I participated in Saturday evening serenades for the young girls in town. I especially admired Adelson. He was left-handed and rather than reverse stringing the guitar, he learned to play all the notes and chords upside down—a very impressive feat. Whenever I saw him playing the guitar upside down I would tell him he was planting bananeiras, as to me it looked very much like standing on one's head.

Anticipating some stretches of boredom, I brought Dad's old trumpet with me to Brazil. Ours was a musical family, so in addition to playing in the local high school band, I played in our family band formed by my father. Once they knew of my trumpet-playing abilities, Dick and Silvia requested that I play for them one evening and invited some of the locals. Silvia told them that I was Harry James, the famous American trumpeter. Although they had no idea who Harry James was, it stuck as my musical stage name during my time in Correntina.

I frequently played with a local brass band that performed on important holidays and, upon request, I did a Harry James Christmas concert. I even portrayed the great trumpeter himself in a local play. All of this was tremendous fun, and when combined with language study, playing cards, serenading the local lassies, and generally socializing in the evenings, I was well on my way to achieving communal acceptance. But soccer would cement my place in Correntina.

Brazilians are as crazy about sports as Americans, with soccer and volleyball at the top of their list. Generally, Brazilians considered Americans to be complete novices who possessed inferior skills and knowledge in both of their national sports. This is where my experience and skill as an athlete became valuable assets. There was a volleyball court at the health clinic compound where people would gather for games on most afternoons once the temperature had cooled and the rain had abated. Initially I was only invited to come and watch. But one day when a player needed to leave I was asked to fill in. At five feet ten, I had the vertical advantage on Brazilians.

Little did they know that I'd played a fair amount of volleyball in high school and college and was quite accomplished at it. As time progressed, my selection by coin flip was replaced by a more straightforward method as teams vied for who would get the gringo that day. If I was tardy, the team that had secured me would send someone looking for me and would refuse to play until I showed up. My athletic prowess also opened another door for me in *futebol*—what we call soccer. There were two semiprofessional teams in Correntina as well as a traveling soccer team selected from the best players. When students like the older Coimbras boys came home for the holidays, there was an annual high-stakes match between the elite traveling team and a team of what they viewed as college brats, rounded out with boys still in school in Correntina.

Because I played volleyball, the college boys asked me if I knew anything about soccer. To their surprise, I replied that while my specialty was American-style football, I indeed had played the game of *futebol* at an intramural level in high school and college, and during Peace Corps training. They conducted tryouts just the same. As a result, they picked me to play fullback, the position right in front of where the opposition would need to score. They told me all I needed to worry about was physically removing any of the speedy little forwards when they approached the goal. Their instruction included some tips on well-disguised tripping maneuvers.

The big contest was finally held before a large crowd of parents and enthusiasts, including Padre André. For the first time in the history of this esteemed match, the underdogs were not miserably beaten but fought back valiantly to a tie. Whether deserving or not, I was toasted as the deciding difference in the match—probably not so much for my footwork skills as for the intimidation and fear factor my presence created for the opposition.

As a result of this soccer match, an emergency meeting was held to decide which of the two town teams I should play on. The team I joined, the Bahia team, won a string of several consecutive victories right up to the last game of the season. We were ahead in the standings, so one of their players feigned an injury and a new player was brought in before this game. Soccer is serious business in Brazil, and this team needed to save face. Many of the locals did not recognize the ringer, a guy named João. Now João is such a common name in Brazil that it is used as a generic moniker for strangers. In the United States, we holler, "Hey you!" In Brazil, they holler, "Hey João!"

Wherever this João came from, he evened the playing field. Since I was the middle defender on our team, João became their center on offense. He was six feet tall and about two hundred pounds with no teeth, thank God. His feet were the size of canoe paddles, and he wore no shoes. He was anything but nimble, but it didn't matter. His sole purpose was to run interference and shadow me as brutally as he could. My shins bore the brunt of that.

It was not that I couldn't handle this giant. I had played defensive cornerback and safety at Minnesota State College. It was not uncommon for a 250-pound guard to charge top speed at me as he led a running back around the end. My job was to take on the block so a teammate could have a clear shot at tackling the ball carrier. The current predicament, however, was not to handle João physically, even if I wanted to do so, but to engage in something called diplomacy.

I fought my instincts concerning his odious behavior and took the high road. Each time he knocked me down, I picked myself up off the ground and gave him a little pat on the back. Normally this would be enough to get an opponent to be a good sport and back off. Not João. He appeared to be rather obtuse; he obviously knew little of diplomacy, nor did he care. We lost the match 3–2.

My primary mission as a Volunteer was to spread goodwill and show the best side of what Americans could be. No matter the material accomplishments we may have brought to the region, we as Volunteers would be remembered forever for our grit and sportsmanship. It was all part of the diplomatic game and the mission of the Peace Corps. On this basis, I personally came out the big winner in the match. I got a rousing cheer from the local fans when I left the field, and for weeks afterwards whenever I met people on the street they would bring up the unfairness of the match and offer their sympathies.

I played for a second season with the Bahia team and felt honored to be selected for the all-star Correntina traveling team. This action again led to a minor diplomatic snafu. Correntina's most heated rivalry was with the town of Santa Maria at the confluence of the Formoso and Corrente Rivers, twenty-five miles to the east. The Santa Maria team had heard about my athletic prowess and alleged that I was a ringer since I was not officially listed on the Correntina team roster when league matches first started and the big game with Santa Maria was played.

It is possible the Correntina boys got a little too cocky looking to spring a secret weapon in the match. Unlike other news in this isolated area, soccer news traveled at the speed of light. The Santa Maria lads won their claim and I was off the team, which deepened the schism between the towns. On a later occasion when Padre attended a game, he chastised the Santa Maria team by saying he had heard that Volunteers were coming to Santa Maria in the near future and he hoped they would be treated better. This was an embarrassment to the players, especially coming from someone as revered as Padre.

Sometime later a gentleman named Wilson tried mightily to recruit me for the Santa Maria team for the 1964 season. Wilson was the director at the Colônia do Formoso, an agricultural colony of the commission south of Santa Maria on the Formoso River. There were actually some commission agricultural capabilities there; they even had two American Allis-Chalmers tractors. One tractor had never seen work in a field, as it simply served as a parts resource for the other. Wilson had gone so far as to petition Dr. Torres to have me transferred there, citing the fact there was no agricultural capability of the commission in Correntina.

By this time, I wanted to stay put and indicated that the Peace Corps would not permit my leaving. This was a bit of a white lie. At that point, thirty of my fellow project Volunteers had moved locations once, twenty-nine had moved locations twice, and seven had relocated three or more times. Wilson never gave up trying. I would spend some time in the colony later and we would become great friends.

My desire to stay in Correntina developed from these many positive experiences. My life became interwoven with the fabric of the community life there. Over time Brazilian friends would say to me, "*Você é mais Brasileiro do que os Brasileiros.*"—You are more Brazilian than the Brazilians. This was an enormous compliment. When a new group of Volunteers came to the valley in 1964, the regional leader in Santa Maria, Pat, paid tribute to me in a Peace Corps newsletter called the *Triangle* by writing that my fame as a troubadour and soccer player had spread throughout the region. I was truly blessed.

9. Open-air confessions

t didn't take long for the relationships and social activities in my new environs to create a constancy that permeated every aspect of my day-to-day life in Correntina. For someone who grew up on a dairy farm where seven-day work weeks were the norm fifty-two weeks of the year, this sort of constancy was not a new concept for me. Rather, a routine that included less work was new to me.

In Correntina people worked just five days a week. What's more, this was the land of Carnival, and the celebrations of all kinds of holidays. These included not only traditional familiar national holidays, but also holidays for the births or deaths of particular saints, some I had barely even heard of. Along with these holidays there was also the declaration of national holidays for the death of important national, international, or religious figures. All of this added an average of another thirty days of leisure to the yearly schedule, far more than I knew on our dairy farm.

The cultural phenomenon that took some getting used to was Saturday market days. As a young boy back home on the farm, Saturdays were the busiest day of the week, especially during the school year. The major task that consumed our Saturdays was barn-cleaning. It was the day to freshen up the housing of the pigs, chickens, and the milk and beef cattle. Most certainly it was not a day to go shopping. But this was Correntina, where Saturdays meant folks would dress in their finest and head for town carrying their wares. Some rose as early as four thirty in the morning to walk sometimes up to ten miles to get to town. The marketplace became in large measure the laboratory where I would come to know the people and their culture and develop the relationships that would become cornerstones of later successes. Over the course of two years, I would travel many miles on foot or by horseback through these valleys with the people I met at the market on Saturdays.

In Brazil people are classified per the census as *branco*—white, *amarelo*—yellow, *preto*—black, or *pardo*—mixed black—ancestry. Across Brazil, slightly more than fifty percent of people typically claim to be *preto* or *pardo*. In the border country between the São Francisco valley and the Central Highlands was an area settled by a different breed of men primarily of the *pardo* race, known as Brazilian bandits. Thus, Correntina was located in what was known as bandit country.

In *Os Sertões,* Cunha describes a race of men who sprung from the *vaqueiros*—cowboys—of the northeast, known as *jagunços,* as follows: 'From the Vaqueiro with his athletic build there sprang the fearless being the Jagunços. Imagine the Vaqueiro's titanic frame suddenly endowed with the tremendous nervous energy of the Bandeirante and you have the Jagunços." [23] The jagunços were bands of mercenaries or private militia employed by *fazendeiros*—large ranchers—as vigilantes to control runaway slaves, or to war with other landowners in disputes over land. Cunha went on to write that the entire valley of the *Rio das Equas*—the Corrente Valley—"constituted the original home land of the bravest and most useless individuals, jagunços, our country possesses." [24]

For a farm boy growing up in an area where families were primarily descendants of white European immigrants, this amalgamation of mixed races and socioeconomic classes was an eye-opening experience. It would be principally at the market on Saturdays where I would come to meet the fazendeiros, the *sertanejos*—sharecroppers—the vaqueiros, and yes, some of the remnants of the feared jagunços.

One of the great challenges at the market was getting to know and remember peoples' names. As time went on and I built relationships, people would greet me at the market and it was nearly impossible to remember all their names; there were far too many Josés, Joãos, Antonios. Also, many of the peasants had no idea what their last names were. The market generally opened by six in the morning and by noon it began to shut down because of the heat. Many of the younger men hit the gin mills, and it was not unusual to have a series of fights and disturbances in the afternoon. The blood of the jagunços still ran thick. On occasion injuries from knife fights would occur, and several times one or more of the participants would show up at our door seeking medical assistance.

Saturday was indeed the big day of the week in Correntina and I rarely missed the market unless I was away. The second biggest day was Sunday, the day for spiritual enrichment and some form of sport or relaxation. I routinely started my Sundays off with attendance at Mass when Padre was in town. Like the marketplace on Saturdays, church was a center for social interaction in the town, so my attendance there greatly enhanced my stature and aided my integration into the community.

While I enjoyed attending Mass, Padre continued to insist that there always be a place for me to kneel at the altar with the town elders or in the front row where he could personally serve me communion. To receive communion, one needed to be free of sin. If I refused communion, therefore, Padre would obviously know something was afoul, and that I would need to confess my sins.

The practice of this sacrament differed tremendously from my home church in Minnesota. Back home, I entered a dark, enclosed, closet-type structure, generally in the bowels of a church, with the priest hidden behind a screen. Not so at Padre's church. The confessional consisted of Padre sitting on a chair contraption with a bench to its side on the front steps of the church building in full view of everyone, which seemed practical in this climate. Padre liked to joke that this style of confession posed no physical barrier for direct communication with the Lord, and the fresh air made for greater consciousness and remembrance of deeply hidden sins.

This sort of *plein air* confession was a two-sided coin of comfort and discomfort. Although more comfortable physically because of the heat, it was very uncomfortable socially and personally because of the crowds. The world of parishioners milled outside the church, waiting until the last minute to enter due to hot conditions inside. Any transgressions confessed to Padre would be well within earshot of dozens of people. Padre often asked, when did I next plan to show up for confession. I told him the fear of confessing in public would assure my adherence to the straight and narrow path while I was in Brazil. I never did take advantage of his offer to confess.

Brazil was the most populous Catholic country in the world, and Catholicism was Brazil's unofficial national religion. Consequently, the Church carried a lot of influence, along with the landed gentry, who controlled politics, and the military. One area of its influence extended to holidays. Certain religious holidays were not only observed by the church but were observed as national holidays, something unheard of in the United States. This applied locally, too, with observances of the priest's birthday and date of his ordination, as well as that of the Bishop and even the birthdays of saints who may have had relevance to the name of the town or some obscure event.

There were also days of pageantry, generally three-day affairs, such as São João Day—Saint John Day, *Bumba de Boi*—Honoring of the Ox, and the *Festa das Virgins*—Festival of the Virgins. For example, during one stretch in June, counting the four weekend days, there were at least twelve consecutive holidays: The Festival of the Virgins and the official days of mourning for Pope John XXIII, both three-day affairs; the Day of Lovers, Brazil's equivalent of Valentine's Day; The Feast of Corpus Christi; and the Festival of St. John. Although extreme, strings of similar holidays throughout the calendar year became the norm.

When to work or not work and which saints to honor or not honor became a major challenge but one I had to master if I were to avoid the sin of not marking a religious day by compulsory church attendance. And since I was dead set on sidestepping confession, master it I would.

10. A useful enterprise

Speaking on the subject of newcomers to foreign service, the noted author and humanitarian Norman Cousins identified the inherent challenge as a dichotomy of worlds. "At first there would be the full flush of exciting response to a powerful new experience ... conditioned by a society of abundance, the newcomers would be plummeted out of the sky into an area where the primary mystery of life is not how it originated but how it is sustained." Many workers suffered what he called "compassion fatigue" or "conscience sickness," and the secret he gave to overcoming it lay in a worker's ability to attach themselves to a "useful enterprise." He added that "their highly developed skills will be meaningless unless their emotional and philosophical equipment is right for the job." [25]

My rapid integration into the social structure of the community was probably atypical. First, I found the local people to be very socially oriented and receptive toward me and Americans in general, and eager to know more about our culture. Also, there were several major factors that accelerated and sustained this process: I was a Catholic in a highly Catholic country; I had a love of sports and capabilities to go with it in a culture where those traits were admired; and I enjoyed and practiced music and engaged in social activities. In addition, coming from a large family, I possessed the ability to integrate easily into family activities and with fellow Volunteers.

Despite my strong start in this foreign land and culture, I knew if I were to thrive on a long-term basis, I would need to find a useful enterprise that would provide a sense of purpose as to why I believed I was there. Everything in my basic nature screamed out that despite all the problems and misdirection suffered in the launch of our project, I would strive to live out a meaningful mission by working to improve local agricultural practices.

In order to achieve this and affect positive change, I would need to pass on knowledge not only in an understandable way but also in a convincing manner through a second-language. Many of the people I would be interacting with were illiterate. They spoke a form of Portuguese composed of a hodgepodge of formal elements combined with colloquialisms.

I spent much time during the first several months surveying the area and improving my language capabilities as best I could. Saturdays at the market provided critical exposure to the local vernacular. I asked our Peace Corps leadership for any economic information the U.S. Embassy might have on the area. They replied that there was none. My inquiry, however, prompted USAID to express interest in collecting such information on the county of Correntina, the sixth-largest county in the state of Bahia covering some 7,000 square miles, and asked if we might put a report together.

Over the next few months, Silvia and I collected the following information: physical characteristics of the region, population profiles, education and health statistics, infrastructure, and extensive review of the economy, which was mostly agriculture-based. Our work yielded some remarkable discoveries in all these areas.

In health and education, the statistics were pretty bleak. The last census to provide a breakdown on education had been conducted in 1948. It listed only 116 people as formally educated. Of these, 104 men and women had elementary educations, five women had secondary educations, and seven men had advanced degrees. [26] Since the 1950s, however, significant progress had been made, and by the time I arrived, there were two dozen or more elementary schools in the county. Padre André's school covered elementary through junior high school grades.

Healthcare remained an area of need. The infant mortality rates were above fifty percent and intestinal and digestive disturbances caused many other deaths. Trachoma was also a major problem among children. Several traditional diseases such as malaria, Chagas disease, typhoid, and respiratory diseases seemed to be under reasonable control through the efforts of the local state health clinic. There were no surgeons in the area, and the mortality rate among women due to childbirth-related difficulties was significant.

I remember well an instance soon after my arrival in Correntina that occurred while visiting Pedro Guerra, the town pharmacist. I accompanied him to the back room in his pharmacy across the street from his house where on a wooden table I witnessed my first death in the area. A woman had just given birth and was hemorrhaging. Narinha, Pedro's oldest daughter and a trained midwife, assisted with the birth. Lacking proper knowledge and techniques for birth control, a practice opposed by the church, the dying woman had borne eight children, one every year. It was a gut-wrenching experience to witness the sobs and wailing of her husband and older children who had gathered. With no surgical facility or doctor, they all knew, well before I had given it much thought, what the eventual outcome would be.

It was not unusual in the countryside to encounter motherless families of ten or more children. These children were typically dispersed among relatives to be raised or made to work as house servants or field hands for people who were willing to minimally feed and clothe them. I would spend a great deal of time at the farm of a bachelor friend named Quinn who supported his mother, aunt, and five orphans.

The issue of infant mortality would be one of the most depressing aspects of life in Brazil. As I travelled the back country through many hamlets that dotted the county, I saw small graveyards filled with tiny wooden crosses for children who had died. Early in my travels, I visited a farm where a robust baby girl was crawling on the dirt floor of the house, with chickens and the family dog roaming through the dwelling. During another visit a few weeks later, I did not see little Maria and inquired about her as she seemed to be the family's pride and joy. The mother told me that Maria was with the *anjos*—angels now. I naively asked if these were neighbors or where it was they lived as I didn't know them. She looked at me a bit puzzled and pointed to the sky, saying little Maria had joined those *anjos* a few days before.

Another disconcerting revelation to me was Chagas disease, known as the "kissing bug disease" because the insects that transmit the disease emerge at night to feed on sleeping people's faces, especially near the mouth and nose. The disease can cause deterioration of the nervous system and enlargement of the heart muscle, eventually leading to heart failure. A person can literally drop over dead at any moment from this disease, an event I actually witnessed on a couple occasions. When someone fell over dead, folks just looked at the victim and said, "The Chagas must have got him."

I was more encouraged in the realm of agriculture, which is what I focused on while doing the economic study for USAID. After all, agriculture was the main economic engine in the county with eighty-three percent of the respondents listing it as their primary occupation. Many of them were vaqueiros, which made sense given there were about as many cows in the county as there were people. [27]

Rice, beans, and manioc, the principal crops, were staple foods. Bananas, mangos, papayas, goiabas, and oranges figured heavily in the agricultural output. Sugarcane was abundant and used for sweets, drinks, and to produce rum whiskey. Some corn was grown for animal feed. Eggs, milk, cheese, and butter were available but limited. As for vegetables, only squash was listed in any existing statistics as an agricultural product of the county. [28]

The dearth of vegetables presented me with an opportunity for agricultural impact at the local level. Family gardens could be developed as small-scale enterprises, providing healthier diets, year-round protein, and supplemental income, especially with the number of rivers in the area to provide irrigation. The biggest obstacles would be lack of seed supply, lack of pesticides to control a large enemy insect population, and minimum horticultural knowledge among the natives.

This would take some serious time and planning—and all the farm boy I had in me—to successfully tackle the challenge.

While I was busy with my assessments, Dick spent his time analyzing what was and was not working with the hydro generator plant. I spent time at the installation becoming familiar with workshop equipment: various welders, grinders and lathes similar to what we had back on the farm. This shop would become the catalyst that allowed us to move ahead on a variety of projects that had been stalled due to needed repair or lack of parts, some of which we could fashion with this equipment. It also served as a crucial element in maintaining our transportation needs.

Due to our hectic arrival in the country and other mismanagement, six months passed before we received the Jeep that had been promised us upon arrival. Once we got one, we quickly became reliant on it. The roads were notoriously unreliable, even for such roadworthy vehicles as Jeeps. On practically every trip, the leaf springs would break in one or more of the Jeep's four suspension points. The nearest place to take any vehicle for repair or to buy new parts was four hundred miles away. Therefore, we would have to remove the springs periodically and separate them, then grind, bevel, weld, and regrind them. Finally, we had to reassemble the set and remount them on the Jeep. This process usually took several hours. During our stay in Correntina, we would perform this procedure at least two dozen times, to the point where some springs looked like a continuous series of welds. Our little shop became the envy of the community where we fashioned parts to fix the school sewing and washing machines, the church organ, the doctor's record player, and other items.

In the first couple months, various workshop projects kept us occupied both physically and mentally. The most challenging of these had to do with the defunct water system in the hydro complex. When the dam was being constructed, officials were not fond of hauling water from the river so they installed a water system at the hydro plant, and water pipes to various parts of the city. But the system was inoperable since the electric motor and the pump were neither properly wired nor properly aligned. The pieces all existed, but no water flowed.

The commission did not have the wherewithal to send someone to rectify the situation. So, over time we built new alignment platforms connecting appropriate units, and then rewired the pumping station both to prevent outages as well as for safety in a wet environment. If locals were oblivious to the dangers of electricity, they were even less in tune to the fact that the combination of electricity and water could be deadly. After a few weeks, we finally got the water flowing to the city. You would have thought the two of us were Moses and had just parted the Red Sea. After we turned on the power and water, little could tarnish our image with the locals.

Our second project involved our good friend, Padre. In addition to spreading holiness among the masses, Padre was a sagacious fellow, first-class entrepreneur, and arm-twisting salesman who had a knack for acquiring needed resources. For example, he had somehow obtained a collection of parts for a saw mill, though none of the denizens of the surrounding area had the knowledge or capability to understand the source or extent of the local mill's functions. During these early months, we spent many hours repairing various components of the mill or fashioning new parts to make it operational. Growing up back home in a land of hardwood forests proved invaluable for a project involving timber-cutting machinery.

Another exhilarating discovery we made at the hydro dam was a large grader sitting in the weeds. The grader had been used to build a road and openings in the cerrado for transmission of electricity from Correntina to Santa Maria and on to Lapa. The sight of the grader evoked visions of leveling fields for irrigation or building and improving roads in the countryside. The only problem was that it needed two new tires, some engine parts, and required a lot of nonexistent diesel fuel. We worked on the grader when we could, but it would be fifteen months before we got it totally operational.

In the midst of gathering information for the USAID report, working on mechanical projects with Dick, and managing a busy social schedule filled with volleyball, soccer, and Portuguese lessons, the inevitable happened. One warm, pleasant evening, I suddenly felt chills. It wasn't long before I was in bed with a fever of 105 degrees and the onset of delirium. This would last through the entire night and leave me in a severely weakened state for a week. My condition deteriorated to the extent that my colleagues fetched the local clinical doctor, who usually did not make house calls, especially on rain-drenched evenings. Dick also visited the telegraph operator early the next morning to persuade him to get the commission plane to transport me to the hospital in Lapa, but there was no plane to be had—it was away for repairs. This was probably the first time all of us realized that serious illness or injury here could be fatal.

Feeling my condition was quite serious, my Peace Corps mates alerted Padre. Silvia, a Protestant, told Dick she recalled that Catholics practiced Last Rites, blessing for the dying known as Extreme Unction. Padre came by and thought I appeared to be on the mend but said he would be at my beck and call if things became worse.

This all led to a bit of comic relief. During a conversation about religion weeks earlier, Dick had professed to Padre that he was agnostic. The two men then engaged in a running, light-hearted dialogue over religion throughout the length of our stay in Correntina. On this particular occasion, Dick sardonically asked Padre what the consequences would be if I truly needed Extreme Unction and did not get it. Padre explained that according to the laws of the church, if an individual knew about Extreme Unction and was in the presence of someone close to death but did not notify a Priest, such negligence would constitute a mortal sin. Padre told Dick, who found practicing the sacrament of Confession on the front steps of the church on Sundays to be a hoot, that if he had not summoned him to perform last rites in my situation, Dick surely would have been obliged to confess open-air style or he would have risked losing his soul. Their joint hilarious laughter was the best medicine I received that day. A week later Dr. Ken, the Peace Corps doctor, arrived and diagnosed my malady as a serious case of acute dysentery.

Just as things were beginning to seem bleak with the combination of my illness and daily torrential rains, we received what seemed to be an endless stream of visitors. The first two were Leo, our new project director, and Dr. Ken. Leo turned out to be an enthusiastic and capable leader. On this particular visit, he came to proclaim that he was there to solve problems and to salvage what was a sinking rat ship when he got the job. Having just come on board, Leo had no idea what I was supposed to be doing in Correntina when I discussed this with him. He did, however, like the CIA agent story the locals had concocted for me but agreed we should let that die.

A few days later, our area Volunteer leader arrived. We always referred to him by his middle name, Clyde, since it seemed to fit his pedantic disposition so well. At that time, he was racing around the valley trying to keep Volunteers from leaving, which proved ironic about a month later when he and his wife would throw in the towel and head home. Clyde had come from Barreiras to the north and had the lovely Ginger with him. Ginger was the nurse from Texas who so infatuated the Bahia Militia during their visit looking for the plow thief. Ginger was finding it difficult to fit in at the hospital and life in Barreiras and was contemplating heading home. Clyde, in an attempt to possibly reverse her despondency, suggested she come to Correntina and spend some time with Silvia.

I recovered from dysentery just in time for my first Thanksgiving in the tropics. Although we were already getting the drift that there were more holidays than we cared for, our new local friends, especially the young friends from the volleyball and soccer teams, insisted that we tell them all about Thanksgiving. They thought it imperative that we celebrate it for tradition's sake, as a welcome to Ginger, and for the fact that I was still among the living. They knew that Thanksgiving and turkey went hand in hand, so they went and scared up a turkey for our chefs, Silvia and Ginger, to cook up.

The rainy season had started a month before, so any feed a turkey was getting was not corn and grain but rather any available garbage. This being the case, the natives engaged in a strange pre-slaughter ritual. Knowing the meat would be tougher than nails, it was important that the tom not go into constriction when he had his head cut off. Also, they thought the old bird should not suffer unnecessarily.

To accomplish these goals, the locals administered a sufficient dose of a local elixir used to solve all ills, known officially as *cachaça*. But just as we refer to whiskey as hooch, moonshine, or white lightning, the most common term for this sugarcane-based brew was *pinga*. Whenever I traveled in the countryside and wherever I stopped, the first thing offered was a shot of cachaça with the invitation, *"Quer provar?"*—Would you like to try it? On good advice, I concocted several good excuses for never accepting the offer.

Cachaça was also used for medicinal purposes, but sometimes it backfired. Around town, in the market, and out in the countryside, it was not unusual to see a significant number of blind people, especially young children. When children came down with the flu, the poor used a shot of cachaça as their medicine of choice to break a fever since it was affordable to them. Unfortunately, if the distilling process went bad the brew turned to methanol alcohol, which could potentially destroy the optic nerve, especially in young children. In the end, I suspect the old turkey felt no pain and never saw the axe coming, whereas I passed on the Cachaça to save my eyes. It was a memorable Thanksgiving.

A few days after Thanksgiving, the commission pilot, Wild Bill, flew into town to take Ginger back to Barreiras at Clyde's direction. Being the one who pulled the strings, Clyde had decided that one week in Correntina was long enough for Ginger, though she disagreed. She found both Correntina and the company of another American woman greatly preferable to her life in Barreiras. As for Wild Bill, he showed up as Romeo reincarnated in a dashing leather jacket—although a jacket was hardly necessary because it was rarely less than eighty degrees in Correntina—shades, and a silk scarf, giving him all the aura of the infamous pilot, the Red Baron. His debonair style and suave lingo were honed to perfection so as to melt the defenses of almost any young lady.

Ginger's resistance to the trip obviously thwarted Wild Bill's best-laid plans to impress and endear her with some of his showy aerobatics. When Ginger insisted she was not leaving, Wild Bill begrudgingly confessed that Clyde had suggested I accompany him on the trip since it was essentially a mail run anyway. Seeing his look of disappointment, I wasn't completely sure I wanted to make the trip with a dejected pilot.

I did make the trip and was able to spend the next week in Barreiras with Volunteer Jim whose training was also in agriculture. Jim, with Ginger temporarily in Correntina, was by himself in Barreiras. Ginger would eventually leave the program and go home. Jim would later be joined by a Volunteer from the Brazil I team who transferred to our group. Since he transferred from the south of Brazil, which is Gaucho country, to keep them distinguished in our conversation once he arrived, we would call him Gaucho Jim. The original Jim in Barreiras was from Rochester, New York, and also was the project clown. Thus, he became Rochester Jim, aptly named after both his hometown and the American comedian Jack Benny's sidekick, Rochester.

Barreiras was a town of 10,000 inhabitants located in a large agricultural valley along the Rio Grande River, where there was a commission agricultural station staffed by two agronomists. We spent several days at the facility doing mechanical work. Rochester Jim had informed the locals that I was an excellent mechanic, news they received gladly since they'd struggled for over a week to assemble a new plow that mounted onto the American-made Allis Chalmers tractor. It was easy to see what the problem was. They only had metric tools, which were not compatible with the American-manufactured parts. Besides the lack of proper tools, the instruction manuals were useless to them since they were not printed in Portuguese. Almost without exception, equipment manuals supplied instructions in the language of the country of the manufacturer. Dick and I would encounter the same situation later when we worked with electrical generators in the Correntina area. The term *jeito* is a handy word in Brazil that more or less means to find a way or come up with a solution, usually through trial and error. They were quite inventive and imaginative and would come up with some type of fix. Now it was my time to work a jeito.

With its agricultural station, modern equipment, and ample seed supply, Barreiras was a desirable station to be assigned to. During my week there, we visited a couple of modern farms with irrigation and spent time with the two agronomists, learning much about Brazilian agriculture. The market in Barreiras was twice the size of that in Correntina. We even had the opportunity to take a long hike, miles from town, where we found an ultra-modern airfield in the middle of nowhere with not a soul in sight, another mirage-type facility in a vast, remote land, much like the hydro installation in Correntina. If someone had told me it was a landing site for a spaceship, I would have believed him. In fact, it was a modern airstrip built in the early 1940s by the U.S. Army Corps of Engineers as a fueling stop to ferry troops to the war in North Africa.

Wild Bill showed up in the commission plane unexpectedly one day and said he was there to fetch me. We were to go to the town of Caetité to open bank accounts. We stopped in Correntina only long enough to pick up Dick and Silvia, and for me to retrieve some fresh clothes before flying on to Lapa to spend the night and then proceed to Caetité.

Bill had tutored me on the basics of flying the plane while traveling back from Barreiras. On the way to Caetité, to my pleasant surprise, Wild Bill asked me to take over the controls for a while. I soon discovered snoozing was not his real objective. Wild Bill was interested in devoting his energy to making time with Silvia. Then on the way back to Lapa, Wild Bill decided to entertain us and, better yet, impress Silvia by doing some wild figure eights with the plane. Again, since we had Silvia with us, the Brazilian machismo kicked in and even though we pleaded that we were not interested in his maneuvers, he proceeded to execute them anyway. It was a breathtaking experience, but there would be worse to come in the days ahead.

I returned from my first real hiatus away from Correntina flush with cash and excited to be back home with my new friends on the first day of Brazilian summer, a new season. The incessant rains continued and most of the local activity centered on getting ready for Christmas. Padre slaughtered a few head of cattle on his farm and distributed the meat to the poor. It was also the anniversary of his ordination and the Feast of the Immaculate Conception, so these holidays gave us lots of down time. There was a lavish party and dance to celebrate the recent engagement of two of my great newfound friends, the mayor's son Adherbal and Yvonne Coimbra of my Brazilian surrogate family. Almost two months to the day after arriving in Brazil, I received my first mail from home. As nice as it was to finally hear from my family, receiving their letters during the Christmas season left me with strong feelings of nostalgia.

In Brazil, I would discover that Christmas was not the same family celebration it was in the United States. Exchanging gifts was not a big deal, neither was the religious celebration, caroling, nor any of that. I had previously fixed the organ in the church, so there were a few songs at midnight Mass. Afterward I played a medley of Christmas tunes on my trumpet at our house for my fellow Volunteers, workers at the hydro dam, and some friends.

On Christmas Day, we had our own little American celebration at home with Silvia putting together as traditional a meal as possible. A few days earlier, Dick and I had repaired a refrigerator for a grocer in town and to show his appreciation he presented us with a turkey, so now Christmas would be somewhat complete.

After dinner, we exchanged gifts. I gave Silvia a bottle of Gilbeys Gin that I had purchased earlier in Barreiras and she was absolutely ecstatic, so much so that by the end of the day, like the turkey on Thanksgiving, she was feeling little or no pain.

Silvia made a bib for me—not sure I was all that sloppy—upon which she had knitted the words "Kenny Weeder Seeder," along with the image of some corn plants. For Dick, she made one with "Dick the Dynamic Dam Builder" knit into it, and a little amp meter stitched onto it as well. Dick gave me a machete to fight my way through the bush in the countryside, and in turn I presented him with tools I had found in Barreiras that he could use at the hydro installation.

To honor the occasion, we jointly composed a Christmas poem to alleviate our nostalgia. In large measure, it summarized the end of our first calendar year in Correntina.

It's Christmas in our little corner of the world,
In the industrial center of southwest Bahia,
Land of promises, plows, pugilists, pump houses,
Pão—bread, Pluto—the dog, pinga—moonshine, and possibilities,

What more could we ask from our little corner of the world?

We don't have Saks Fifth Avenue,
>   but we don't have anyone to shop for,
We may not receive any gifts from home,
>   but we didn't send any,
We don't have a Christmas tree,
>   but we do have a henpecked garden and two bananeiras.
We don't have Bing Crosby singing "White Christmas," but
We have Merrill (Dick) singing, "Down by the Old Mill Stream,"
We don't have snow and ice, but we've got mud and rain.
We don't have Aunt Jane (Dick's good cook aunt)
>   but we have a Betty Crocker cookbook,
We don't have Santa Claus or a chimney, but Papa Noel
Will come in the door if he can get past Pluto.
We may not have candy canes or cookies,
>   but we have a drunken turkey.
We may not have our friends or family but we have each other:
Pluto, Paulo (diminutive Commission manager), the Motorista (the
stuttering Commission Jeep driver), chickens, termites, roaches,
spiders and Raid (our pet Duck).
So drink a toast with Brazilian coffee
left over after exports to the U.S.
Aren't you glad that Christmas is here?
And that it comes but once a year!

Thus ended an incredible year and first few months in Brazil. The year was capped off with a graduation at Padre's school and a play; I provided trumpet music at both events by request. They loved my performance of our traditional processional song, *Pomp and Circumstance*, which was a first at a local graduation. We enjoyed a small New Year's Eve party at our house even though the festivities were interrupted by a blown fuse. Dick crawled up in the attic to replace it only to be stung by a scorpion. We immediately summoned the doctor, who administered a shot, but Dick would be out of commission for a couple of days. Somehow it seemed like a fitting end to the year and a reminder that plenty of challenges lay ahead.

11. An adventurous year

The New Year got off to a somewhat dismal start. One morning, Wild Bill came roaring in for a mail drop, which was usually a highlight, but unfortunately the delivery included bad news for all three of us. My mother's letter told me of the sudden passing of Millie's father in early December at fifty-three years of age. It was one of the most helpless feelings I have ever experienced in my life. I could not run to a telephone and call her, and a letter would take weeks to arrive. Dick received news that his favorite uncle died a few weeks before, and Silvia found out that her best friend back home was dying of bone cancer. She would most likely never see her again. It was times like these when we felt the distance from home most sharply.

This was one of the great moments of soul searching and loneliness for me as a nineteen-year-old farm boy. After all the turmoil of our arrival in Brazil—being placed in a location with no job definition or support, my recent bout with severe sickness, and my mates soon to leave for Rio de Janeiro for extended weeks of training— I would be alone in the backlands. Two-thirds of the almost thirty Volunteers that would eventually leave the project early had already called it quits, many for lesser reasons than I faced. If there was ever a time for me to throw in the towel, this was it.

I immediatcly sat down and wrote a letter to Millie concerning the sudden death of her dad.

"Millie, I received the bad news. It is bothering me so much I cannot think straight … if there is anything I can do to help please let me know. If it means going home now, I will gladly do it for you. Whatever happens in this world, you come first. I guess I was a fool to leave home now and throw away everything."

Neither Millie nor my parents had yet heard anything from me. In a letter dated December 25th, which I received some weeks after Christmas, Millie told me about her dad dying at home, alone with her. Tragically, this came just four years after the sudden death of Millie's youngest sister at age eight. In spite of the trauma, Millie encouraged me to stay and finish the Peace Corps mission, something we agreed was important to both of us. She believed our writing could sustain our love, and our relationship, over the remaining months.

Adding to all of this drama, Millie mentioned that my parents had received a startling call from Washington just days after her dad's death. Fortunately, the call turned out to be good news. The State Department informed them that I had arrived safely in Brazil. Millie said she had been reading news accounts of several plane crashes in Brazil. Given the fact that no Peace Corps families had heard of our whereabouts since departing in October, someone must have persuaded the government to take action and inform families.

Millie said, "If it had been bad news, I would have wished to die myself."

Despite losing her dad, Millie concluded the letter with a bit of levity: "I am so worried that something will happen to you, like getting too tan. Different ones here ask me how you like it there and I tell them you are crazy about the place and plan to stay. So please don't live up to what I am telling everyone. You are in my prayers every night."

Reading that, I surely was not going to tell her about Ernesto taking off in the Aero Commander inches above the cotton gin.

But there were bright spots. Dick got word that he was to attend a short seminar on hydro development in Rio. Then our good buddy Ton Toni, the *commission motorista*, who had been downriver in Santa Maria, brought back a trunk from the United States Information Service, USIS, filled with almost a hundred books, including classics like *Huckleberry Finn, Tom Sawyer, Gone with the Wind*, and *War and Peace*—all translated into Portuguese. Since I'd read most of them in English, they would be a great aid in improving my Portuguese. This trove of literature would also be a start of the first library I would eventually establish in the county. More trunks arrived in the following days, filled mostly with work supplies and kitchen tools we'd shipped from the United States over three months earlier. Life was improving.

When Dick returned from his seminar, he brought a German engineer with him who resided in Brazil but worked for the German company Siemens, whose turbine and generator were installed at the hydro facility. He would be the first of a memorable cast of characters that paraded through our lives early that year. We were grateful for their visits because they broke up the monotony of the mundane routine we'd established by working on the water station, continuing repairs on the saw mill, and inventorying everything that might be needed for the hydro dam and the electrical network in town.

After the German arrived and settled into the house directly across the road from us, he joined us for dinner. He was quite an interesting chap, around sixty years of age, with typical Germanic features of blond hair and blue eyes. He would not be the first German we would encounter in the backlands of Brazil. He always wore sunglasses and kept his window shutters closed. World War II had ended less than two decades earlier, and widespread rumors hinted that former Nazis fled Germany to hide in South America, particularly Argentina and Brazil. So naturally we were suspicious about this secretive German. The man loved to chat and tell stories, but he never offered any information about Germany, the war, or his background or family. We eventually concluded that it was best not to ask.

No love was lost between him and the Brazilians at the hydro installation, including the manager Paulo Pimento. The German detested all of them, viewing them as lazy and incompetent. As for the Brazilians, they hated when the German came to town because of his imperious and pedantic behavior. This included to some extent Dick, whose knowledge of engineering was not something that interested the German. Of course, the locals tolerated him as best they could since those who worked at the hydro dam greatly valued the prestige and pay of their jobs, especially given the lack of such opportunities in the area. As for Dick, he was out to learn all that he could about the hydro installation whatever the costs and thus demonstrated an admirable level of equanimity during his visits.

The German had worked on several hydro projects throughout Latin America, including Bolivia. He told us about two hydro dam structures he was associated with that collapsed before they were operational. One collapsed on the day that it was inaugurated with the president of the country and other high-ranking government officials present. Evidently, the president threw the switch to release water flow into the canal that carried it to the turbines, and when the canal was almost filled, it totally collapsed. The German blamed the fiasco on government corruption, particularly how the government awarded contracts. In building the canal, the contractor used only forty percent of the amount of cement that should have been put into the concrete and pocketed the remainder of the money. Such public humiliation would be hard to forget. I was glad they had not shorted the cement in my fabulous swimming pool in Correntina.

A Frenchman in town to conduct irrigation studies around Correntina joined us for dinner on occasion. His listening skills matched or exceeded the talking skills of the German, who tended to dominate the conversation.

I remember one notable dinner conversation with the Frenchman. Our new regional Volunteer leader, Georgia Buck, a former Volunteer who replaced Clyde, came to visit. We dined at the local boarding house. Given the moniker Georgia Peach by two of the Volunteers in Lapa because of his smooth Southern mannerisms and political skills, our new leader told the Frenchman about his frustration in dealing with Brazilians, how those in prominent positions always wanted something from him, especially transportation. "This is a big burden, and makes it very difficult to get projects accomplished," Georgia Peach complained.

The Frenchman paused, then asked, "Why do you do it?"

Georgia Peach replied, "To get anything done and gain acceptance, it is important that they like you."

"If you persist with this obsequious philosophy, you will have a long and miserable stay in Brazil," said the Frenchman. "I do not believe it is so important that they like you. What is more important is that they respect you."

He went on to explain his views on human nature. "People will take advantage of you if they think you are soft-hearted. And they will continue to do so as long as you allow it. You will gain respect if you do what is right, even if at times it may offend some people."

I should explain that at this first meeting with Georgia Buck, we didn't know yet about his Georgia Peach moniker, and the Frenchman observed that we addressed him as Bucky. "Don't you Americans have a phrase?" the Frenchman asked. "Something to the effect that you have to buck up when the going gets tough?" Well it sounds like it is time to buck up!"

All of this sage advice would go far in shaping our future approach to working in Brazil. I came away with a lot more than dinner that evening. \29

A few days later, we received another visit from Leo, our project leader, who was accompanied by the irrepressible Dr. Pepper, the commission chief, and Dr. Ken, our Peace Corps doctor. They came to survey our project progress and to announce the news of more intensive training sessions in mid-February for both Dick and Silvia, six weeks long this time. Only one of these sessions struck me as legitimate, the hydro training for Dick, of course. As for more health training for Silvia—well, that seemed a bit more suspect. Apparently, the Peace Corps theorized that some of the women in the group, the bulk of whom were nurses or health workers, weren't achieving much in the backlands and needed to become more familiar with Brazilian approaches to public health and nursing. A more realistic agenda came to light through the little news we got. Although it had only been a couple of months since our arrival in Brazil, the majority of the Volunteer women were an unsettled bunch, and this program opportunity in Rio de Janeiro was as much about restoring their enthusiasm and drive as it was about imparting useful knowledge in the health sector.

Before he left, Dr. Ken administered necessary injections to protect us from new maladies. Later while visiting the saw mill with our guests and Padre to view our efforts in restoring it, Dr. Ken asked Dick and me to come out behind the saw mill, out of earshot of the others, for a little health chat on behalf of the Peace Corps. Obviously cavorting at the local bordellos was not a practice the Peace Corps condoned but human nature being what it is, they felt it was better to be safe than sorry, so Dr. Ken offered us condoms. Dick and I both declined his offer, telling him we did not believe they would be necessary.

Later Dick said to me: "I found the trip out behind the saw mill a bit strange. I always thought the old adage, 'taking someone out behind the wood shed,' was meant to be a form of punishment and here the Peace Corps was offering us the means to go pleasure ourselves!"

85

The trio left and it wasn't long before Silvia was gone also. Two more visitors, Ed and Eileen Willis, a married couple, among the oldest Volunteers in our group, arrived right after the condom incident to visit the hydro facility and assess whether it would be a better Peace Corps fit for Ed, who had worked for years at General Electric. While we hosted them in Correntina, we learned about still more moral challenges the Peace Corps leadership faced.

Ed and Eileen told us about a situation among the Volunteers in Jacobina, four of whom were no longer with the Peace Corps. One male and two females had been summarily dismissed after the Peace Corps learned about sexual indiscretion and cohabitation. The young man it seems was sleeping with both young women, though neither of the women knew he was sleeping with the other. Perhaps he needed to break up the boredom of having nothing more enterprising than managing a harem to consume his time, but the secrecy eventually became unmanageable and the love triangle collapsed.

One of the female partners, a violinist, reacted with a vengeance. While her supposed beau was pleasantly engaged with the other woman, the violinist parked herself outside the bedroom with a large butcher knife in her hand. She demanded they come out, ready to perform some surgery on her young male lover. Apparently, none of the other four Volunteers in the house, one of whom was trained in psychiatric nursing, could convince her that revenge was out of the question. She did not leave the door until Peace Corps authorities flew in to intervene. They somehow got her to change her tune, and then sent all three packing for the United States.

Jacobina must have been a town filled with love, because the male psychiatric nurse later fell in love with the daughter of a South African miner living there. The Peace Corps at the time would not allow marriage, so despite his gallant effort to save the violinist, the psychiatric nurse was also sent home. Of the three remaining, two were nurses and decided to transfer north to work in a hospital near the coast. That left only Sprinter Charlie, my soccer cohort from training in Oklahoma. He stayed the course in Jacobina but fell in love with a pretty Brazilian woman named Dag. When they got engaged, he followed all the rules of the church and local custom. A couple of years after Sprinter Charlie left the Peace Corps, he married Dag.

A week or so after Ed and Eileen left, Dick and I were able to spend some time with Padre. He hosted us for dinner one evening and shyly disclosed that he was leaving the hinterland for about one month to get some much-needed rest. Padre sensed that Dick, who had developed a paternalistic attitude about my safety, did not like the idea of me being alone in Correntina. Padre, with typical insouciance, said that he was proud of me; that I had become socially integrated into the community; that I would do just fine in the absence of my Peace Corps colleagues and my Padre. Then he laid down the ultimate threat, assuring Dick that if I got into any trouble, the confessional would be waiting for me when he returned.

I was not sure of the implication, but Padre was astute enough to know that loneliness can lead to romance and romance to other difficulties. We shared with Padre the Jacobina story of romance gone astray. Conversation eventually drifted to a topic that troubled Dick.

"You know here in Correntina there are a significant number of young bastard boys and girls who are mulatto with blue eyes and blond hair," said Dick. "I notice when people want one of the bastards to do something, they waver their hands and say, 'Hey *Alemão, vem aca*,'—Hey German, come over here. "What's the story, Padre?" Dick asked.

"When the Germans were here they were no better than the Latin lovers, and it is a disgrace," Padre replied. "I do all I can to treat these children like everyone else and accept them in my school."

While we were on the subject of the Germans and the paternity scandal, Padre said to me, "I heard you attended the birthday party last night for Janette."

Janette was a woman I knew in town. I admitted I'd been there and said, "Janette seems to be out of place, Padre. Even though she's in her early thirties, she's a knockout beauty. She's the closest thing to Sophia Loren I've ever seen anywhere. She always attends the dances and picnics. And besides being beautiful, she has a wonderful personality."

Hearing that such a beauty lived in Correntina perked up Dick's ears. He chirped in, "So what's the story? What is she doing here and why isn't she married?"

Padre explained, "It's a sad story. While the Germans were here, Janette was the *namorado*—steady girlfriend, or perhaps even the *noiva*—fiancée, of one of the German engineers. When he left, he promised he would send for her, but he never did. She waited and waited but she never heard from him again. Some suspected he had a wife back in Germany. Janette was heartbroken and rarely left her house for a couple of years. It took her a long time to recover."

Padre continued, "There was no one of Janette's social stature in the community or region to appreciate such beauty. Of course, you also have to take into account the chauvinistic nature of Brazilian men. In this culture, being engaged is a definitive commitment to marry. There was a lingering suspicion among local men that her relationship with the German may not have been entirely platonic. He may have deflowered her." Padre raised his index finger. "Brazilian men are no less prone to sleeping with unmarried girls than the Germans, but they would never knowingly marry a girl who was not a virgin, or even suspected of not being a virgin."

The tragedy of the story was that in poor Janette's case, no one really knew the truth. Janette, her family and close friends, were mum on the subject. She would have been better off to move away to a larger city and start a new life. She had her mother to care for. If there indeed had been a moral transgression, Mom's silence may have carried a heavy price for Janette. Whatever the case, Janette now played volleyball with the rest of us, attended all the *festas*, and seemed to be making the best of her life and fate.

Padre said he was happy that Dick was interested in Janette's story. Padre evidently had been giving some thought to Dick and Janette after hearing about Dr. Ken's visit with us behind the wood shed i.e., the saw mill. "Dick, you would be a good match for Janette." Padre smiled. "You're blond, blue-eyed, and an engineer! The only thing you're not is German. This makes you the perfect man to assuage Janette's woes and keep yourself on the proper path."

Padre looked at me and quickly added, "Ken, I know you go to Mass regularly. You are faithful, and you have the lovely Millie back home. You've shown me photos of her. She is surely worth the wait."

Then he turned to Dick and said, "I know of no romantic inclinations of yours." Padre reminded Dick that Valentine's Day was coming in a couple of days, and that, although it's not observed in Brazil, Saint Valentine's was a big day for romance in the United States. "Maybe you should deliver a valentine to Janette's door."

Dick's face turned crimson, which sent Padre into one of his uncontrollable fits of laughter.

We all had a good laugh, but Dick and I agreed to work hard to keep each other on the straight and narrow. We much preferred to have the salutation, *"Hey Americano vem aca."* reserved for our spiritual calling in Correntina.

The day finally arrived when Dick had to make it to Lapa to catch a plane for Rio. He telegraphed ahead for the plane, but Wild Bill was nowhere to be found. It was the rainy season and there was no other way to get to Lapa except by vehicle along the questionable road on the north side of the Corrente River, or by boat from the next town down the river.

We left early in the morning with Ton Tonio piloting the Commission Jeep. Seat belts were still a future phenomenon so one had to hold on for dear life given the deteriorated condition of the road and no roof on the vehicle. At Santa Maria, we negotiated passage on a small river boat. The boat was supposed to leave in the early afternoon but did not get underway until early evening. As was typical, the operator always waited until the last possible person or package was crammed on board before leaving, no matter what the advertised timetable. There was barely room to stand, let alone to find a place to lie down for the all-night journey.

The boat made two stops along the way, one in the small town of Port Novo and the other at Sítio do Mato, where the Corrente converged with the São Francisco. Ten hours after leaving, we pulled into the landing in Lapa.

It was indeed a long night, although we got some sleep on the porch on the back of the boat. Due to the crowded conditions, though, we spent most of the trip lying on the roof next to the smoke stack just to stretch out. Sleep on the roof of the small boat, with the noise of the diesel engine and the smell of its fumes, was difficult enough, but Dick and I took turns staying awake so the one sleeping did not roll off into the water. When daylight came, we had a good laugh. Our faces, arms, and clothes were jet black from the diesel fumes. We shuddered to think what the insides of our lungs looked like.

In spite of its fast current and minimal backwater areas, this river was home to huge anacondas and voracious piranhas, just like other rivers in the area. Paulo, the chief at the hydro installation, had once presented me with a beautiful fifteen-foot-long skin of an anaconda he had shot along one of the area rivers. The gift would serve as a constant reminder of what lurked in these waters. Later, I would purchase a twenty-two-foot-long python skin from a local hunter who killed the snake in the *mata*—bush around Correntina.

After arriving in Lapa in the early morning, we had to make our way in the dark from the river to the commission compound on the east end of the city. There were no lights and the area around the river was fraught with beggars and derelicts of all sorts, not to mention lots of wild, starving dogs constantly on the hunt for food. Many were undoubtedly rabid. We weren't so concerned about the people as the dogs, so we picked up a piece of firewood as soon as we could in case we needed it for protection. It was 4:00 a.m. when we made it to the compound. Not wanting to wake any one, we slept on the hard tile floor of the front porch.

Sunrise woke us. The resident Volunteers were amazed to see our blackened faces and wondered whether we thought we had to travel in disguise during the night to be safe. We each took a good shower to remove the grime before we joined the others for breakfast.

Two new Volunteers had recently arrived. Jim and his project mate, Loring, were relocating from the Brazil I 4-H group in Carazinho in the southern State of Rio Grande do Sul. Jim was the reason I had made the trip to Lapa with Dick, so I struck up a conversation with him at the table. I would assist him in finding his way to Correntina and then on to Barreiras. He already had a Peace Corps Jeep and, although I had never made the trip from Lapa to Correntina by vehicle before because the route was deemed impassable, somehow Jim and I were going to make the trip by Jeep and I was to be the guide. This would truly be a case of the blind leading the blind.

Jim was a California boy who majored in animal husbandry at Pierce College, and he had that classic California fun-in-the-sun look the Beach Boys made famous. His charming manner and stand-out good looks would be sure to create excitement with the local girls. Jim said that he was enjoying the weather here even though it was hot and humid. He indicated that the weather in southern Brazil at this time of the year could get darn right cold; the only place in Brazil that received occasional snow. Someone at the table asked Jim how cold it got down in Rio Grande do Sul.

"Well I don't know if you will all understand this," Jim replied, "except possibly Ken, who grew up on a Minnesota dairy farm so he is probably familiar with what I'm about to tell you."

Table chatter subsided as everyone listened.

"A few weeks ago, a dairy farmer came to me and told me that in the freezing temperatures his cows' tails froze off and they were now bob-tailed," Jim said. "The farmer had read that in the U.S. it gets mighty cold. So he assumed this was quite a common phenomenon for farmers there, especially in the upper Midwest where most of the dairy farms in America are located."

Then he looked around the table at us and asked, "Folks here think we Americans have the answer to everything, isn't that right?"

We all shook our heads in agreement.

Jim continued, "I'm from California. I don't know anything about cold weather and cow tails freezing off, so I wasn't sure what to tell the poor soul. But knowing the standards folks here told us to abide by, I wanted to provide an intelligent answer for him. My college major was animal husbandry and I'd made the mistake of telling folks this. So as not to appear the fool, I gave it some thought and finally told him what I thought he'd have to do."

He paused until someone asked, "What did you tell him?"

With the straightest face possible, Jim said, "I told him he would probably have to sell the cows wholesale as they could not be re-tailed!"

We were all listening with such great intensity to Jim's story that it took a minute for his answer to sink in. And then we all broke out in roaring laughter because we all knew that we'd been had.

"Yup," Jim said with a grin. "It gets mighty cold down there in Rio Grande do Sul and that is why I decided to come north."

It appeared I would have an interesting week ahead of me with Jim. After breakfast, he and I drove Dick to the airport in Lapa to catch one of the two weekly flights to Belo Horizonte and on to Rio de Janeiro. It would be a month and a half before I would hear from or see Dick or Silvia again in Correntina. It seemed the art of survival was now totally in my own hands.

12. The road less traveled

Jim and I were ready to hit the road. The only potentially passable route in the rainy season ran along the north side of the Corrente River. Travel by roads was always unpredictable and a little treacherous in those parts of Brazil, but our four-wheel drive Jeep gave us some confidence.

We left at sunrise and drove to the banks of the São Francisco to load our Jeep onto the commission's motorized launch for the twelve-mile ride up the river to Sítio do Mato at the confluence of the Corrente. I was extremely thankful that the launch was available, and that Dr. Torres was kind enough to arrange its use for us. Otherwise, we would have had to drive twelve miles up the east side of the river and get a hand-powered launch to take us across at Sítio do Mato.

The area along the east side of the São Francisco was low and swampy. In the rainy season, the road would flood up to two feet deep, so stakes were set on both sides of the road to mark its position for travelers. The deep, swampy area running along the perimeter of these stakes was known for poisonous snakes. One wrong maneuver and that would be the end of our journey, unless we were lucky enough to be rescued by a team of oxen before the snakes got us.

But this was less of a problem than the gypsies. A gypsy colony lived in the area, and local stories circulated about gypsies moving the road stakes to purposely redirect a passing Jeep or truck into the swamp. The gypsies waited for unsuspecting travelers to end up in the swamp and then robbed them of all their goods, sometimes kidnapping or raping women and young girls. As a couple of young bucks, we sought our share of adventure, but this was not the type two greenhorns like us needed.

At Sítio do Mato the American Presbyterians had established a mission. The current resident missionaries were Reverend Al Reisner and his wife. There were not one but two Cessna 172s at the mission, along with a well-kept airstrip and generator-powered lights on the runway for late night arrivals. Two airplanes certainly seemed like a luxury, but I soon realized that this was born more out of practicality. Like everything else in Brazil, replacement parts were hard to find, and I imagine mechanics to service an aircraft were even more hard to find. On many occasions when Al flew to Correntina, the other plane was away for repairs or sitting idle awaiting parts. Reverend Al's missionary work not only included the conversion of sinners, but also transportation of gravely ill or injured people to the hospital in Lapa. It was comforting to know he was close by if Wild Bill was not available.

Al was away when we stopped at the mission, but Mrs. Reisner told us she heard the road was in very rough shape and didn't know if we could actually get through with all the rain. She had not heard of any vehicles arriving lately. When we left, Mrs. Reisner said she would have Al telegraph Correntina upon his return that evening to confirm we had made it safely. If he got no reply he would send someone to look for us.

Mrs. Reisner's words proved prophetic. Despite the four-wheel-drive feature, our Jeep became mired in mud up to the axles on two separate occasions, requiring assistance for us to extricate it. The first time, several local pedestrians helped us push the Jeep out of the hole we were in. The second time, the road was so bad that an oxen cart loaded down with cotton bales had tipped over. There was no passing it, even if we had wanted to spend time clearing trees and brush to create a route around the mess. Instead, we spent an hour helping the drivers haul all the cotton bales off to the side of the road before righting the oxen cart. The oxen then managed to pull the cart out of the mud.

Once we had the cotton, oxen, and oxcart out of the way, Jim made a charge but to no avail. The Jeep quickly sank down to the axles. Jim was a dryland California boy accustomed to driving only on good roads, which he also found in the south of Brazil. I suggested I make the run instead, but in his machismo, he insisted he do it. Afterward I chided him that I knew a girl who could have done a better job driving than he did.

This offended him a bit. "Ja, what makes you think so?" he asked.

"Well," I said with a grin, "my high school sweetheart drove a regular school bus route at age sixteen over rural roads often in little better shape than this. When the National Jaycee Safe Driving Road-E-O held a teenage driving rodeo, she had to drive an obstacle course and complete many other challenges. At ages seventeen and eighteen, among a dozen finalists entered, only one of which was a gal, my Millie won both times.

Jim said, "Well you should have brought her along!"

I replied, "I wish I could have, back home the boys call her the "Tomboy of Third Street" and I think she would have fit right in here, especially driving this Jeep."

The good news was that there were four oxen on hand. We hitched them to the front of the Jeep, and with several of us pushing, we managed to get the Jeep onto solid ground. Once we were well out of trouble, we spent the next hour helping our newfound friends carry their cotton bales through mud up to our knees, then reload and tie the cotton back onto the cart.

I could not have known it at the time, but a little more than a year later, shortly before I returned to Minnesota, my girl Millie purchased a sleek black Plymouth Valiant Signet convertible—Chrysler Corporation's answer to the popular Ford Mustang introduced in the 1960s. Millie's dad had owned a Chrysler dealership until his sudden death, and he'd also taken out a $10,000 life insurance policy with Chrysler. When he passed away, the proceeds were divided equally among his five surviving children. Millie used her proceeds to buy the Signet, which had the compact profile of the Mustang, adding to its sporty image. Unlike the early Mustang, with a straight six-cylinder engine, the Plymouth had a 182 horse V8 engine, and a four-speed manual transmission with a revolutionary European style Hurst shifter. Chrysler had designed the combination specifically for big block V8s—though not necessarily for a compact car.

Well, Millie knew her cars. Chrysler only made a few hundred of the Signet model. After her repeated success at the Safe Driving rodeo, most young men would not want to suffer further humiliation by challenging her to a drag race.

We could have also used all that horsepower in our current state of peril. We finally arrived in Correntina at midnight, a trip of fourteen hours over sixty arduous miles. We were dog tired and covered in mud from head to foot. As we pulled up to the house in the hydro compound, the thought of even a lukewarm shower this late in the day was an immensely comforting thought.

When we went to the river the next morning to wash the Jeep, Correntina was a ghost town. There was hardly a soul on the streets. It finally dawned on us—Carnival started that day. For the next three days, the town would remain deserted until late afternoon when the residents would finally arise from sleep and prepare for the party that would go on all night until the wee hours of the morning.

Jim and I participated in some of the festivities in the evenings, but only hung around until midnight. As young gringos, we became the object of many lovely young ladies' attentions. Evidently this festival turned out to be a time for maidens to let their hair down and be more aggressive than normally allowed, especially with their identities artfully obscured by masks and costumes. We may have thought that our recent road trip was fraught with danger, but this was even more serious. Revelry or not, Brazilian men keep a close watch on their paramours. They were well aware of the ladies' demonstrated interest in a couple of Americans who might be tickets to Hollywood and American dreams. Brazilian Carnival could be fun, just not for us in this place at this time since we had no masks or costumes that could adequately disguise who we were.

After a couple days of partying and taking the grand tours of Correntina, Jim was anxious to move on to Barreiras. Like my other visitors, he greatly admired my one-of-a-kind swimming pool and asked if I would mind having an assistant in case Barreiras did not work out. His request flattered me. I told him he was always welcome to make the trip back and spend more time at my "resort." I think he appreciated the invitation. But for the present, it was on to Barreiras, and that would require some gasoline, a precious commodity in our region. With only three vehicles in the entire county, there was no gas station around, so we relied on the local supply, which was available in twenty-liter tin cans. Normally it was shipped upriver to Santa Maria and then trucked to Correntina. The mayor had the only truck in the area, and his son the only Jeep other than the Commission's, so it was easy to figure out who ran the gas business in town.

Not only was gasoline in short supply, so was its quality. First of all, gas cans were poorly labeled with only raised embossed lettering indicating their contents, generally gasoline or diesel, but occasionally kerosene. Add to this the illiteracy of most workers and the selection process became a shot in the dark. Even more bizarre was the fact that if they ran out of a particular fuel, few of the workers knew one type of petroleum from another or why it mattered, so they would fill cans with whatever was on hand.

The second major issue was that the tin containers made visual inspection of the quality of the contents impossible. It was not unusual to have a gas can filled at a ratio of three-fourths gasoline to one-fourth water—not a good mix for any vehicle. However, since water and gas do not mix, pure gasoline could be drained into a vehicle's gas tank through the technique of siphoning. Not for the faint of heart, but it worked in the clutch.

Siphoning required a clear plastic hose and ideally two people—one to hoist the can of gas up and the other to siphon the gas and manage the hose. The siphoner would insert the hose into the can and suck on the hose to produce a draw of liquid before quickly transferring the hose into the tank to fill it with gas. To control flow throughout the operation, the siphoner would cap the hose end with a thumb, always watching for a bubble of water, which signaled an immediate stopping point. No water must enter the tank. Water had to be drained onto the ground.

By no means was siphoning efficient since it involved a considerable loss of gasoline. The whole process carried many hazards, not the least of which was inadvertent ingestion of gas. Smokers especially had to be careful. If they lit up a cigarette after siphoning without thoroughly rinsing out their mouths with water, the results would not be pretty, especially for their faces. Most likely they'd be sent home as unrecognizable to family members back in the States. And then there was the undesirable net result of gas yield, equaling roughly half of the purchased amount. Despite all its drawbacks, however, siphoning was the best solution we had for fueling our vehicles in the backlands. We did our best to fuel Jim's Jeep and the next morning he left, hoping the gas we had siphoned would get him to Barreiras by sundown.

With Gaucho Jim's departure and all the excitement of my trip to Lapa behind me, it was time to get back to work. During this period of solo operation, I continued restoring the saw mill and monitoring the water system. I also made numerous forays out into the countryside to familiarize myself with the local agricultural environment and to meet prospective farmers whom I hoped to work with. I usually made these trips on foot or by horseback, sometimes up to five miles or more.

Upon first arriving in Correntina and knowing we would not have a Jeep for some time, I had looked into buying a horse and riding equipment. I grew up with horses and enjoyed riding.

When I discussed this idea with Padre he looked at me like I was crazy. He reminded me of the half-dozen or so good riding horses in his pasture along with an arsenal of riding equipment.

Roads being little more than pathways, Padre often went by horse to the small outlying villages to say Mass, and on numerous occasions to minister to the dying. Thanks to his generosity, I never lacked for saddle transportation from that point on. "If you need a horse just come over and tell old João my caretaker and he'll have one all saddled up for you when you get here!"

Not only did my riding skills improve at this time, but by necessity so did my Portuguese. I did gain one English speaker for a short spell by the name of Dr. José. He'd grown up in Correntina, then went off to study medicine and practice surgery in Salvador, Bahia's capital. As a way of giving back to his community, Dr. José made periodic visits to the area to visit family and provide medical services to as many citizens as possible. He did this on a table in the back of the drugstore, the same place where I first had witnessed the death of the woman in childbirth months earlier. During the doctor's absences, Pedro the pharmacist and his mid-wife daughter were the next best substitutes. When Dr. José operated in the evenings it ended up being somewhat of a social event with a few select friends sitting around to observe him in action. One evening I happened upon Pedro, who invited me to come meet Dr. José at the pharmacy. He added that the doctor spoke good English and wanted very much to meet me.

I found Dr. José hard at work in the backroom. It was readily apparent that the poor gent on the table had sustained a horrendous wound to the face. There was a gaping hole that ran along the side of his face from his jaw just to the right of his nose and up to his right ear. His face was swollen and bloody. Then I heard the story behind the wound. The preceding day, bandits had attempted to rob the victim's farm. In his haste while chasing them, he dropped his gun. It accidentally discharged, the shot hitting him at close range.

Lighting conditions in this makeshift operation room were quite primitive. Lights were normally shut off in town by ten o'clock at night, so usually I carried a large flashlight on my long walk home. I had it with me then. Thus, I became the source of Dr. José's surgery light. The good doctor's presence in town that night was certainly a positive stroke of luck for this patient considering the damage to his face.

A couple nights later Dr. José operated on a child with the onset of trachoma. During training, we'd had some public health coursework on the ravages of this disease. Trachoma is the world's leading cause of preventable blindness. Left untreated, the eyelid eventually turns inward and causes the eyelashes to rub the eyeball, resulting in intense pain and scarring of the cornea. This ultimately leads to irreversible blindness, typically between thirty and forty years of age. I knew this was the case as it was not unusual to see a significant number of people of this age who were blind and who'd had to resort to begging as a livelihood.

For Dr. José, the highlight of his operations was practicing his English. While he prepared the little gal for her operation, he went into significant detail so I would understand exactly what was happening. There were a half-dozen others in the room, none of whom spoke English, and it fascinated them to hear us speak English just as much as it did to observe surgery. The procedure was hard to watch. Dr. José administered a local anesthesia in the muscles of the upper eyelid and attached sutures to it, which inverted the eyelid so he could remove the diseased area and re-expose the eyelids. In most cases the cornea would heal after some time, especially in younger patients.

All of this was routine for the good doctor. He was meticulous about explaining everything to me in excellent English. I soon found out why. As he finished, he informed me that come the next night he would give me a pair of gloves and I could have a go at performing a trachoma procedure while he guided me. I doubt I've laughed harder, leaving all the locals curious as to the source of my outburst. I soon got the impression, though, that the doctor was dead serious. For one nanosecond, I entertained the idea for its humanitarian value, but then common sense kicked in and I quickly dismissed it. I replied that one screw-up would land me in jail. I wasn't interested.

It was business as usual the next night for the doctor. This time he performed hernia surgery on a man without anesthesia. At first, he feigned disappointment in me for my refusal to become his intern, but then he chuckled and said he understood the potential implications. Dr. José eventually left town for the coast and his normal practice.

While in Correntina, he certainly demonstrated the need for a full-time surgeon. I hated to see him go, but my life then resumed a somewhat welcome routine.

About a week later I received a letter from Phil Mahle, a Volunteer from my hometown serving in Sierra Leone, Africa. It seemed that his experience in Sierra Leone was not much different from ours in terms of start-up hassles with the Peace Corps. Phil's project goal was to build a school. Fortunately for him, English was the working language in Sierra Leone.

Next came a letter from Walt Mischke, the first of us four hometown lads to join the Corps in 1962. Walt spoke of his difficulties in finding his own useful enterprise but also of his dogged determination to remain at it.

Like the Brazil I project, Walt's project in Venezuela was also an adopted 4-H project with the aim of establishing 4-H clubs in his region. But the project seemed riddled with problems. Only thirty of the original forty-three Volunteers were left in the country. Local agents would not cooperate with the Americans. Leadership was shaky at best with the recent firing of his Peace Corps boss followed quickly by the 4-H Center representative quitting. An ex-Army man from Peru had been assigned to take over the project. Their twenty Jeeps were reduced to fourteen in three months due to six wrecks; one of those vehicles had also sustained a bullet hole in the back door; and one AWOL Volunteer was found at a beach on the coast of Venezuela some five hundred miles from his duty station.

Walt concluded his letter with, "I'd like to hear about your flawless program." [30]

Letters from fellow Volunteers from my hometown gave me a better perspective, and a more appreciative attitude, about my project work and life in Brazil.

By now, the soccer season had started. Late one afternoon as I sat at home licking my wounds from the match, there was a knock at the door. I hobbled over to see who my visitor was and opened the door to find it was none other than my buddy Dave, the Plow Thief. The old boy looked none the worse for wear. He'd originally been stationed in Januária, a large town where there was both a commission agricultural station and school. Being one of the few individuals in the group with a formal education in agronomy, Dave made a sensible fit there.

But I'd heard a rumor that he had relocated to a small, isolated town a hundred miles or so south of me. This was in fact true. It was this visit by Dave that led up to my episode with the Bahia State Police, however, Dave's visit was not totally unproductive. Our most important discussion centered on the need for seeds. Dave said he'd heard that Purdue University had a joint program with the University of Paraná in the south of Brazil and if necessary, we could drive there and confiscate those seeds. Unfortunately, the State of Paraná was more than one thousand miles to the south. Since I was ineluctably frustrated, like Dave, with our slow progress with agriculture and desperate for seeds, I told him I was up to the task if it could be arranged even if it took a big chunk of time and our own cash.

After all the excitement of Carnival, the back-room operations of Dr. José, and the visit by the plow thief, I got back to my work routine and life settled into my new normal. I knew I would be traveling to Rio in the near future to meet Dick and drive our Jeep to Correntina, so in addition to keeping things running in town I was starting to spend a fair amount of time out at the Coimbra farm a mile south of the hydro installation on the Corrente River. It was on an upland area that the ancient irrigation ditch ran through, which was made possible by the same drop in elevation that allowed for the hydro installation's operation. With its irrigation, it would become my little experimental farm where I would plant new varieties of corn, cotton, and vegetables. It was also located on a main path that locals used to get to market on Saturdays, so work being done here was visible by many people.

The first day of Brazilian autumn arrived without much fanfare, especially compared to the busyness of the early months of the new year. One day working out on the farm, I heard Wild Bill fly over and thought this might be my lucky day to head to Rio. I hustled back and had almost reached town when I saw the plane heading away down the valley. No plane ride for me. I plodded back to the house feeling somewhat dejected. Shortly thereafter I heard Ton Tonio's Jeep coming up the road, and lo and behold who walks into the house but Silvia.

Luck was not with me that day, but it sure was with Silvia. Spring had sprung for her, just like back in the States. First and foremost, she was leaving Correntina and was thrilled to death by the prospect of being transferred to Rio to work in the *favelas*—slums. Perhaps the even bigger news, though, fell into the romance category. In the short span of six weeks she had become engaged to none other than Dr. Ken, our mild-mannered Peace Corps doctor. Dr. Ken was slated to leave Brazil in December, at which time he and Silvia planned to marry and return to the United States. I had rarely seen anyone as excited as Silvia, who obviously was not all that happy in Correntina. She would now join a contingent of women from those early Peace Corps days who found the rigors of service and surroundings too difficult of an adjustment, a group that numbered nearly half of all the female Volunteers who originally came to the valley. Not everyone found their useful enterprise with the Peace Corps in the backlands.

While I had no luck getting a plane ride to Lapa, Wild Bill and Silvia did have mail for me. A letter from Millie related a bit of medical news that rivaled the hilarity of the operation I performed with Dr. José. Millie mentioned that she had returned to school in Minneapolis, but her dad's sudden death was still causing her severe anxiety. She recently had been taken by ambulance from her dorm to the hospital. Not knowing that her dad had died suddenly, and that she had discovered his body, the examining doctors asked if her anxiety attack was due to the fact that she might be pregnant. Apparently, because of the stress of her father's death, she had missed her cycle for a couple of months. The comedy of this diagnosis seemed to temper her anxiety and get things back to normal, including the frivolity of her writing. Silvia laughed heartily when I told her of Millie's diagnosis, finding it every bit as comical as the Dr. José episode. It was also a good shot of comic relief to lighten my mood after months of isolation and continued delays.

Silvia assured me that Dick had almost finished his training in Rio, though she did not know the nature of his work there. A bona fide workaholic, Dick was anxious to get the dam up and running. Instead of spending time at Rio's scenic beaches, Dick would be taking advantage of his training. Soon, I heard from Dick. He and the Jeep were ready to go whenever I could get there.

Two days later, the plane still had not come. I'd lost all confidence that it was going to show up, so I decided to take matters into my own hands and head for Lapa where I could catch a flight to Rio. This meant I would most likely have to catch a boat downriver in Santa

Maria for the trip to Lapa. Unfortunately, the commission Jeep was also not available to take me to Santa Maria. Lady Luck did come my way however. There was a trucker in town who had come to Correntina from the west and was driving to Lapa the next day. His truck would be loaded with people and cargo, but given that I was the Americano, the driver guaranteed me a spot on the truck.

Finally, some good news: I was going to Rio. After all the delays, I would have been ready to walk the seventy-five miles to Lapa in the rain and mud if necessary.

13. Marvelous city by the sea

So, while I would not have to relive the perils of sleeping on the roof of a boat, possibly falling off into anaconda and piranha infested water—since Dick was not along to stand guard—I would instead experience my first truck ride, which I had been warned also had its own unique risks. The shine of my adventure had begun to wear off a bit, and I started to realize this experience was not a trip but a journey. From what Silvia had told me upon returning from her time in Rio, I was but one of only a handful of Volunteers who had not left their original location in the valley to travel somewhere else, move permanently, or go home to the United States.

Although I had developed a great affection for the people and the place where I resided, I knew innately at times that I was of a different people and place. I believe these words of Tom Carter, who served with the Peace Corps in 1963 in Peru, applied to every Volunteer: "There comes a day when all this suddenly becomes apparent, all at once. Things are no longer picturesque, they are dirty, no longer quaint but furiously frustrating and you want like crazy to just get out of there, to go home—it happens to one and all, usually about the third or fourth month—more Volunteers quit and go home at this stage than any other." [31]

The Peace Corps had an inkling of this when it built into its programs a month's vacation time for each year of service. Their oversight, however, was the requirement to have one year of service at post completed before taking R&R. Four months would have been a more productive option. Seeing Silvia's enthusiasm and renewed energy after her hiatus in Rio, I felt a break would be good for me. The Peace Corps still had provided no clear definition of my official assignment in Correntina and no Jeep to get around. Others had left their posts for far less than this.

While the Peace Corps was playing on my emotions, I still felt great anguish over Millie's emotional suffering back home. She felt in large measure responsible for her dad's death. Naturally, I thought I should be there with her. Besides my isolation, not to mention all the other difficulties, the sentiment of Peru Volunteer Tom Carter consumed my thoughts. Then I received a letter from Millie that went a long way to assuage my concerns about sticking with the program to the end.

"A single day cannot be found where my thoughts have not been with you and I miss you far more than you could ever know. I am so sorry I cannot tell you the words you may want to hear, but as you know from the past I just do not write everything I feel; I really do try but am a bit shy by nature, as you know. So you must realize that whatever I might say I mean it ever so much—and more than I say. Maybe it is not the right thing for me to feel this way, but I have just never thrown myself at any fella unless I was awfully sure of my feelings for him. I really do not mean for this to sound rash as it does but please try to understand me—it is hard I know. In other words I have never held so much respect and love for a fella as I now have for you. I hope nothing ever changes me on this and I somehow believe it won't. I want to be with you so much and it will not be long before you will be back with us. I worry whenever I read of the many planes that go down in Brazil. Your letters mean so much to me. I know I could not get along half as well without them. I do miss you so very much. All that is important to me is to know you are safe, in good health and are happy in your work. Knowing you will be here with us someday makes it so much easier. Take extra good care for me. Love Always, Millie."

After reading this heartfelt letter I knew there was no way I could not stick with the program, given the great faith Millie placed in me. Her words would go far toward sustaining me in the remaining months, including my journey to Rio.

I had made the trip to Lapa by air and by river, and now I would attempt it by land. As usual, my departure was delayed by too much dickering over fares and the trucker looking to squeeze as many passengers as possible on board. Padre came to see me off at the last moment and had with him the plans for his pet project the maternity hospital. I am sure he thought while I was in Rio Dick and I could persuade the American Embassy to throw in a pile of money for this good cause. I thought to myself, I bet he would also appreciate it if I asked them at the same time if they had a spare Jeep sitting around, as Padre had asked me previously to contact the Catholic Church in the States to see if I could get one for him.

I rode in the bed of a truck crunched in with what seemed like a hundred other passengers on the way to Santa Maria, and what a ride. Navigating through the deep ruts and mud nearly resulted in tipping the vehicle over multiple times. At each near catastrophe, the screaming of women and children on the truck became unbearable. Such overloaded trucks moved constantly throughout northeast Brazil since the intermittent droughts caused people to always look somewhere else toward a better stake in life.

The loss of truckloads of people like this was not unknown due to various hazardous conditions, whether faulty mechanics of the truck, washed-out bridges, or overall terrible quality of the roads. We waited in Santa Maria until late afternoon, leaving some folks there and the driver negotiating with others to fill his load. It turned out we were taking the Road from Hell that Gaucho Jim and I had taken several weeks before. It was now late March, so the rains were less frequent, and the road was drying out a bit. We arrived in the little village of Porto Novo two hours later just as evening fell. There were no lights in town other than candles, and the streets were inhabited by wild dogs, beggars, and drunks, which was typical of many of these small, isolated villages.

Before I left Correntina, Padre had asked the truck driver to look after me. The driver blatantly ignored Padre's request and proceeded to get totally drunk. He wanted to find the nearest house of ill repute and make an evening of it. He invited me along, but I told him no thanks and managed to find a boarding house with a cold shower, which was like heaven after a hot, sticky day crammed onto a truck with too many people, some of whom probably hadn't showered in months. My supper of rice and beans wasn't much, but it just felt good to have a place to lie down.

We left Porto Novo for Lapa at five o'clock the next morning, even though the driver was severely hung over. I think he felt some remorse about ignoring Padre's request the night before and didn't want me to rat him out, so I got to sit in the middle of the cab on the trip from

Porto Novo to Sítio de Mato. That was the good news. The bad news was that I had to hold the back window in place since someone had kicked it out the day before. We also ran over an emu\32 stuck in the mud in the road. The driver wasn't stopping for anything.

By mid-morning we arrived at Sítio da Mato. Rather than wait for a barge to come and ferry the truck down the river to Lapa, I got one of the locals to paddle me across the river where I caught a ride on another truck heading there since I did not want to miss the departing afternoon flight. Not waiting for the ferry may or may not have been prudent as there was always the possibility of running into the notorious gypsies that inhabited the eastern bank of the São Francisco in this area.

Once in Lapa, I cleaned up at the Volunteer house and then headed to the airport to board the flight to Rio with a stop in Belo Horizonte. Flight connections rarely happened on a tight schedule, but it was my lucky day. After arriving in Rio, I checked into the Rex Hotel, the usual Volunteer hangout in the city and not far from the Peace Corps offices and the U.S. Embassy. I met Welder Bob and Electrician Perry, two Volunteers who were in Rio looking at relocation possibilities, and they joined me for an American movie and fast food, the perfect way to spend my first night back in civilization. We went to see *Sanque da Apache*—translated as Blood of the Apache, but *Geronimo* to us. While in Rio, I would also see *Exodus, Mutiny on the Bounty, X-15*, and a couple other movies. After the show, our fast-food destination of choice was usually a joint called Bob's, a favorite of all Volunteers wanting to get a little taste of the USA. Rice and beans and the hinterland were soon forgotten as I feasted on a hamburger, French fries, and a milk shake topped off with a banana split.

On my first full day in what Brazilians call the *Cidade Maravilhoso*—Marvelous City, I engaged in a whirlwind of activities. After a morning at the Peace Corps office, Leo, my project director, took me to the opulent dining room at the American Embassy. He said he was extremely proud of what we were doing in Correntina and the stability and patience we were demonstrating in an isolated location while the Peace Corps was attempting to figure things out. I told him the story of Plow Thief Dave and my episode with the Bahia State Militia; he was incredulous but said it did not surprise him.

After lunch with Leo, I went to the commission headquarters to find Dick. This was the first time I'd seen him in six weeks, and indeed

I had wondered if he would ever return. He had a desk and all the trappings of permanency. I soon got the feeling that most of the staff had no idea that he was not a permanent fixture and would soon be leaving. Dick had been there so long he even had business cards with the commission address on them. He may have entertained the thought of staying, but I think he was anxious to get back to Correntina and make his mark getting the hydro installation operational.

Then there was my newfound buddy Dr. Pepper, the commission chief. He had apparently become a big fan of mine as he had the opportunity on a couple visits to see that we had many positive things going on in Correntina, and he delighted in telling his staff about them. Given Dr. Pepper's bubbling bonhomie, I mentioned Padre's needs: equipment for the maternity hospital, a Jeep, more funding for the school, and a few other things. Hearty laughter spilled out of him. Evidently, whenever Dr. Pepper visited Correntina, Padre relentlessly begged for these things.

After his laughter subsided, he said, "Gosh, I don't get the guy. I already got him the Saint André statue in Correntina, the only small town in the valley so honored. I told him, since his namesake, Saint André, was the patron saint of fishermen, he should bring Padre luck finding these things somewhere else, like the church. They're the ones with all the money!"

Three days after arriving in that indescribably beautiful city I celebrated my birthday, astonished to think that I was turning twenty years old in Rio de Janiero, a world away in both distance and perspective from anything I had known back home or in Correntina. It was a time and place never to be forgotten. I started the day off by having breakfast at the American Embassy with Dr. Ken and some other Embassy brass. Ken took me through the complete medical plan to keep us healthy and alive in Brazil. He thought I looked in fair shape after the many months I had lived in the backlands. Of course, he had to tell me all about his engagement to Silvia and said he would probably be seeing me more often, if he could convince Leo to come there to visit.

Ken had a big chuckle thinking about what the lustful males in Correntina would conjure up next since the concubine had fled the area. The lustful males were of course Wild Bill and Dr. Strangelove—

the name we gave to Dr. Torres, the area commission director, who also took a liking to Silvia. Apparently, Silvia had told him all the stories. Later that morning, Dick and I went to pick up our Jeep, which he'd already been using for about two weeks. When we reached it, we were met by an unfortunate sight. Someone had smashed the window and stolen Dick's briefcase, which contained all the information he had been gathering. He was heartbroken.

That evening I had an unforgettable dinner at a Hungarian restaurant on Copacabana Beach with Dick and Ann, the Peace Corps secretary. I got the feeling that Dick may have felt something for her and this was not the first time they had dined together. Was there something in the air, and both of my old acquaintances from Correntina would fly off on the wings of romance? After dinner, we took a long stroll along Copacabana Beach. The exquisite dinner, the beautiful beach with its crashing waves, and time with good friends was a dream I never wanted to end.

The next day, Saturday, sports highlighted our agenda. Late that afternoon I headed out to Maracana Stadium—the largest soccer stadium in the world with a capacity for nearly 200,000 fans—with Perry, a fellow Volunteer. The Brazilian National Championships were being held in Rio, and this particular match was one of the biggest games of the year, featuring two perennial rival teams: Santos from São Paulo and Botafogo of Rio de Janeiro. Two nights later I attended the second match in the series, accompanied by Perry and Bill, another Minnesota Volunteer. In this match, a young phenomenon named Pelé on the Santos team scored three goals. His superior talent foretold his future rank as the greatest soccer player in the world.

Having seen Pelé not once but twice would be way too much for the soccer aficionados in Correntina. I suspected that when I returned to the backlands I would get a lot of touches. By this I am not referring to touches of the ball in the next match, which is a statistic in soccer regarding ball deflections away from a star player. No, the sort of touches I expected would be from all sorts of folks in Correntina who would just want to touch me because I had been in the presence of the soccer great, Pelé.

The evening after the first match, Perry wanted to stroll down Copacabana Beach and take in the wonders of the nightlife. During our walk we passed the Manhattan Club. Perry said it was one of the most expensive and exclusive clubs on the beach. He said he'd heard it was a hangout for high-roller Americans and other foreigners. We had thoughts about having a look inside but the club screened its guests, and by all appearances we were definitely not high rollers. If only we had attempted to enter, I surely would have experienced one of the most bizarre meetings in my life.

The nature of this bizarre missed experience came to me forty years later in 2002 when I was making a return trip to Brazil. I discovered quite by accident that in 1963 this club was owned by an American named Frank Fritzlaff. In 2002, I would meet Frank in a rest home in Plainview, Minnesota, my hometown, which also happened to be Frank's hometown. Just think of the odds in life, that there I was standing on possibly the most famous beach in the world in front of a swanky nightclub and the person who owned it was from my hometown of fourteen hundred souls!

The story of Frank's coming to own the Manhattan Club is long and sordid. In the rest home, he had several autographed pictures of some of the club clientele from the early 1960s, including the Russian astronaut Yuri Gagarin, the first man to orbit the earth. Frank told me the Manhattan Club at that time was also a hangout for mobsters who had fled the United States for crimes, especially financial crimes such as stock embezzling. Frank sold the club in 1963 and returned to America, only a few months after I passed by strolling the beach in Rio. He said he sensed the overthrow of the Goulart government coming and feared he would lose everything he had.

Dick and I spent the next few days preparing to leave Rio. This included a visit to a Sears and Roebuck store to buy tools and some other items for the months ahead in the interior. I also found a store that sold seeds and acquired some. There were more meetings and visits to the dentist, but after ten days we were ready to leave on our journey back to Correntina.

We were held up a day, however, getting official Brazilian paper-work for the equipment we would take with us. Without these papers, we could be arrested as thieves, joining the illustrious company of my buddy Dave. This would take no less than a half-dozen stamps from a half-dozen different agencies. With so much busyness filling my time, I made it to the beach only once for my very first saltwater swim-ming experience.

W ith paperwork finally in hand, we left the city around noon with our much-coveted Jeep and equipment. Rio de Janeiro lies on the eastern side of a range of relatively high hills known as the Serra da Mantiqueira, and it was necessary to pass through these hills for forty to fifty miles on a road that was very steep and winding. Rain fell heavily and the visibility was not very good. To compound the problem, there were a considerable number of trucks coming down the mountain.

This stretch of road was considered one of the most hazardous in the country, resulting in a large number of accidents due to periodic road and bridge washouts. The asphalt was thin and could give way in seconds, creating large holes and deep pits in the road that, when filled with rainwater, could cause a vehicle to flip instantly. A few months earlier, a Peace Corp Volunteer in the Brazil I group was killed on this same stretch of road when he was hit by a runaway semi-truck. Dale Swenson was a 4-H agent in Wisconsin when he joined the Peace Corps. He grew up on a farm in Amery, Wisconsin, not far to the east of my hometown in Minnesota.

Brazil law required that an individual be buried within twenty-four hours of death, or the body needed to be taken out of the country. Director Leo told me that in Dale's case, with the need to retrieve the body after hours of delay in notification, and completion of all necessary government paperwork, they got his body on a plane and out of the country with only minutes to spare. One of the results of this was an edict from the Peace Corps that no Volunteer, except in the line of local work, was to drive on major highways alone. Accompanying Dick on the drive to Correntina therefore, may have been the only reason I had been given the opportunity to come to Rio. It's sad and sobering to think Dale had to die for me to finally make it out of the backlands for a brief taste of civilization.

Our ambitious goal was to cover the first seven hundred miles to the Bahia city of Victória da Conquista in two days, taking turns driving on asphalt highways the entire distance. We were on target to do so when we encountered our first hiccup on the trip. Dick was driving as we passed through a small town with unlit streets in the early evening darkness. A man ran into the road just as we approached him. Thank God, we only bumped him with the side of the Jeep. At first, the man seemed to be fine. A crowd quickly gathered around our vehicle, however, soon followed by the local police. An officer checked out the old duffer, who fortunately did not seem to have any broken bones or other serious problems, but if the policeman had not escorted us through the crowd, I am not sure what would have happened.

We had to give a lengthy explanation of who we were and what we were doing with all the equipment we were carrying. While the paperwork delay in Rio had frustrated us, we were now thankful we had it. The ruse to get through the crowd was that we were going to the police station, which we did. I think the cops were looking for a bribe to get us on our way. Equanimity was one of Dick's outstanding characteristics. He was pretty skilled at handling the exigencies of unusual situations, especially pretending, when it was necessary, not to understand. After the crowd dispersed and darkness fell, the police released us. But it was clear we could not stay in that town.

Given the delay caused by this unfortunate event and our brief incarceration, we had no choice but to continue on, though night travel was against Peace Corps policy. Either we found a place in the bush to hide the Jeep and sleep in it or we pushed on a few hundred more miles to Victória da Conquista. We chose the second option and arrived at our destination late at night, found lodging, and went to bed tired and hungry.

The next morning, we left bright and early to make it to our bank in Caetité—300 miles of dirt roads and bridgeless rivers to cross. João Goulart had won the presidential election a few months earlier, and he had done nothing yet to solve the country's financial ills or control inflation. We needed cash, and the sooner the better. With the exchange rate accelerating the way it was, Dick thought it was handy that we had our Jeep to haul all the currency we would need.

Since we were in the vicinity and Lapa was still a haul of one hundred miles on terrible roads, we decided to veer southwest twenty-five miles to the town of Guanambi. Guanambi originally had five Volunteers, but upon arriving we found it to be a ghost town with nary a Volunteer to be found. Of the original five there was a health worker with a degree in psychology and public health, a professional nurse, and two college graduates in agriculture: one in animal husbandry and one in agronomy. And Georgia Peach.

We discovered later that the animal husbandry guy, a Connecticut boy, and Georgia Peach, before his ascension to regional leader, had a relationship as trying as that of the Yankee and the King in Mark

111

Twain's *A Connecticut Yankee in King Arthur's Court*. The Connecticut lad's demeanor was rough around the edges while Georgia Peach was a smooth operator. Like the peasants in Twain's work who took the interaction between King and Yankee as the work of madmen, at some point the rest of the local Volunteers took these two for the same and decided to move on somewhere else. Georgia Peach, of course, by now had maneuvered himself into the role of King of the Lapa region. The Connecticut Yankee, therefore, was now living alone in Guanambi but for some reason was not around when we arrived.

We intended to push on to Lapa, but while hunting for the missing Volunteers we ran into the local commission director. He turned out to be a very hospitable chap and implored us to stay for the evening, even offering us dinner at his home and a tour of the area the next day. True to his word, in the morning the director gave us a tour of the Guanambi compound, an agricultural station. It was obvious that he enjoyed our company and wished we would stay longer. With a functioning ag station, what was not to like?

But we had to press on and hit the road again, arriving in Lapa at noon. Volunteers had been setting records all year moving around the valley, but their movement paled next to that of our director, Leo. We had just seen him in Rio a week before, and there he was in Lapa accompanied by Jack Vaughn, the Latin America director of the Peace Corps. In 1966, Vaughn, though a Republican, would be appointed by Democratic President Lyndon Johnson to replace Sargent Shriver as the second Peace Corps director. We stayed the night in Lapa and had a pleasant visit. Leo brought the macaroni and cheese and Vaughn provided the entertainment. A highly decorated Marine in WWII and a boxer, Vaughn regaled us with interesting stories. He'd won three Golden Gloves titles and had sparred in Detroit with Sugar Ray Robinson, Jake LaMotta, Willie Pep, and Sandy Saddler—all famous boxers that I often watched on television in the late 1950s.

In the morning, Dick and I departed early, got a lift across the São Francisco River, and began the final seventy-five miles of our journey to Correntina. At Santa Maria we had to cross the Formoso River, not always a simple matter. Two pontoons provided the launch, both with wooden platforms but no motors of any sort. Each pontoon was powered manually by two very strong men, and our first task was to locate them. Then we would have to tackle the issue of negotiating with them. If ours was the only vehicle around to cross, the price could be exorbitantly high as it was an arduous job and they did not want to have to do it more often than necessary. The high price was intended to encourage customers to wait around for an indeterminable length of time to see if any other vehicles showed up.

Noon came and no extra customers appeared, so the men ate lunch. One additional Jeep arrived before they finished, and another one shortly afterwards, so we finally had a full load and disembarked. To watch these two men maneuver a floating platform with three vehicles on it across a fast-moving river was a thing of beauty. It was one of the finest athletic feats I had ever witnessed. We would observe this procedure many more times before we left Brazil and would never cease to be amazed at the skill and craft it required, given the weight of the cargo and the speed of the river's current.

After a thousand miles of travel, we finally arrived in Correntina by late afternoon. We drove to the hydro dam and unloaded our equipment, then took the Jeep to the river for a good washing. Through our journey, we had gained a striking sense of independence and, in some respects, a feeling of greater security knowing we could reach our destinations without having to imperil our lives by riding with the likes of Ton Tonio and crazed truck drivers.

14. The president's ambassadors

We had arrived back in Correntina on the day before Easter. In some cultures, Easter Saturday is called "Joyous Saturday" or the "Saturday of Light." People in town were indeed joyous that we were back home and also that it would most likely be the beginning of a time of light, as Dick arrived with all his newfound knowledge concerning the hydro installation. It was a wonderful sensation to be home among my new friends. Silvia was right, spending a few days away created a new sense of purpose and enthusiasm to take on any future challenges.

Coincidentally, it was the fiftieth birthday of Paulo Pimenta, the current hydro manager, and a big celebration had been planned for the evening, making our return only grander. Paulo was an unforgettable character. He barely reached five feet tall on tiptoes, had lost most of his teeth, and sported an enormous belly. Normally he wore only a pair of shorts and sandals. If not for the large stomach and bald head upon which he never wore a hat in the intense heat, Paulo and Ton Tonio, the *motorista*, could have been brothers. He looked like one of the seven dwarves who had escaped from the snowy forest of Fantasyland to the fringes of the jungle. If I had to characterize him as one of the storybook dwarves, it would have to be Happy since he was a bundle of energy and always smiling. A nasal condition made his Portuguese even more nasalized than the average Brazilian; combined with his lack of teeth, this made him difficult to understand. Although possessing an obtuse management style, Paulo did have one hell of a bark, however, and possessed all the traits of a controlling personality, like someone with a Napoleon complex. *Pimenta* means pepper, so like the other Dr. Pepper, my diminutive friend and commission chief in Rio, this local Dr. Pepper loved to pepper people with commands and dictums.

Everyone wanted to know about our travels to the marvelous city by the sea. When I told them about attending the Botafogo-Santos soccer games and being in the presence of Pelé, I got the exact reaction I'd anticipated. For the next several days young people hovered around me and just wanted to touch me, as if some soccer magic would be transmitted to them. From that moment on I would indeed be a living, breathing icon.

We were anxious to get back to work but would have to wait. Besides Joyous Saturday and Easter Sunday, Monday would be a government holiday since it marked the official installation of President Goulart. Politics was a big deal in Brazil, and with Goulart being a member of the Brazilian Labor Party and popular with the masses and poor, average folks intended to celebrate. Basically, it was another day of revelry with little productive work.

In spite of the holidays we had plenty to focus on. Prior to Dick's absence, our work goals centered on the maintenance of diesel electric generators in outlying villages. Now that we had a Jeep, folks would be clamoring for us to get their generators in running order. Padre said that a couple of these towns were nearing riot status out of fear that we had left town for good. The problem with maintaining these units was that they were like the proverbial dog from every town. There were units from Israel, Czechoslovakia, Poland, England, and a couple other countries. Some were based on the English system of measurement and others on the metric system, a situation that required two different sets of tools. We purchased a set of English tools while in Rio since there were none at the hydro shop. As for spare parts, typically there were none. Using our resources at the hydro station, we were able to fix broken parts and occasionally fashion replacements. For a couple units, we found spare parts on future trips to the coast.

It was always amazing to observe the excitement of the people once they had lights again after many weeks or even months of relying solely on candles. Electricity was magic to these folks, and because we could make these units work they held us in high esteem, on the order of mystical wizards. If there were a key to the city, we would have received it.

As a matter of fact, a key to the city was the focus of our next major project. Earlier in the year, Padre's parishes in Correntina and Santa Maria became part of the new Diocese of Lapa, and Correntina would host a Bishop for the first time when the new Bishop visited. More celebration. In honor of this special occasion, Padre conscripted Dick and me to fashion a large metal key to the city for this church dignitary. While we employed our metallurgical skills, the town was abuzz with excitement and preparation. Given the level of planning and panoply for the event, one would think the newly elected President was coming to town. Things never looked so good. Roads were repaired, buildings were whitewashed, the band was practicing, and parades and feasts were arranged.

During all this activity, Leo and Dr. Ken arrived by air. We suspected that the nature of their trip was to briefly reunite the engaged couple, Dr. Ken and Silvia, to see if the relationship was holding. Apparently it was. When it came time to leave they could be found only after an extensive search. But the real mission of the visit had to do with the Peace Corps bringing thirty more Volunteers to the valley for a new project. Leo indicated that our success in Correntina had spawned regional jealousy. The mayors of Santa Maria and Santana now desired their own Volunteers. Leo wanted us to go to these towns and meet with their mayors for assessments. Whatever his intent for coming, Leo was absolutely fascinated with our making of a key to the city, and he took at least a dozen pictures. He had fun with this and said he wanted to send the pictures to Peace Corps headquarters in Washington to "show the kind of innovative technical and creative work the Peace Corps was doing."

It was too bad Leo did not stick around for a few more hours, as later in the morning the mayor's son, Adherbal, brought us a big can of silver paint to apply to the newly fashioned key. Being a creative sort, Adherbal suggested that since we were gaining a near mystical reputation in the area as electrical and mechanical wizards, maybe we should paint everything we fixed or made with this silver paint. He added that the locals might even equate us with the Lone Ranger and his horse Silver, who rode into towns, solved problems, and then rode off into the sunset with a hearty "Hi-Ho Silver!" Obviously, Adherbal was watching one too many western flicks that were occasionally shown at the local theater, in English of course with no subtitles, but all the locals had the phrase Hi-Ho Silver down pat. We appreciated his enthusiasm but thought it best to use the paint sparingly.

Adherbal also informed us that the lone truck in the area that was supposed to serve as the Bishop's carriage into town was mechanically incapacitated in Santa Maria. Could we rescue the truck? And could our shiny new Jeep fill in as the Bishop's new carriage from Santa Maria to Correntina? It was a difficult request to refuse, so we hightailed it to Santa Maria. Once we had the Bishop safely in Correntina, Padre gave me a full range of assignments, including acting as ambassador, chauffer, trumpeter in the band, and official photographer. Thank goodness for my trusty old Argus camera.

Because we were now considered big cheeses in town, Dick and I were part of all the pomp and circumstance: the opening ceremonies, the inaugural dinner, and all official events attended by the Bishop. We were formally introduced at these events as the "United States of America Ambassadors" and representatives of our good Catholic President John Kennedy. Dick jokingly told Padre it was so exciting and impressive he was almost ready to convert to Catholicism just to be part of the religious pageantry, noting that I, as a good Catholic, was allowed to kneel right up at the altar with the Bishop. Padre offered to give Dick special dispensation for the occasion if he wished. Dick's response? "Let me sleep on it."

After a high mass on Sunday all the festivities came to an official close, but our commitment remained ongoing. The Bishop left for Coribe, the next largest town about forty miles to the south on what could best be termed a cattle path. Our Jeep was once again commissioned into service as part of the entourage that traveled with the Bishop. The grand caravan comprised all the vehicles in the entire county. The only vehicle missing, including our Jeep, was the Jeep belonging to Ton Tonio, the commission motorista. Ton Tonio was incensed that he had not been invited and threatened to leave the church. Padre was not too fond of his driving antics and said he did not recall ever seeing him in church anyway.

A fter the festivities, we resumed our work. There was no question we had enough to do. There were still several generators in outlying villages to repair. And there was Padre's saw mill, which had sat idle during our civic diversions. Our perpetual task there involved the manufacture of building products for various projects, such as houses, two new rural schools we'd designed for the mayor, and Padre's pet project—the St. Alfonso Maternity Hospital. These projects required not only door and window jambs but also studs, boards, and slats for suspending roofing tiles.

A funny incident loosely related to the maternity hospital occurred about this time. One Saturday Padre decided to hitch a ride to Lapa for maternity hospital business with the commission plane since it was in town and there was a spare seat. Before takeoff, he realized he'd left the building plans at our house. I was away with the Jeep in the countryside, so Dick literally had to run the plans out to the airstrip from the hydro complex. Running was no problem for Dick. With his long legs he generally moved around town at a brisk pace that locals had to hustle to keep up with.

At the two exit roads from town, there was a barrier in the road called a *mata burro*—literally kill the donkey. It was a three-foot-wide hole in the ground covered wood planks spaced four to six inches apart. An animal's foot could fall between the planks but a vehicle could traverse it fine. Since the airport was no more than a pasture that ran over the hill, the *mata burro* was used to keep the real donkeys out of town.

Well, that day a two-legged donkey did not pay close attention as he sped across the barrier. In Dick's race against time to get the plans to Padre, his foot caught on a plank of the *mata burro* and he took a tremendous tumble, his leg penetrating between the planks. The airplane's arrival always drew a healthy crowd, so among those who witnessed the tumble were the commission director, Padre, and the pilot, Wild Bill. Dick easily could have broken his leg but only severely skinned it and badly twisted his ankle. Wild Bill would not have to make a medical transport.

The incident took top billing in community news that day and when I returned I was told at least several dozen versions of what had happened. One person related that after Padre and Wild Bill realized that Dick was not in need of hospitalization, they laughed almost to the point of requiring hospitalization themselves, and it was questionable whether Wild Bill could regain enough composure to fly the plane. Padre of course knew his Latin and was a keen student of science including the study of flora and fauna. On one occasion, he told me Dick reminded him of the cartoon character the Road Runner. In Latin, the species was called *geococcyx californianus*—California earth cuckoo. Dick being a Californian, Padre could not resist on occasion declaring when he saw Dick rapidly approaching, "Here comes the California Cuckoo!"

Dick soon recovered from both his gimpy leg and lost sense of pride enough to continue with our projects, and Padre had one more hilarious episode to add to his growing repertoire of "Gick stories." Within days, we received a telegram from the office in Rio telling us that we needed to take our Jeep in for a scheduled checkup. It was a bit mind-boggling to think we needed to take our Jeep in for a warranty checkup that required a fourteen-hundred-mile trip to the coast and back over mostly terrible roads. Other than the drive from Rio, I doubt we had put a hundred miles on the Jeep. Certainly, whatever repairs they might make would be mainly for naught.

We left the next day and did not arrive on the west bank of the São Francisco River until after dark, too late to use the commission launch to ferry us across. There were a couple of mud huts on our side of the river where one could spend the night, but Dick and I craved the excitement of Lapa, which was a sad commentary, for Lapa was such a putrid place. So we hired a gentlemen with a dugout canoe to take us across the big river in the dark. This was a risky venture, as there are numerous sandbars, possibly unfriendly piranha, and bad currents. We took our boots off and prepared for the worst but were determined to sleep in a normal bed rather than on a dirt floor.

We used the launch the next morning to retrieve our Jeep, and then we were off on 250 miles of dirt road to Victória da Conquista where we had been just a month before. An hour down the road we picked up a woman in a small village who was hemorrhaging, similar to the woman I first saw die in Correntina months before. We took her and her husband to the hospital in Caetité.

Halfway from Caetite to Victória da Conquista, we picked up a soldier who was headed for Salvador, which made for smooth sailing when it came to roadblocks that sprung up occasionally. Carrying firearms is illegal in Brazil, so the military police set up roadblocks periodically to check vehicles, and also to look for other contraband.

We spent the night in Victória da Conquista before pushing on. The soldier was still our guest, so we continued our fine chat. He had been posted in the interior for a year and was destined for reassignment in the capitol—what he called the "dream of every soldier." He considered the interior of the country to be tough duty and could not fathom how we, as Americans who were used to the good life in the

120

United States that he had read about, could possibly survive in the country's interior. He was even more incredulous when we told him we would be living in Correntina for two years; he assumed we were doing some temporary studies in Brazil.

This young man had never been west of the São Francisco River. We told him it differed greatly from the area east of the river. It was not so flat and arid and had lots of beautiful blue rivers, but it was quite isolated. He said it was that sort of isolation with little or nothing to do in the towns that eventually made it so depressing.

"About all you could do is find a girlfriend to spend time with, but then you would be considered engaged and possibly not be able to escape town without marrying her," the young man said. "Her family would want you to stay in the area where you would be trapped forever. From that point on it would only be drinking cachaça that would provide any solace in life."

We couldn't fault him for his realistic view of life in the interior. By nightfall, we arrived in Salvador, said goodbye to our new friend and checked into a hotel. The next morning, we dropped the Jeep off at the Willis garage, then Dick and I did some shopping for various needs as well as some banking. Who should I encounter at the First National Bank of New York in Salvador, but Plow Thief Dave of all people. Obviously, the state militia had no idea he was in their jurisdiction. Unlike us, Dave was not there to service his Jeep. He had just decided to come to Salvador to obtain necessary items and to visit the Ministry of Agriculture to see if, in his words, "there was any lifeblood in this government organization." Along the way he had picked up Georgia Peach, also known as the nemesis of the Connecticut Yankee, two of the missing Volunteers from our previous stop in Guanambi.

The Plow Thief and I found a small café and had a bite together. Because I had not seen him since his infamous visit to Correntina, I recounted the story of the Bahia State Militia showing up at my door, explaining they could just as well have shot me and that I damn near died of heart failure. Dave could not stop laughing over the whole incident. Little did I know when he stopped at my house with the stolen plow, he had a strong suspicion that someone might come looking for him, so once he left Correntina he did not linger on his way back to the safety of his "fellow convicts" in Montalvania.

The fact that he did not mention a word of his suspicion to me at the time, in addition to my shock at the militia showing up on my doorstep with loaded weapons, made his laugh all the louder and longer. In his proper Ivy League and highbrow style, he said, "I wasn't trying to be a fallacious fellow but my fealty, my friend, might have been compromised." Of course, I had no idea what in the hell that meant.

That afternoon Dave and I went to the State Ministry of Agriculture to see what assistance they could provide. Like me, Dave also had a hard time getting seeds and other equipment for his work. I told him I got seeds in Rio when I was there and informed him that I had planted some of them on the Coimbra farm, but the germination was horrible. Most of the seeds produced nothing.

The Ministry of Agriculture had a lot of research data and knowledgeable people but little in the way of practical assistance such as the seeds and insecticides we were looking for. Dave was still obsessed with the road grader I'd shown him sitting in the weeds in Correntina. Enamored by its prospects for leveling land for planting, he said, "We could create a veritable agricultural revolution in the backlands and be famous!"

Later we visited the Caterpillar tractor dealership to see what they had for spare parts. An open checkbook would have been nice for making repairs on the grader back in Correntina, but that was not the case. That evening, Dick and I met back at the hotel room. While there we received a telegram from the Peace Corps office in Rio. They knew we were going to Salvador for a Jeep checkup and they were looking for Georgia Peach from Guanambi. The telegram said his sister had been killed in a car accident in Georgia and that he should make arrangements to fly home immediately. This caused a strange sensation. Such tragic events were much more likely to happen in a vast, underdeveloped country with poor transportation, communications, and medical facilities, than in our safe, modern homeland.

We found Georgia Peach attending a movie. He quickly made arrangements to head to the States, although he was scheduled to return to the interior the next morning with Dave. Dave decided he would go solo, an action that was strictly against the rules. I encouraged him to wait another day and we could caravan back since he was only one hundred miles south of our destination, and maybe I could even pay a visit to Montalvania. Dave declined. He'd been in

Salvador for more than a week and was anxious to get going. He was also leery of waiting around, knowing how things could be delayed with potential repairs for our Jeep.

Dave was right. We did not get our Jeep until two days later, but at least we were confident of its road readiness. Before reaching Victória da Conquista, however, the engine started to miss badly. Although it would cost us yet another day, we found an automotive garage and decided to let them figure out the problem since it was still under warranty.

It was all dirt and dust from there on, but we made a good two hundred miles and decided to give Guanambi another shot. This time the Volunteer known affectionately as Connecticut Yankee was home but that was about it. He did not have a lick of food in the house and there were no restaurants open in the town. Since our only sustenance during the trip had been bread and Guarana, a soft drink, we needed food. We found a little grocery store where we got canned meat, peas, bread, and fruit. Over our meager meal, we updated Connecticut Yankee with what news we had, and he did likewise. His solitary existence there was pretty lonely.

Unfortunately, he would not complete the tour with our project group. He was eventually sent home. It seems he might have felt a bit like Twain's *Connecticut Yankee in King Arthur's Court* who said, "I saw I was just another Robinson Crusoe cast away on an uninhabited is-land, with no society but some more or less tame animals, and if I wanted to make life bearable I must invent, contrive, create, reorgan-ize things; set brain and hand to work and keep them busy." [33]

Generally, reasons for early termination of Volunteers were kept silent, but late hour conversation fueled by too much beer or cachaça had a way of loosening tongues. One story told months later was that at some point our compatriot, apparently unlike the real Connecticut Yankee, did not have it within himself to "invent, contrive, create, reorganize things," or find solace here with "some more or less tame animals," despite his degree in animal husbandry.

Rumor had it that his involvement with a local woman resulted in her becoming pregnant. Worse yet for him, the new mother-to-be was the town mayor's daughter. This was a real problem. Out-of-wedlock births for Peace Corps Volunteers were an absolute no-no. It was the ultimate disgrace for Brazilian families, especially the fathers. Typically, the solution was marriage as soon as the pregnancy became known. If a marriage could not be arranged because of a fleeing husband-to-be, the young woman was often sent east to Salvador or another distant town to live with a relative. Mother and baby could never show their faces in the hometown again. If there were no relatives to take the mother in, the alternative was to send her to a nunnery where the child would be given to an adoptive family. The mother would serve the Lord in celibacy for the rest of her days as punishment.

Fortunately for our good buddy, if indeed the story was true, his girlfriend may have explained his plight before telling her father. Connecticut Yankee had told us Guanambi was a lonely place and, like the soldier we'd recently met, it was not where he wished to spend the rest of his days. Or possibly before the pregnancy could no longer be kept a secret, he decided to flee in the night for a safer haven to avoid angry pursuit by the girl's prominent father, who had both his reputation and family honor to defend. The mayor would be on the Connecticut Yankee's tail to bring him to justice either at the altar, to save the good name of the family, or dead in the Sertão somewhere, never to be heard from again. After all, his daughter's unwed pregnancy was the ultimate shame and disgrace—worse than horse stealing—and no one, including the authorities, thought of justice by murder as anything but proper for the aggrieved father.

So we left our compatriot behind in Guanambi and set out for Lapa, hoping to get to Correntina the same day, but having to cross those rivers made that unlikely. Normally we would have crossed the river at Lapa and taken the more direct dry season route, but we decided to stop in the town of Santana along the old Road from Hell. We needed to go there at some point anyway to chat with their mayor about receiving future Volunteers, as suggested by Director Leo. According to local rumors, the mayor of Santana was a sympathetic Communist. This might be a bit challenging, as it meant he was a Worker's Party aficionado and supportive of the local peasants; not necessarily all bad.

The mayor came by our hotel after dinner to meet with us. He'd heard a lot of good things about our particular projects, especially from the folks in Correntina whom he knew—Elias França the mayor, in particular, as well as the ubiquitous Padre André, the troubadour of the Corrente Valley. Apparently, we had by now shed the Imperialism label give to most Americans. The mayor was indeed a big supporter of peasant farmers and their plight. It seemed his sympathy for the peasants was all that was needed to brand him a Commie, a revolutionary. All in all, the mayor struck us as one of the more educated chaps we had met.

We left Santana the next morning and headed southeast toward Santa Maria. The Road from Hell was still in terrible shape with lots of deep ruts left from the rainy season. Although it was only about twenty-five miles to Santa Maria from Santana, it took us three hours to make this final phase of the journey. There were places where we had to stop and fill in ruts to pass or cut a new path requiring removal of scrub brush and small trees. It seems a bit strange to say we only averaged eight miles or so in an hour. A good horse would have gotten us there in less time.

After another long and eventful journey, it was good to be back home.

15. Dog days of winter

I read once that the phrase "dog days of summer" originated with the ancient Romans. Back home, the dog days ran from mid-July and lasted at least a month—supposedly the period of least rainfall in the Midwest, and the hottest, sultriest days of summer.

In Brazil, however, it was winter and there had been no rain for several months. The landscape was brown and dry with trees stripped bare. Dust clung to every building and tree, and the roads were little more than pools of dust. There was no feed on the land for cattle; they became skinny, sullen wretches whose every rib bone could be counted, the fortunate ones already sent to slaughter.

Not only did plant and animal life suffer, but languor seemed to be the state of people as well. The air was hot and asphyxiating and the humidity low. It could drop to as low as ten to fifteen percent, causing a lot of respiratory problems. The town seemed to have passed from existence. People stayed indoors out of the heat and dust for fear of contracting the *gripe*—flu, so there was little activity on the streets. Truly, the dog days had arrived.

It was indeed the dog days of winter for our old dog Pluto. Shortly after returning from our travels we went to Santa Maria for a couple days to rewire their water pumping station with materials we obtained on our trip. Usually upon arriving home at any time of day or night, Pluto would come running from behind the house to greet us; not this time. Our neighbor João Amador came over and told us that Paulo (Dr. Pepper II) had come by late the day before with a rifle and shot Pluto. João said he noticed Pluto was foaming at the mouth and having trouble with his balance, so they assumed he had rabies. A rabies bite in the backlands meant death, nothing else.

This was truly the most depressing time of the year in Brazil and I found myself engrossed often in beautiful memories of home to overcome the morass of it all. While Minnesota winters can be harsh—temperatures averaged eleven degrees in the winter of 1962-1963, with many days failing to climb above zero—there is also contrast and beauty winters produce, which is not found in the stark Brazilian landscape; no day-to-day change for months. When long Midwest winters ultimately abate, they produce a phenomenon known as spring fever and a time of new beginnings.

"Everything suggests spring and I am really having the spring fever something awful," Millie wrote. "A couple of evenings back I went out with the most handsome fella—he was almost as good looking as you. We went to the Flame Café (a popular country western music venue in Minneapolis) and saw country western star Stonewall Jackson. Well, we finally reached my place before midnight and he had a ways to drive so he left right away."

Millie's letter sank me into despair far deeper than the foul mood my current situation had put me in. I wasn't sure if I wanted to read on or just burn the letter. Reasoning that Millie was being honest at least, and curious to know more, I continued.

"We have three new girls at the dorm. They came for the first time to my tiny room and went immediately for your picture which is on my mantel. Some weeks ago I was home in Plainview and your mother called and said she had some neat slides Ken had sent and she invited me out to see them. One of them in particular caught my fancy. It was a photo of you sitting on a Jeep crossing a river. You were sitting there in a James Dean like pose as if right out of a Hollywood movie. I loved it so much I asked your mother for the slide, and had a large photo made of it. The three new girls went all bleary-eyed and crazy upon seeing the photo and wanted to know if that was the same handsome guy they just saw give me a big hug and embrace when he dropped me off at the front door. I told them that the picture was indeed that handsome guy. I really had fun with my big brother Don tonight who happened to be in the city and you now have some new admirers, if you should chance to come by."

Until I got to the end of the letter and discovered Millie's handsome admirer was her brother Don, and she was just having fun with her new dorm mates, my heart skipped a beat or two and added to the general malaise that gripped me.

Homesickness felt worse than reminiscing about the joys of spring and summer. My thoughts often went to Whitewater State Park where

I first set sight on Millie ten years earlier. Easily the most idyllic place in the area, the park held many great memories: beautiful river, oak studded hillsides, and a swimming beach. Remembering Whitewater filled my mind with a sense of contentment that helped to lessen my despair during the bleakness of Brazil's dog days.

In the summer, when school was out, Millie chauffeured busloads of youngsters to Whitewater for swimming lessons. Millie loved the water and she said she had dreams of becoming the next Ester Williams. In the 1950s, Ester was known as "America's Mermaid" for popularizing synchronized swimming in Hollywood films. Ester, like the Nelsons, was another Hollywood neighbor of Millie's great uncle, whom she idolized from her visits to California.

It gradually dawned on me that another beautiful spring and summer back home would pass before I returned to my family and my sweetheart. My journey had become more emotionally trying over time, but it was never more difficult than when I realized I still had a long road ahead.

Feeling somehow responsible for the death of old Pluto, João managed to find a younger replacement for us a few weeks later. When he brought the dog by he told us that they had named it *Duque*—Duke. At first, I thought this was quite an honor. This was the revered title given to only one person, possibly the greatest Brazilian leader of all times: Luiz Alves de Lima e Silva, *Duque de Caxias*—Duke of Boxes. The Duke fought in the War of Independence in Brazil and led Brazilian forces in the Ragamuffin War, the Platine War against Argentina, and in the bloody Paraguay War. He subsequently became a baron, a count, a marquis, and finally the only person ever titled a duke during the reign of the King Pedro II in Brazil. John Wayne had nothing over this guy.

In Portuguese, I told João that having the name of the famous Duque de Caxias for the dog was quite an honor, thinking he would be duly impressed with my knowledge of Brazilian history. João, who did not speak English, shook his head and said, *"Não, sabe Duque in Inglês,"*—No, Duque. Well, we knew *Duque* in English was Duke, but after he repeated it a few more times we came to understand that he was trying to say "doggie." Apparently João had asked someone who knew a little English how to properly refer to a canine. After the rabies scare with old Pluto, neither Dick nor I were especially crazy about the idea of having another dog. Once we realized that we were not treading on sacred ground, and the animal was just a doggie and not the reincarnation of the famous Duke, we told João as politely as possible we would be honored to have him name it Doggie, but it would be best to leave the dog in the care of his young daughter, who had already become fondly attached to it.

Dog days or not, there was work to be done. In addition to our usual workday responsibilities, the school term was underway. I had promised Padre that I would teach evening classes in English, math, and some history and geography. Although not a teacher by any stretch of my imagination, one year of college in the United States (the equivalent of a master's degree for a teacher in Correntina) put me at the top of the faculty.

Although we were anxious to gain momentum in our work, a succession of festivals and holidays would stall our progress. First there was the three-day Festival of the Divine, with many beautiful events including re-enactments of the Crusades, theatrical productions, fireworks, and parades. This was followed promptly by the Festival of São João, which was followed by three official days of mourning for the death of Pope John XXIII. A week later there were national holidays for the Day of Lovers—Brazil's Valentine's Day—and the Feast of Corpus Christi.

The biggie, though, was the Festival of the Divine. In this festival, a local resident plays the emperor, which is a great honor. Accompanied by virgins, the emperor goes to the church to designate a successor for the coming year. The procession includes the crème de la crème of local beauties.

Like most small towns in America, the font of local gossip and insight into political correctness was the local barbershop. It was no different in Correntina. The barbershop was also the gathering place for local sages and pundits. We came to refer to them as the barbershop boys. During the Festival of the Divine, the barbershop boys assumed we would find a young woman to our liking among all the virgins.

They normally informed us whenever another peasant girl joined the local brothel. On this occasion, brothel newcomers were evidently untouchable until we had exercised our first right to turn our noses up at one or all of them. The barbershop boys believed there had to be an explanation for everything in life. When we refused to pick even one girl from the crème de la crème during the festival meant to them that we were either misogynistic, gay, heading for the priesthood, or taking pleasure somewhere else. The barbershop boys well knew, however, that somewhere else for me was back in Minnesota with Million Dollar Millie. I had previously shown them her photo, which elicited rave comments at the time. They, however, reminded me of the plight of Janette and the German. I could have a paramour. No one was going to rat me out. And they insisted, they would cover my tracks when I left Correntina.

There were indeed a number of beautiful girls in the festivities that would tempt most red-blooded young American males. The Catholic girls of course were all virgins. I was careful not to shoot any photos of them and set off alarm bells at home because I sent my film to Millie who passed it on my mom to develop. I used Kodachrome film, which at the time could not be developed in Brazil. Millie seemed to have a sixth sense, however, about writing something appropriate to help keep my eye on the target. "Some dreams die hard," she had recently written.

On the occasion of Millie's grandparent's fiftieth wedding anniversary, Millie's great uncle—Millie's grandmother's brother, the one who lived in California—and Millie's great aunt—also named Millie—traveled to Minnesota. Millie was a popular family name. They encouraged my Millie to think about moving to California to live with them, much as her aunt Millie had done twenty years before. Millie confessed that she still had a secret affection for Ricky Nelson, the big-time music star, whom she had dated in Hollywood years earlier. If I did not return from Brazil, she said she might just consider moving to California, and hopefully Ricky might still be available.

"On April 20th unfortunately, Ricky married Kris Harmon, daughter of legendary football player Tom Harmon," she wrote. Millie said she hoped, contrary to what her dad had told her when I left for the Peace Corps, that I would still be interested in a small-town country girl when I came home, as small-town country girl no longer seemed to fit Ricky Nelson's interests.

"Obviously his new big hit song, *There'll Never Be Anyone Else but You for Me*, was not written in my memory, although the words have become my mantra that keeps me going day to day hoping for your return."

As Ricky was no longer an option, Millie asked that I take special care to come home safely, concluding by saying she hoped that I knew she was joking about Ricky, "but it doesn't hurt to dream." A little humor was good for my soul at the moment, and I think I got the message.

Right on the heels of all the dog days holidays I decided maybe the best thing to do was to hightail it out of town before something else delayed our work. While we had lots of mechanical projects on our plate, I was determined not to lose sight of my agricultural plans. With this in mind, I headed for the commission agricultural station at the Formoso Colony on the Formoso River some fifty miles away to visit my old soccer nemesis, Wilson.

Arriving in the colony, I was met with pandemonium. Evidently a wildcat had somehow entered the compound the previous night and stolen a couple pigs. Therefore, the day was consumed with improving fencing and pens and discovering who was at fault for not locking up the pigs. The theft had occurred on Sunday, and Wilson said it most likely involved someone drinking a little too much cachaça the night before and nodding off on the job.

During my visit, Wilson did his best to convince me to move there to work with him. This was very tempting as they had a tractor and other equipment I did not have, and I enjoyed Wilson's company. Fortunately, other Volunteers were coming in a month or two as part of the Brazil III project and they would be stationed in and around Santa Maria, including at the colony. Wilson was wondering if I would simply just trade places with his designated new arrival since he still had soccer on his mind. But why take the chance? The new Volunteer might not be an athlete.

The next day Wilson asked if I would drive to Lapa to pick up Dr. Giovanni, a government official working with settling landless peasants. Upon arriving back in the colony with Dr. Giovanni, we had a most interesting meeting with a group of peasants, each of whom was slated to receive a free forty-acre plot of land from the federal government. Several conditions were attached, one of which was to provide proof of identity in the form of a birth record, marriage license, or some other official document. None of them could produce any of these documents.

The peasants were assigned numbered plots and needed to write down the number. But few among them could write, and those who could write, wrote a number between one and ten, even though there were forty lots assigned. This created considerable confusion and led to heated arguments over who had been assigned which lot. Names did not help since many of them had common names, and some did not know their surnames. Another condition dealt with house restrictions, such as prohibiting the building of a pigpen next to a home since this was a common practice and one of the chief sources of disease among the rural poor. People did this primarily to keep a close eye on the pigs and protect them from marauding thieves such as the wildcats, as well as foxes and even humans.

One of the more intelligent landless fellows took serious umbrage at this condition and got in an intense argument with Drs. Giovanni and Wilson. In frustration, he finally turned to me and asked if we had to do this in the United States. I proceeded to tell him that indeed we had to build our pigpens some distance from our houses. It seemed that he had heard the United States was the land of the free and we could do pretty much as we pleased. While he did not want to listen to or believe the good doctors, somehow my position on the matter made sense to him and he agreed to build the pen away from the house.

We assured him that we would supply wire mesh fence instead of the flimsier but typical woven stick fence and that he could erect it to a sufficient height to keep out marauding animals. When this intelligent chap asked me how Americans prevented intruders, I told him we used fencing that had a current passing through it called an electric fence. He wondered if this fence would keep out marauding human thieves. I replied that if enough electricity was run through the wire it would not only keep them out of the pen, it would kill them. He and the others loved this idea.

I noticed Dr. Wilson just smiling and shaking his head, and I knew maybe I had taken this a step too far. Wilson informed them that although no such innovation was planned, the colony would get electricity in the near future from our hydro complex in Correntina. For now, they would just have to take turns sitting up at night to guard the pigs. After a week's time, I headed back home. Wilson would not let me bring his only functioning tractor to Correntina, but he promised to do what he could to help find some seeds and other things I desired.

Silvia had already left Correntina, so we signed the lease for a house located in town on the village square, the church only twenty yards from our front door, and the town and county offices right next to the church. Diagonally across the square was the market, and right across the river sat the saw mill, Padre's rectory, the school where I would be teaching, and Padre's farm with horses.

The house had been vacant for some time and needed a lot of work. It lacked water, electricity, a toilet or shower, and furnishings. The roof leaked when it rained, and it had only a wood burning stove to cook on. So that was the bad news. The good news was we rented it for a whopping five dollars a month. The additional good news was that the house had a large back yard that I hoped to turn into a greenhouse. The additional bad news was that the yard had formerly been used as a horse corral, and there was a dilapidated building at the end of the alley that would have to be disassembled. At least the yard was protected by a wall, so I wouldn't have to worry about chickens or dogs destroying the fruits of my labor.

Given all the work required, the structure presented an excellent opportunity to create a multipurpose project: repair and upgrade the house while training locals in the practical trades of plumbing, electrical wiring, and carpentry. Even finer woodworking skills could be taught since we needed beds, bookshelves, a table or two, and benches to sit on.

These dog days of winter made it a good time of the year to be doing this work. It had cooled down slightly, enough to cause the locals to wake me up one night and come outside. They wanted to know if what was happening in the air was what we called snow, but it turned out to be a rare bout of fog. The dry, dusty conditions induced hibernation throughout town. Fewer people came to the market since there was less to sell, with most land fallow and livestock nothing but skin and bones. Many of the students my age were away at school, so social activity was also at low ebb.

*T*he only big social event that winter was the marriage of the mayor's son to Yvonne Coimbra. Sometime earlier, Adherbal and Yvonne had asked me to be the best man for their civil wedding ceremony. This turned out to be the social event of the season if not the year, but I didn't bring much for fancy clothes along to Brazil. Keno, a brother-in-law of the Comibra's, was the town's tailor and he was willing to make a suit for me. We spent a lot of time selecting just the right fabric, the best in town. Keno wanted perfect results to the point of going beyond the old carpenter rule of measure twice and cut once. His fastidious approach yielded a gorgeous suit and an exquisite fit. I told Keno there was only one thing missing. He asked me what that was. I told him I could not find the tailor's label *Keno of Correntina*.

He laughed loudly but I said, "I plan on taking this to Rio, Salvador, and even to America with me. When folks see this, you will be the rival of Oleg Cassini and Pierre Cardin!"

Whether or not my compliment made any difference, I am not sure, but Keno did not charge me for the suit.

The grand wedding took place as planned with leading citizens from Correntina and the surrounding towns present. Dr. Oswaldo, Correntina's new and first-ever county prosecutor, performed the ceremony. As best man, I was required to sign the marriage certificate. Dr. Oswaldo said this posed a complication since the certificate would be the first legal document in the county ever signed by someone not born in Brazil. After checking with state officials, he eventually found a way it could be done—quite an honor for me all the same.

The barbershop boys reported that some of the ladies in town who followed American movie stars featured in Brazilian magazines said Dr. Oswaldo was a spitting image of the famous American actor Clark Gable. I agreed they had a valid point. He had the little mustache, jet-black hair, and was indeed a handsome dude. The boys said they thought his presence would take the pressure off Dick and me, but especially off me after women saw me in my fancy new suit.

Since we had the only hardtop Jeep in town, it became the official wedding vehicle for the newlyweds and bridesmaids. Dick chauffeured, even without a suit. When people did something in Brazil that was not proper or up to standards, they were chided with the words *sem vergonha*. Interpreted, this can take on several nuances ranging from shameless, disgraceful, or scandalous to the point of mortification. The barbershop boys, although not a pernicious lot but prone to frivolity, jokingly told Dick he was *sem vergonha* and they would chip in to buy him a suit before the next big event rolled around.

Speaking of weddings, before the dog days of winter subsided we received news that Doctor Ken and Silvia were married in a beautiful ceremony in Rio. Although we had lived through months of trials with Silvia, heroically protected her against the advances of lechers, and upheld her reputation against the onslaught of innuendos about her real occupation, we were left in the lurch and not invited to the wedding. We sure would have enjoyed another visit to Rio.

While these two lovely weddings overshadowed the dog days we experienced in Brazil, they reminded me that the summer months back home were the most delightful of the entire year, days spent swimming, boating, fishing, playing summer sports. There were always lots of weddings and family gatherings, something I missed dearly.

After the tragic loss of her young sister and her dad, Millie and her family finally had something positive to celebrate, the fiftieth wedding anniversary of her grandparents. Fifty years of marriage was a major achievement, and family members from across the country gathered to celebrate. But once again, a joyous occasion turned into a tumultuous disaster. A sixteen-year-old cousin from Washington State played with an uncle's rifle, assuming it was not loaded. He pointed the firearm at his five-year-old brother and foolishly pulled the trigger, killing the boy instantly. In the Peace Corps, I thought I was living in the Wild West, but it was Millie's family who could not shake tragedy. Once again, my heart went out to them, though there was little I could do to assuage their grief.

As time progressed we saw less of our project management personnel, in spite of our various project problems, significant attrition, and the country teetering on the brink of a revolution. One reason for this was expansion. The Peace Corps had several new projects groups training for Brazil, a full seven that would grace the country before our project terminated. The first of these, deemed Brazil III, had just arrived and been stationed in the valley, boosting the number of Volunteers to six assigned downriver from Correntina at Santa Maria, Santana, and the Formoso Colony. Among these new Volunteers were a skyscraper builder from New York, an Alaskan commercial fisherman, and a pipe-smoking cowboy from Texas.

Upon their arrival, I traveled to their locations to orient them to their new surroundings. The new Volunteer stationed in the colony was the commercial fisherman named Rick, so I took him and the Texan to introduce them to Drs. Giovanni and Wilson. I knew Wilson's primary interest in my coming to the colony was to play on his Santa Maria soccer team against their hated rivals in Correntina. I had previously declined, figuring that the new prospects would most likely be good athletes. I noticed Wilson assessing pint-sized Rick and the lanky, bow-legged Texan. I think he felt that, while these two

Volunteers may have possibly excelled at fishing and bareback rodeo riding, soccer was not likely their forte. I gave Wilson a wink of the eye and he returned a giant but shy smile. Sometimes a gift does not contain everything you wish for.

Not long after our new colleagues arrived, we drove to Lapa to meet some of the other new Volunteers and to take in the largest annual area event, which was the celebration of the day the priest who lived in the cave with a cougar supposedly saw the image of Christ. August sixth also marked the Catholic holy day of the Transfiguration. A miracle reported in the New Testament, Jesus underwent metamorphosis while praying on a mountain, and became radiant with glory. It amazed me that in Lapa there was a big rock—a mountain—and inside the mountain, in a grotto, a priest living with a cougar reputedly saw the image of Jesus. What a coincidence.

During this event, the town swelled from a population of 10,000 to more than 100,000 pilgrims. Hordes of people gathered along the river reminded me of photos of the Ganges River in India in an old encyclopedia I stored under my bed back home. People bathed and washed their clothes in the river, and most likely it provided their source of drinking water and served as a latrine. With the throngs of souls gathered, the President decided it was a good time to visit the region. The original purpose of a presidential visit was to officially inaugurate the hydro dam in Correntina, but government officials visited Correntina and decided against that plan. Perhaps they wanted to avoid the donkeys and the cotton gin on our so-called airstrip. Whatever the case, they decided to the chagrin of the locals that if an inaugural switch was to be thrown, it would be done in Lapa.

The President went by the nickname Jango. My fellow project Volunteer, Airman Jim in Lapa, wrote the following passages about Jango's visit and our encounter with him: "A gathering of locals collected outside my house awaiting the President's arrival. After a meeting with the Commission Chief Dr. Lascarus, President Goulart was escorted on foot to the meeting place, leading the entourage himself. As he approached head down, looking neither left nor right, I and another Volunteer, Ken Fliés, impulsively stepped out with our hands extended to greet the President, saying in Portuguese, '*Bom dia Senhor Presidente. Muito Prazer*'—Good day Mr. President. It is a pleasure to meet you.

"With undisguised indifference, he raised his head cautiously and gave us the once-over. Being unable to ignore our outstretched hands, he replied by nodding slightly and giving us in return a limp, damp hand to shake that felt like cold fish and, without a word, continued on his way. His bodyguards, no doubt taken aback by our effrontery, had made no effort to intervene." \34

During the afternoon festivities, Jango's itinerary called for a visit to the holy site. Inside the cave, stalactites dripped water that was considered holy, plus there was an area called the *Sala das Milagres*— Room of Miracles. Given the tenuousness of Jango's presidency at the moment, he might have been looking for a miracle or two. Airman Jim observed Jango's march to the cave from the vantage point of a small plane joined by none other than our friend Reverend Reisner.

"We flew over the town, circling especially over the church plaza where Goulart would make another appearance. Below us in the narrow cobblestone streets leading to the cave and the plaza, thronged thousands of pilgrims. We circled at less than a thousand feet going round and round the hill, losing sight at times of the festivities. On about the fourth or fifth pass we saw the President's car drive up and then, on the next pass, we saw a column of smoke rising from the plaza and people running frantically away from the scene. Something awful had happened.

"We immediately thought there had been an attempt on the President's life and hurried to the airport. We soon learned that the smoke we had seen had been caused by a box of fireworks having blown up after a rocket misfired. A number of pilgrims were badly burned by the resulting explosion. The President was rushed to the airport and flown off in great haste. The injured were left to fend for themselves in a place where medical facilities were sorely lacking." \35

The getaway from Correntina was short but historic for us; for President Jango as well, I suspect. Jango no doubt understood his religion. The Feast of the Transfiguration was a celebration of Holy Trinity: God speaking from heaven, God the son being transfigured, the Holy Spirit present in the form of a cloud. The blast Jango had witnessed could be interpreted as a message from heaven. The transfigured son possibly represented the President's own life, and the cloud of smoke he had witnessed was the Holy Spirit telling him to get the hell out of Lapa. An astute historian, Jango might have remembered that not many years before on the Day of the

Transfiguration, Hiroshima was leveled by an atomic bomb. Known in church circles as the Little Epiphany, the fireworks explosion was more than Jango cared to deal with in a backwater town like Lapa.

It was late afternoon before we could get a lift across the river, its banks lined with a massive tent city as far as one could see. When we got to Santa Maria, there were five trucks with pilgrims and a Jeep waiting for the muscle men to ferry them across the Formoso River, so it was ten-thirty in the dark of night before we made it across and midnight before we rolled into Correntina.

W ell, it was back to the mill and to work on the house. I finished removing the structure from the back yard and continued building hotbeds for a greenhouse. We received a bonus with the new batch of Brazil III Volunteers. Two of them were roving mechanics who periodically relieved us of some of our mechanical workload, allowing us to focus more on the hydro installation and agriculture.

Soon after our return, director Leo paid us a short visit, this time with his lovely wife. Mrs. Leo apologized for not staying longer. She said, based on what she'd seen so far on her trip through the São Francisco Valley, that this was the prettiest place by far. She even chided Leo for not having done a better job of planning to stay the evening. And once she viewed my fabulous swimming pool, she reprimanded him all the more, saying if she'd known about the pool, she'd have brought her swimming suit. Perhaps to avert a family quarrel in our presence, Leo told her the five of us would all stand guard if she wanted to go for a quick skinny dip. It was a nice try but modesty won out.

Obviously there had been too much excitement surrounding the old swimming hole because within a short time, the canal sprung a leak in the cement wall. The floodgates had to be raised to lower the water in the canal below the crack and there would be no electricity for anyone for the next day or two while repairs were being made. This did not make for a village of happy campers. When the leak first occurred, we had images in our minds of the story the German had told us months earlier about the lack of the proper amount of cement and the collapsing hydro dams in Bolivia.

By now one year had passed since we had left our homes in America. It had been a year of incredible adventure and experience never to be forgotten. What better way to mark that milestone than by a special delivery I received in the mail about this time. It was addressed to me personally from the President of the United States of America:

The White House
Washington
July 29, 1963
Dear Mr. Flies:

   You have recently completed your first year of service in the Peace Corps.

   At home and abroad the Peace Corps has been recognized as a genuine and effective expression of the highest ideals and the best traditions of our Nation. You and your fellow Volunteers have made that judgment possible.

   I am proud of your participation and I trust that in your second year of service your conduct and performance will continue to reflect credit upon you and the Peace Corps.

Sincerely,
John F. Kennedy

16. The elusive pig chase

At the one-year mark of our arrival, Peace Corps leadership brought Brazil II Volunteers together to see what was and was not working, though it was too late to arrest the attrition that continued to shrink the size of our group. With our project spread over a 15,000-square-mile area along 1,800 miles of the São Francisco River, only those Volunteers stationed in the central region of the river would gather in Juazeiro, a city of 10,000 inhabitants located 500 miles upriver from Correntina. A dozen Volunteers had been originally posted in Juazeiro. Only six remained.

The commission planned to build the new Sobradinho hydro dam in Juazeiro and Peace Corps Volunteer technical assistance was a crucial piece of the grand scheme. Four Juazeiro PCVs were geologists. Unfortunately, one had already returned to the States, two others had relocated, and another was busy distributing Food for Peace commodities and teaching kids to play basketball. Juazeiro also had a major agricultural station but most of the agriculturalists had moved off to smaller towns in the region.

It would be refreshing to see old friends, so after making travel arrangements by telegraph Dick and I made our way across the three rivers to Lapa. Neither of us had been to the bank for some time, and with the extra spending because of our move into Correntina, we needed cash. Dick took an immediate flight to visit Dr. Torres, now stationed in Juazeiro, and to look at plans for the Sobradina dam, so I agreed to make a trip to the bank in Caetité and bring money to Juazeiro with me.

About twenty miles into my trip to the bank, disaster struck. The Jeep started to sputter and lose power and finally gave out altogether. Suspecting a fuel supply problem, I spent time alongside the dusty road diagnosing what turned out to be a punctured carburetor float, and it needed to be replaced. I had no idea how the float ended up with a hole in it. Obviously, there was more than just water and gas in the fuel. After waiting a few hours, I caught a ride with a trucker headed to Lapa. I had to leave the Jeep on the road, always a dangerous practice as by the time I returned the wheels could be gone. As a small precaution, I took the tire wrench with me and hoped for the best. I managed to get the float soldered at the commission shop, snagged a ride back to the Jeep, replaced the float, and finally made my way back to Lapa. Continuing on to Caetité in the dark would have had its hazards.

I left once more for Caetité early the next morning. In retrospect, my ordeal the day before was a walk in the park compared to my second trip to the bank. In a distance of sixty-five miles—technically beyond the fifty-mile solo limit allowed by the Peace Corps—I stopped no less than a dozen times to clean the gas line. Buying gas in Brazil was always a risky venture. I finally made it to Caetité and a garage where we proceeded to remove the gas tank and clean it out. Sure enough, there was a significant amount of water in the gas. I had burned my hand on the manifold trying to clear the carburetor, but fortunately Volunteer Art, who had recently moved to Caetité, bandaged it up for me. When I arrived back in Lapa around dusk, I was amazed at how well the old Jeep had functioned with good gas and a clean tank.

The next day I left on a commercial flight to the major town of Barra, halfway to Juazeiro. Director Leo had requested I visit a new Brazil III Volunteer named John, both to share my experiences and to assist in his adjustment. It was the weekend, so Barra was as good a place as any to enjoy some R & R. Also, two of my dear Correntina student friends and fellow volleyball aficionados, daughters of the pharmacist Pedro Guerra, were students in Barra studying to be teachers. Just like the times back in Correntina before the Guerra girls returned to Barra for school, we played several spirited games of volleyball, danced, and sang. When I visited their school and word got out I could sing, I was conscripted into service as a vocalist to perform the United States national anthem in recognition of its 150th anniversary in 1962.

I spent considerable time with John. His enthusiasm left me feeling encouraged and renewed. I left Barra again in the trusty old DC-3 puddle jumper headed to Juazeiro. Somewhere midway on the flight near the town of Xique Xique—Ouch Ouch—\36 I thought I heard excessive engine noise. Since it was no more than a hundred miles to Xique Xique, the pilots had not bothered to shut the cockpit door and flew only a few thousand feet off the ground. At first, I assumed this was the source of the extra engine noise. Well, not quite.

As I looked out my window, I suddenly noticed the commission plane with Wild Bill at the stick laughing and waving to get my attention, Dick at his side. The wing of his plane was literally right under the wing of our plane. He flew this way for a while, gesturing and saying something in Portuguese that he must have assumed I could lip-read. He was trying to tell me he'd come to pick me up. The DC-3 pilots appeared quite enamored with Wild Bill. Through the open cockpit door, I could see they were having a good laugh over his antics, flicking the DC-3 wings a bit from side to side to signal him or chase him off.

For some unknown reason Dick and Wild Bill thought that they were supposed to pick me up in Barra and fly me to Juazeiro. They flew down to Barra, but I had already left on the commercial DC-3. I was just happy when Wild Bill finally decided to be on his way. Looking over into their plane, I could see that Dick was in dire panic and pleading with Wild Bill to get the hell out of there before a downdraft caused the wings to collide. Being a skilled engineer, Dick probably had a good idea which plane would come out the loser in the encounter. This turned out to be one of the truly most bizarre moments of my time in Brazil.

*T*he first evening in Juazeiro was consumed in storytelling. In every crowd, there seems to be a champion raconteur. In this instance it was Big Ben, who was stationed in the small town of Itacuruba, which he referred to as the "rectum of Brazil." Ben spoke Portuguese perfectly and was a keen observer of the Brazilian landscape and society, having spent the first seventeen of his twenty-one years living in Brazil. With excellent command of the language and superior storytelling skills, he could leave you in stitches as he knew the subtleties of what was really being said by the Brazilians.

Ben said the first Peace Corps house in Itacuruba had been so shoddily built that the bathroom wall collapsed while one of the female Volunteers was taking a shower, and the whole town got to view her "glorious butt." Being a gentleman, Ben did not want to further embarrass her by mentioning her name. Many of the Peace Corps women had moved around a bit. Some had left the interior to work in the slums in Rio. He left us to wonder and speculate exactly whose glorious butt it was.

Ben's second memorable story dealt with livestock breeding. He said, "I remember with awe the day one of our female Volunteers instructed a bunch of terrified Brazilian technicians and scientists how to attach an artificial sperm collection device on the penis of a very large and mostly pissed-off bull." Again, no details of the heroine were disclosed to ensure her anonymity, but we had our suspicions. As Ben hinted, there were only a few women in the group with a "brass set to do that."

Big Ben left his best story for last. This one involved a young Volunteer from the Deep South. Just eighteen, fresh out of high school the previous June, he went straight into training for our project. A new high school grad might work for the military but not the Peace Corps. First of all, the young man was a poster child for the stereotypical Southern redneck. Second, he was a rebel to the core, with a bit of a temper to boot. If you were interested in a fight or wanted to revive the Civil War, he was your man. In Alabama, during the James Meredith unrest, he was ready to abandon the project, hop in a car with locals, and head to Mississippi to fight with troops sent there by President Kennedy. In addition, he had the deepest Southern drawl of anyone in the group. He was not especially adroit with Portuguese and his drawl only accentuated the problem. Ultimately this combination of feisty disposition and language deficiency got him deselected from the project. His daddy had political connections, however, so the young man was promptly reinstated and sent to Juazeiro.

Considered a redneck by some Volunteers, he fancied himself a Southern gentleman and a ladies' man. He did not lack hubris. In training we were told that the quickest way for a male volunteer to learn Portuguese was to get a girlfriend, so immediately upon his arrival in Brazil he took this to heart. But there was a serious flaw in that advice. What the instructors in Oklahoma failed to tell everyone was that in Brazil there was no such thing as a steady girlfriend, like Millie, my girl back home. In the backlands, going-steady meant you were engaged to be married. Perhaps out of ignorance, this young man soon acted upon the misguided advice of the instructors in Oklahoma and hooked up with a young Brazilian girl. According to Brazilian customs, the girl's family wanted their honor protected, hanky-panky or not.

Whatever the motivation, a true Southern gentleman was imbued with a sense of honor. When called to task by the family, he agreed to take the local girl's hand in marriage instead of fleeing as other Volunteers sometimes did when faced with the same quandary. Somewhere in the chain of events leading to marriage, all of this was brought before the local Bishop, an American, who might have understood and sympathized with the young man's predicament, except that when it came to the Catholic Church, the Bishop was a hardliner. Already upset with the young man for disregarding local dating customs, the Bishop was especially concerned to learn that the Volunteer was a strict Southern Baptist. The Bishop told our storyteller, Big Ben, that there was no way he was going to allow a fine Catholic girl to marry a hard-shell fundamentalist Southern Baptist.

Acting as interpreter, Big Ben assisted the young man through these perilous waters. Ben did all he could to assuage the reservations of the Bishop; he advised the Volunteer to enjoy the moment. After all, according to Ben and the other local Volunteers in Juazeiro, the girl was quite good-looking. Ben told the young man that if he had any misgivings about Catholicism and his family's attitude toward it, he could always go his separate way with the religion issue when he returned home after his tour. The Volunteer followed Big Ben's sage wisdom and decided to convert to Catholicism, making the Bishop a happy man.

Ultimately, the young man was forced to confront any doubts he might have had about his conversion sooner than he expected. While the young woman's family and the Bishop were happy with the wedding, the Peace Corps was not. Rules concerning Volunteers getting married were vague. The Peace Corps Director could use marriage as an excuse to get rid of a troublesome Volunteer. Rules were rules, and the unauthorized nuptial provided the Peace Corps an opportunity to demonstrate who ran the show. There would be no string-pulling by the Volunteer's father this time. No longer a Volunteer, the young convert and his bride were sent packing back to the United States.

It was a long night of camaraderie. Everyone seemed to have a story to tell about some unusual peril or hilarity. My contributions about

Padre, Plow Thief Dave, and Wild Bill the Aviator ranked right up there with the best of them.

The next day we received an invitation to attend a more formal storytelling event—a play put on by a traveling troupe from the capitol in Salvador excoriating American exploitation in Brazil. The education establishment at this time was a bastion of radicalism and had a lot of Communist sympathizers, especially university students. Most of them came from more affluent families. The general impression we had after a year in Brazil was that once their university days were over, most of these students would fade back into daddy's business. There were only a few real Ché Guevaras in the world.

Before leaving Juazeiro, I had a personal conference with Director Leo. He promised me that before the upcoming planting season in October I would get seeds and other support items the commission had yet to deliver. Leo told me Purdue University had a project in southern Brazil that was producing vegetable seeds and that he had made arrangements to provide these to us. I said this was good news and then shared with him Dave's proposal to take matters into his own hands. Dave too needed seeds, and he'd heard of the Purdue activities in Parana State. I explained Dave's plan for the two of us to drive one thousand miles to Paraná to get those seeds. I quickly added that as desperate as I was for seeds, one brush with the law over plow thievery with Dave was enough for me. Leo gave me a forlorn look and told me he was well aware of Dave's questionable style in such matters, but he would get us the seeds come hell or high water. He said he did not need to deal with a couple Volunteers in jail or worse. He had enough problems already.

It wasn't long before spring arrived in the tropics and we left the dog days of winter behind. With the promise of seeds, I could return to Correntina with new energy and excitement. This time I would travel with Gaucho Jim, the Connecticut Yankee, and Sprinter Chuck on an eleven-hundred-mile trip across the backlands by Jeep in search of hogs at an experimental farm near the coast.

Leo had informed us that the pigs were available, and since Gaucho Jim and the Connecticut Yankee were both animal husbandry majors the pigs made sense for them. Working with Dr. Raul, the new chief at the hydro dam, we had already obtained a Holstein heifer in Correntina, possibly the first of its kind anywhere in the interior of

Brazil. Familiar with both Holsteins and hogs on my family farm, and being game for anything that smacked of progress, I signed on for the mission.

Two days earlier Gaucho Jim, Sprinter Chuck, Dick and I visited Volunteers in the small town of Corípos north of Juazeiro. On the return trip to Juazeiro, Gaucho Jim's Jeep ran out of gas. And that's when he confessed the gauge did not work and he had no spare gas on board. Obviously, he'd given little heed to my instructions back in Correntina about the vagaries of the gas business. Sprinter Chuck and I spent several hours along a desolate road with the Jeep while Jim and Dick hiked many miles to Juazeiro for gas. They did not return until midnight. Needless to say, we saw to it the gauge was fixed the next day.

With reasonable assurance that the Jeep was in good repair, we set off in the early morning hours, to avoid the intense afternoon heat, on our journey across the heart of the *Sertão*—hinterland, country that's made up of what is called the *Caatinga*—scrub forest. It was the most despicable land I had seen in Brazil for man or animal. The worst of it in the native etymology is referred to as the *caatanduva*—the ailing forest.

In *Os Sertões*, Euclides da Cunha writes, "In the backlands, even prior to the midsummer season, it is impossible for fully equipped men, laden down with their knapsack and canteens, to do any marching after ten o'clock in the morning. On the tablelands, the day is blazing hot, with no shade in sight; the barren earth refracts and intensifies the sun's rays owing to the exhausting effect of a very high temperature, all the vital functions are accelerated in an amazing fashion, and the result is sudden collapse. [37]

About halfway through the Caatinga we stopped in the town of *Senhor do Bom Fim*—Man of Good Ends. The mayor there wanted Volunteers and Leo asked us to check in on him. No one seemed to know how the town got this name or who the namesake was. It most likely was not the bad man who formerly lived in the town of Canudos, a short distance to the west.

Canudos was the ultimate destination for fully equipped men referred to by da Cunha. In the backlands, during the years of 1896 and 1897, a fanatical religious mystic named Antonio Conselheiro established a colony that attracted several thousand devoted followers, mostly runaway slaves seeking a new and better life. The

Brazilian government considered this growing movement dangerous and took actions to destroy it. Even using cannons before resorting to hand-to-hand, house-to-house warfare, the Brazilian army took ten months to destroy all 5,200 homes in Canudos and kill all of its residents. [38]

After lunch and a visit with the mayor, we waited for the worst of the heat to wane before pressing east to the town of Jacobina, the locale of the now infamous ménage á trois and home of the town's lone Volunteer survivor, Sprinter Chuck. After a restful night without incident, we set out in the early morning for the coast. Upon arriving in Salvador, we shopped for needed items and went to the Agricultural Ministry of the State of Bahia. As foreigners, it was necessary for us to get permission to acquire pigs.

The next morning, we drove to the ag station forty miles northeast of Salvador in Catu. The whole idea behind our quest was to acquire breeding stock in order to develop a better strain of pigs in the interior. Like the peasants in Formoso Colony, everyone in the countryside seemed to have a pigpen right next to their house. Most of the pigs in the interior were inbred, skinny, and of very poor quality. They also had so many worms and parasites that they never seemed to gain any weight. Eventually the peasants just killed the old pig and ate it before it totally turned to shoe leather.

Being pseudo-veterinarians, we intended to promote good health in these new pigs, especially with the aid of some Merck Manuals supplied to us by the Peace Corps upon our initial placement in the backlands. These tomes were guidebooks for lay people that listed solutions for any malady that might assail man or animal. With the information they provided, we could diagnose ills, prescribe medicine, administer shots, and even attempt a procedure or two if we saw the need. The crucial point to remember was that the blue Merck manual was for humans and the red manual was for animals.

When we finally reached our destination, it appeared we were in luck. There were pigs aplenty, but the officials in charge said none of them were the right age, whatever that meant. This mantra seemed to be well-rehearsed by anyone of authority at that facility whenever we attempted to determine which pigs we could take.

Again, this was one more of the many faux pas we experienced in trying to get any sort of program going. So it was not only the commission that was inept and underfunded, but also the State of

Bahia. We all got the distinct feeling that they did not want us to be doing this work, thus demonstrating their unwillingness to service the wilderness areas of the state. Our little swine sojourn from Juazeiro to Salvador was all for nothing—it ended up being just a wild pig chase.

We left late in the afternoon and headed for Victória da Conquista 270 miles away, finally arriving at midnight. I drove most of the distance since Gaucho Jim did not particularly trust the Connecticut Yankee behind the wheel. I think both men had enjoyed the big city of Salvador too much the night before. Fortunately, this stretch of road was asphalt, so I drove late into the night, once again in violation of the rules. There was always the worry about road bandits when traveling late at night and we were not allowed to carry weapons of any sort. We felt we could handle the situation since there were three of us, even though two were dead to the world for most of the journey.

After a few hours of shut-eye in Victória da Conquista, we left again the next morning. The road from Victória da Conquista to Caetité was dirt, ruts, and holes, and by the time we arrived the Jeep had broken springs on one side and the bolts connecting the springs to the frame had sheared off. Thankfully, there was a garage in Caetité. Like most garages they did not have a set of springs, but they had bolts, so we could attach the spring back to the frame, making the ride at least bearable.

The Connecticut Yankee left us in Caetité and headed to his post in Guanambi only eighteen miles down the road. It would be the last I would see him in Brazil. He invited Gaucho Jim and me to stop by and spend the night, but I remembered my previous stops in Guanambi when we almost starved to death trying to find food in the town, so I decided to pass. It was Saturday and Jim and I wanted to get to home.

We spent the next day in Lapa. Dick was there as well making arrangements to go to Rio de Janeiro yet again for more hydro training. Yes, for the third time. I sure wished I could have found an excuse to go with him for a few days. Unfortunately, I had a lot of things to do back in Correntina and was already feeling guilty about having been off chasing pigs. While Dick was excited about his travels he could see that we were a little weary and forlorn from ours. Dick asked, "So how did the great pig chase go?"

Jim replied, "You would be better suited to call it the 'grease pig chase.' Those boys in Catu were a slippery bunch."

17. Gardens of delight

On October 1, 1963, Gaucho Jim and I took off for Correntina driving separate Jeeps. From Correntina Jim would continue on to Barreiras. This time we would not be on the Road from Hell, but on what we called the Southern Road. Rather than follow the Corrente River twelve miles upstream, we would follow the power transmission line directly from Lapa to Santa Maria.

It hadn't rained for months; incessant dust so thick it was like driving through sandstorm. Red-legged *seriemas* (the real inspiration for the long-legged Road Runner cartoon character, not the short-legged California cuckoo) could run up to fifteen miles per hour along and across the road, faster than a human; big lizards called *tatus* occasionally ambled in front of my Jeep causing me to brake hard. Gaucho Jim had to be doubly observant so as not to rear-end me in the blinding dust cloud.

After a twenty-day absence, I finally made it back to Correntina. The next day we washed our Jeeps in the river and Jim headed north. After so many days away, the town looked worn and old. The dryness of the air, dust hanging on the trees, and the emaciated look of most living things, including people, seemed worse to me than a harsh northern winter. Only the beautiful mellifluous blue river that never changed in color or volume, as if it flowed from some magical place, broke up the ugly brown landscape.

Although the trip north had interrupted the progress of our projects, the time away from post re-energized our spirits, particularly when we witnessed the enthusiasm of other Volunteers who had also survived their first harrowing year in Brazil. Our move into town from the hydro installation created many exciting opportunities, as did the arrival of a telegram from Leo announcing that the coveted vegetable seeds from Paraná were on their way. Leo indicated that he had also telegraphed the Plow Thief—even Leo was now using this moniker for Dave—but got no response, and that if he showed up in Correntina with plans to drive to Paraná, to tell him to hold his horses, stay put and wait for seeds to arrive.

The most urgent project was to complete our move from the hydro complex to the new house in town. As usual, I was the pied piper with more than enough help from a passel of boys who competed for the privilege of riding in the Jeep back and forth between the two places. There were also friends who showed up to get in on the action, one of whom was my buddy Quinn from out in the countryside. Since I had been away for some time, Quinn was out of touch with the latest news.

When in town, Quinn liked to come over to visit and generally found a way to stay for dinner. He was a typical Brazilian ladies' man who thought that his status as a young, unattached male with a nice farm and ranch he could be the perfect remedy for Silvia's Correntina-induced melancholy. When I disclosed to him that she had flown the coop permanently, he just frowned and shook his head. Not one to be defeated easily, he expressed that he had also taken a liking to our maid. I told Quinn he had been away too long and that I had more bad news for him. The maid was engaged to be married and she was often accompanied home after dark by her fiancé and a family member, usually one of her brothers. Messing with someone's girlfriend, fiancée or wife was an unpardonable offense in the backlands, for both parties involved. The telegraph operator in Lapa, our main communications conduit to the outside world, had recently killed his wife for such a transgression.

After my last supper in the old house, I would have to eat at Donna Vivi's boarding house until our new place was ready. Two days after I moved into town, Dick returned from Rio with gifts in hand: the long-awaited vegetable seeds that I had sought for almost a year. He was accompanied by Dr. Raul, the new director for the hydro installation and a well-trained electrical engineer. With Dr. Raul's arrival, Dick could focus more on the saw mill. Likewise, with the Brazil III roving mechanics now looking after generators in the outlying towns, I was free to focus more on teaching school and developing my agriculture projects.

My first priority, therefore, became building the enclosed greenhouse in the back yard of our new home. This represented a sort of catharsis and new beginning for me. Seeing my enthusiasm when he stopped by, Padre encouraged me by explaining *hortus conclusus*, a walled garden referred to in Latin literature.

Padre said that a walled garden formed boundaries, as opposed to unbounded direction. He said that sages have long believed that man gets away from the blows of the world and finds the wealth of his psyche, his paradise, in a walled garden. I had indeed suffered my share of blows attempting to achieve my professional goals in Peace Corps based on my upbringing and training. Was it possible that my dogged determination and grit were about to find their fulfillment in this garden?

Like the medieval gardens of Persia that Padre described to me, my garden would also be walled in. The house formed its front boundary, two high masonry walls the side boundaries, and a high wire mesh fence along the alley formed the rear boundary where everyone could peer in and see exactly what was taking place. For the next few weeks I was consumed with demolition of the existing structures, hauling in manure and black dirt from Padre's farm to reinvigorate the soil, and planting the beds with new seeds. The rains usually came around the end of October or early November, so my goal was to have seedlings ready to transplant.

In addition to working on my *hortus conclusus*, I put together a program for expansion of vegetable garden projects in the countryside. The vegetable seeds I received were in bulk packages of around ten pounds each, some dozen varieties in all. Upon receiving these I set up a little production line in my new house. Working with the entourage of young lads who typically followed me everywhere, we made little triangular packets out of paper, measuring about three inches a side. Next, we placed sufficient amounts of each seed into these, one variety to a packet. Then we put these small packets into a larger package along with precise instructions I wrote up in Portuguese detailing how to prepare the soil, plant the various types of seeds, and maintain the plants—watering, pest control, and so on.

In subsequent weeks, we would empty the large bags of seeds and assemble three hundred larger packages for distribution. During the production process, it was easy to spread the word about the upcoming availability of these seed packages in the county, whether through my visits to the market, my trips throughout the countryside, or my store in my house.

I was on a mission. Now all I needed was some rain. It began to rain in late October, the first time in six months. I hoped the rain would mark the end of the torturous dry season and the beginning of a growing cycle leading to harvest. Although there were no planned Halloween festivities, there was a lot of celebrating in the streets. I never knew rain could be so wonderful. Everyone just stood out in it and let themselves be drenched in happiness. It was a day for celebration for sure, but not for long. My elation at the rain ended abruptly when I returned home and discovered that many of our roof tiles were cracked. We had at least a dozen leaks, soaking things. We had updated the electricity and plumbing in the house but never thought about the roof. We cursed the damn buzzards that regularly landed on the roof and destroyed tiles.

It would be another couple weeks before the rains came on a steady basis. Then I could begin to plant vegetable gardens, as well as corn and cotton plots. Once the rains started, they could be intermittent, with occasional breaks of a week or so without precipitation. Anything planted before steady rains would require replanting unless there was irrigation. I began planting in locations where I knew water was available. This included Padre's school and farm, the Coimbra farm, and with Dr. Raul at the hydro complex.

Working in my *hortus conclusus* and focused on what I believed to be my original mission in Correntina, agriculture, I was also looking forward to taking a trip to the Amazon. With all of this, I almost lost track of time. Then I received a letter from Millie reminding me that I was on the downhill side of my journey. Things were indeed looking good. "Ken," she wrote, "it has been over a year since I've seen you, but if this one goes by like the last did I'm sure you will be with us once more, for a while at least. So many things could be happening, and I am constantly hoping it be willed that you might be back here someday soon. Please be cautious and take good care for us please. Thinking of you often and miss you."

I was a bit perplexed by her comment, "for a while at least." The only thing I could think of was a number of local boys back home, in accordance with my mother's warning and prophesy about Vietnam—in hope she could disrupt my Peace Corps ambitions— were leaving home to join the military. In the 1960s, men of Draft-age were granted a four-year deferment to attend college. But in the early days of the Peace Corps, there were no guarantees that after two years as a Volunteer, the local Draft board would give me an extension on a college deferment. In other words, a year after returning, I could be eligible for the Draft. Six of the ten boys in our family would go on to serve in the military during the Vietnam War.

Once the rains came in a steady pattern I began planting the hybrid corn and cotton seed. Around this time, I received a few bags of these seeds from Barreiras as a promised reward for the mechanical work I had done there the previous year. I would plant these in locations without irrigation; the rains would be essential to their survival. The mayor, who had a piece of land along the main road coming into town from the lower valley, was a great supporter of my planting program. He gave me a hectare of land (about 2.5 acres) to plant in hybrid corn, and he also planted a hectare of regular corn right across the road so everyone coming into town could see how the two compared. He didn't seem to be a big proponent of my corn, since the picture I showed him of mature plants demonstrated that hybrid plants were much shorter than the traditional corn grown in that region. Everything there seemed to be judged on size, be it pig, cow, or grass. Food value was a novel concept.

The idea of cotton, however, tripped the mayor's trigger. One of the main projects of his administration had been to build the infamous cotton gin, the installation I feared the Aero Commander plane would hit on takeoff. In two years of existence, the gin had never been operational. The mayor was pursuing every avenue to acquire ginning equipment; he was a very astute and progressive businessman. He also knew there were two American mechanics in Correntina—me and Dick—and a couple of roving American mechanics to assist in putting the gin together for nothing.

The previous week, a man had come through town. He said he was building a cotton gin in his town many miles to the south and offered to provide ten thousand pounds of cotton seed to plant in the region if we could find growers. We assured him that we could. The mayor did not believe he would come through with his offer; nor did I.

During subsequent interactions with the mayor, I was reminded of this man with the ten thousand pounds of seed. Mayor Elias was always looking to make big money. About this time, he started trying

155

to convince me to stay in Correntina after my Peace Corps service. He felt we could make a fortune together. He even intimated that he would look into getting me a good chunk of land that would be mine over time, at no cost. I was left to wonder if this tale was not as tall as the ten thousand pounds of cotton seed the salesman offered.

I continued on through the latter part of the month planting all I could since I planned to travel in December. But late one November afternoon, my planting momentum came to a sudden halt; a day I would never forget.

I had just finished teaching classes at the school. As I approached the north end of the Corrente River Bridge, Ton Tonio, commission motorista and local gumshoe, came storming across the bridge in his Jeep and stopped me. He told me that his mother-in-law had been listening to his radio when she heard President Kennedy had died. Knowing that Ton Tonio was a bit of a fabulist by nature, I replied that I knew the President's father, Joe Kennedy, had suffered a serious stroke some time ago and I suspected if there was any credence to Ton Tonio's message, it was most likely that his mother had heard a report of Joe Kennedy's passing. Ton Tonio had already gone to the hydro installation and told Dick what his mother had learned and then dropped him off at our house in town.

When we moved into the city, we purchased a radio. By the time I reached home, Dick already had tuned into the Armed Forces Radio station and listened to announcers recounting the tragic news of President Kennedy's assassination in Dallas.

What transpired throughout that evening to well past midnight left us speechless. A continuous line of people filed through the house to express their condolences. The fact that President Kennedy was Catholic meant a great deal to Brazilians. With his Alliance for Progress and the Peace Corps, Kennedy was the first president in decades to pay much attention to Latin America. By the time of Kennedy's death, we were highly regarded in the community, and we accepted the generous outpouring of sympathy from so many visitors as an expression of their great respect and love, not only for the President but for us as well. We would never forget the many kind words, food, and other gifts that were brought to our door that evening and in the days ahead. The President of Brazil declared three days of official mourning throughout the nation.

Another prevalent sentiment among many townspeople was a genuine fear that we would be leaving Correntina. After all, the Peace Corps was Kennedy's revolutionary program, and not all politicians supported it. A new administration might not retain the program. Like most Americans in the United States, we listened over and over to the report of that horrible day's events and did not want to believe it could be true. It was almost morning before we got any sleep.

The following Saturday, I went to the market to take my mind off the turbulent events. Many of the people from the countryside first heard the news of President Kennedy's death when they arrived in town. As word of the tragedy spread among the rural populace, the only thing that many of them really understood was that "Kennedy" had died. I mentioned previously the difficulty for most Brazilians to pronounce my name because of their inability to pronounce the *th* sound. To most of them, my name was Kennedy.

Because of this unfortunate linguistic problem, the rural folks who didn't read or had no radio and only got news secondhand thought I had died, not President Kennedy. Upon greeting me at the market, they appeared overcome by wonderment until they finally understood what had really occurred. Padre was aware of the mistaken identity by many of the poor from the countryside since many had gone first to the rectory in anguish, certain that I was dead.

I spent most of my time at the market that day receiving condolences from the friends I had made in the countryside. Many of them had to touch me or shake my hand to assuage their doubts that indeed I was alive. Even later, when I returned to my house, people kept streaming to our door to express their sympathies and drop off some small token of their appreciation and respect for us. They were persistently concerned that we might not remain in Correntina. Padre even dedicated a special Mass as a tribute to President Kennedy, mentioning in his homily his gratitude for the Peace Corps program sending us to Correntina.

Those four tumultuous days seemed like an eternity as we attempted to understand and resolve the meaning of what had happened, and how to chart a new course for the future. In the end, resolution came for me with the knowledge that our work as pioneers of the Peace Corps program was the most fitting embodiment of what President Kennedy stood for. If we could do all that was possible through our efforts to ensure that the Peace Corps survived, that it would be preserved as a unique instrument of foreign policy, there could be no greater legacy on our behalf to his memory.

Over the next several days, the town crept back to normal life and I got back to agriculture work. One night we listened to the Thanksgiving proclamation President Kennedy had prepared before his death. Sobering as it was, we gained solace and inspiration for the months ahead from a passage from his stirring message: "Yet, as our power has grown, so has our peril. Today we give our thanks, most of all, for the ideals of honor and faith we inherit from our forefathers— for the decency of purpose, steadfastness of resolve and strength of will, for the courage and the humility, which they possessed and which we must seek every day to emulate. As we express our gratitude, we must never forget that the highest appreciation is not to utter words but to live by them." \39

Since I had been in the Peace Corps for more than a year, I planned to use some of my allotted vacation time, leave Correntina for a few weeks and to travel to the Amazon. In anticipation, I spent as much time as possible in the countryside getting corn, cotton and vegetable projects in place. And before leaving, I arranged to have them looked after. One evening I returned to town to find a surprise visitor at my house, the illustrious Plow Thief Dave. We sat up until midnight discussing the Kennedy assassination and its ramifications, my forthcoming trip to the Amazon, and our agricultural projects. Although Dave longed to accompany me to the Amazon, as usual, he was short on funds. He also had a lot of projects underway and wanted to stick around to ensure their progress.

Dave was in Montalvania by himself and didn't have someone like Dick to keep an eye on things while he was gone. He confided that it was "hard to know which of the convicts to trust" in Montalvania. He asked Dick to send him a telegraph if anything major happened, like some strange epidemic or insect infestation, and he would come have a look to see if there was a remedy. That was rewarding to hear, as Dave knew his stuff. He was en route to the hamlet of Inahumas to the north but remained vague as to his mission. Then again, I did not particularly want to know the details. A couple days later he was back in Correntina, penniless of course and out of gas. Always prepared for possible emergency situations, Dick and I kept a reserve of fuel. I suspected Dave caught on to this quickly. Perpetually in need of gas, for Dave, all roads led to Correntina.

Dave always maintained secrecy about his comings and goings, and after the plow incident I was comfortable with my ignorance. But that was about to change. Later that same afternoon he returned with a doctor from Montalvania. This was no ordinary doctor like my old friend Dr. José. This doctor lived in the convict colony. According to Dave, the doctor was a very capable soul but had run into some bad luck and thus found his way to the security of Montalvania. Dave told me the whole story.

The good doctor, being well-educated and intelligent, had recognized Dave to have similar qualities. One night over a few too many beers he bared his soul and swore Dave to secrecy. Dave emphasized that he had told no one else but knew he could trust me not to share the doctor's story, even with Dick.

The doctor came from La Paz, Bolivia, where he had performed an abortion for the daughter of a well-connected, wealthy family. The operation resulted in the girl's death. Well, this doctor had performed the operation as a favor to his close friends, another prominent Bolivian family whose son had gotten the young woman pregnant in the first place. Her family swore vengeance on the doctor, and he fled deep into the interior of the Bolivian mountains, then into the equally desolate interior of Brazil. He learned of Montalvania and decided that the convict town would be about as safe as any he could find. It was definitely unusual that he would venture this far from Bolivia, but our "end of the world" may have been the first speck of civilization he'd encountered.

Dave liked to contend that he was much more deprived than I in his little hamlet. I told him that was impossible. He at least had a first-rate surgeon, fugitive or not, to give him the chance of surviving a serious injury or illness, whereas that was not the case with us. I offered them a room at my place but they already had rooms at Dona Vivi's boarding house. I suspected Dona Vivi had heard of the doctor in her usual fashion—from one of the many out-of-town customers who gathered around her big dining room table for evening meals—and invited him to town.

It was Saturday and I needed to spend time at the market for a scheduled seed distribution, so I temporarily forgot about Dave and the doctor. By late morning that all changed. A boy came by the house to tell me that Senhor Dave wanted me to go to a house where he and the doctor were up to something. I immediately followed the boy to one of the poorer parts of town and entered the appropriate house where I saw Dona Vivi, Dave, and the doctor huddled around a woman on the dining room table. This was the only table in the place and would have been used for everything, including butchering chickens.

It was obvious that an operation was in progress, but surprisingly it was Dave who had his hand inside the woman's incision instead of the doctor. Dave explained in English that the doctor had just performed an abdominal operation and had invited Dave to perform an exploratory probe while he pointed out a couple things. And to think I balked at doing a mere trachoma procedure with Dr. José. The doctor was explaining to Dave where the woman's fallopian tubes were. He also revealed that whenever he did this type of operation on poor women who already had large families, he would tie the tubes off so the women could not have any more children.

The doctor sternly instructed Dave to let me know that I absolutely must not tell anyone else, particularly Padre, or I would be taking up residence in the convict colony along with the rest of them. In Catholic country, doing something of this nature was akin to murder in the eyes of the church. Another interesting aspect of the operation was that Dona Vivi was a very devout Catholic. I got the impression, however, that she had no idea secondary sterilization was a part of this operation. Thank God, she did not speak a lick of English.

It was hard to judge what was right or wrong. I remembered very well witnessing the death of the woman in the back of Pedro Guerra's pharmacy from the effects of possibly one too many births. Traveling regularly in the countryside and seeing all the orphaned children and small crosses in cemeteries was a constant reminder of the other side of this issue. So, mum it was. To do otherwise was too risky. I may already have been put on the state militia's watch list because of my relationship with Dave. And I surely could not risk being excommunicated by the church.

Dave and the doctor left town the next morning after a few more operations. This was a good thing in more ways than just saving me from possibly explaining other transgressions that might surface. My trip to the Amazon was at hand and there was work to finish. As I attempted to make necessary arrangements to leave, my efforts in

160

getting people's attention were further interrupted when the circuit judge arrived for the start of a murder trial. Fortunately, this diversion was short-lived. By the end of the day the jury had acquitted the murderer. I think this had much to do with the local governments' general unwillingness to undertake the costs associated with incarceration. They would much rather give the accused time to pack up and get out of town, which some might have seen as a remarkably practical solution.

In making my final preparations to head out for a month, most people in town thought that, as a twenty-year-old, I was far too adventurous to be taking a trip up the Amazon. Admittedly, it was a trip few Brazilians would ever contemplate taking. But I was young and not to be deterred. The challenges of the Amazon might be a welcome respite from all the recent happenings in town.

18. The *Wolf* and the Amazon

From early on, the adventures of great explorers fascinated me, stories about men like David Livingstone in Africa; Teddy Roosevelt, who almost died in the jungles of Brazil on the *Rio das Dúvidas*—the River of Doubt—now named the Roosevelt River; and Percy Fawcett, who disappeared along with his eldest son in 1925 during an expedition to find *Z*, an ancient city that he and others believed existed in the Amazon. Being so close to the Amazon and not seeing it seemed a sacrilege. While in Juazeiro back in September, I and two other Volunteers—Bill from Minnesota and Bob from Connecticut—decided to make the Amazon our next great adventure. We decided to meet in the major coastal city of Recife in November.

To get there, I would need to travel through Santa Maria, to the compound in Lapa, then on to Caetité for a necessary bank run, east to Victória de Conquista, then to Salvador, and finally north to Recife. At the compound, I ran into the notorious Dakar Dougy. When it came to pushing the envelope, Doug had gained a reputation only slightly down the scale from the Plow Thief. Among his more stellar feats, some months earlier he had traveled to West Africa. Apparently, he was in a bar in Recife and met some Air Force men heading across the Atlantic to Dakar. Doug decided to make the trip with them since he was none too busy, apparently still searching for his own useful enterprise. He spent several days there before they returned to Brazil. Mum of course was the word about this among the troops or Dougy would have been taking another flight back to the States with no return trip.

Discovering that I was headed for the Amazon, Dougy thought he should come along. We all were aware of the official policy of notifying the Peace Corps whenever we traveled more than fifty miles from our duty stations, but Doug shrugged it off. "Hell," he said, "if I could make it to Africa, spend ten days there, and get back with no one in the administration being the wiser, the Amazon should not be a problem."

After my recent episodes with the Plow Thief and other antics of Doug's that he regaled us with while we sat around the table in Lapa, I was not enamored with the idea of his joining us on the trip. Doug did not give up easily, however, and accompanied Dick and me on to Caetité and the bank. With the current exchange rate, I withdrew one million cruzeiros from the bank. I was a millionaire! Dick dropped us off at Volunteer Art's house in Caetité, and Art took us to our next destination.

We found the bus station in Victória da Conquista and caught a ride to Salvador where I could get a flight north to Recife. Art headed to Rio to take his vacation in the more civilized south of Brazil, Uruguay, and Argentina. Doug suddenly thought Rio and Argentina sounded more exciting than the Amazon and decided to head south with Art.

At the airport, I finally boarded a DC-6 filled to capacity. We headed down the runway but never became airborne. Our plane skidded off the tarmac into a field. Passengers screamed and were in full panic. The pilot eventually taxied the bird back to the airport where people mauled each other, fighting to escape with their carry-on bags. I sat patiently, probably in shock myself, seeing no purpose in battling the rabid crowd. The stark reality expressed by Millie in her letters about her fear of air disasters in Brazil suddenly hit me like a thunderbolt.

While everyone cleared the plane, I struck up a conversation with George, an elderly man still seated several rows in front of me. We determined we were both Americans, exited the plane and struck up a great relationship while waiting for further instructions. After some time, the airline decided to give it another go with the same plane and crew. I asked George his thoughts on re-boarding the plane. He told me he was an Air Force pilot and had lived through two crashes. He said, "Lightning rarely strikes twice in the same place."

This gentleman was Dr. George Leiby, a medical doctor who served as the assistant surgeon general during the Second World War and was also a high-ranking officer in the Air Force Reserve. George was in Brazil working with USAID to set up a chain of health clinics in the poor areas of northeast Brazil. He was enamored by the idea of the Peace Corps and invited me to come and stay with him and his wife in their beautiful oceanfront apartment in Recife. In his youth, during World War One—he lied about his age and entered the Service at sixteen—George was especially intrigued by my mechanical skills as a young lad and the work we were doing in Correntina. With a wistful tone, he told me to continue enjoying these pursuits as he would give anything to be able to engage in such youthful endeavors once more. He reflected that those times in his life were his greatest joy.

George's apartment was in the affluent ocean side suburb of Boa Viagem. His wife, Louise, was a South Carolinian and suffered from multiple sclerosis. She was formerly a pianist with the Boston Symphony Orchestra. George raised California redwoods in a backroom, eventually to plant in Brazil. He worked problems in integral calculus as a hobby. "Just to keep my mind sharp," he said. After a quick tour of Recife, we returned for dinner; and what a dinner it was. Louise served Southern fried chicken, lettuce salad, pork and beans, strawberry shortcake, and milk. It was all absolutely heaven, especially the milk, which I rarely had in Brazil.

Later that evening, I met up with Bill and Bob to plan the next steps of our journey. They had rented an apartment near the beach. Both were stationed in the far north of the São Francisco Valley, so I had little direct knowledge of what transpired in their worlds. Bill had originally been stationed in the commission agricultural colony of Paracatú, a few hundred miles southwest of Correntina in the State of Minas Gerais. Paracatú turned out to be disaster central; an original ten Volunteers now numbered zero. Bob's situation wasn't much better. His duty station of Petrolândia was also a major commission agricultural facility; its original ten Volunteers were now down to three.

Because we had a lot of catching up to do, storytelling filled the night. The best of these, recited by Bill, rivaled the episode of the *ménage à trois* in Jacobina I'd heard months earlier.

According to Bill, a Volunteer named Becky was an artsy type with a Master's Degree from the University of Illinois who served in the small town of Colégio and, either out of ignorance or loneliness, she became involved in an affair with the town's mayor, a married man. He went around wearing two pistols and had recently put down a revolt in his town. Given the violent reputation of the man she had taken up with, the Peace Corps contrived an excuse to have Becky come to another town where they "kidnapped" her and sent her by private plane to Rio to await processing out of the country. And from there the story got even more bizarre.

Fearing that Becky would attempt to escape back to Colégio, Peace Corps staff sequestered her in the home of Director Leo in Rio, who was away at the time. Lo and behold, who showed up at Leo's home a few days later but Becky's pistol-packing lover hell bent on taking her back to Colégio. Leo's wife was able to convince them that to flee would be a stupid thing to do as authorities would be in hot pursuit. Becky took this advice and returned to the United States but somehow was able to get the proper documentation, return to Recife within three days, and marry her lover, who either conveniently overlooked the fact he already had a wife, or, given his political connections, quickly disposed of the previous marriage. Bill said, "Word is she's living the life of a Brazilian peasant woman with this philistine and seems to be happy."

After an evening of great storytelling I returned to George's apartment. The next day I attended a church service for Americans with George and Louise, where George introduced me to a very interesting elderly gent who was the U.S. Vice Consul in Recife. After hearing about some of my Peace Corps exploits in the interior of Bahia, he told me the story of his shooting a flying snake. Thirty years before, this man traveled on an expedition across Brazil to the remote areas in the State of Mato Grosso near the Roosevelt River.

After a night of camping, another young man on the expedition apparently did not store his boots properly or check them before putting them on the next morning. When he slipped his foot into the boot, he felt something very warm and he froze. Seeing the look of anguish on the young fellow's face, this man realized what might be happening. He told the lad to keep pressure on whatever was in his boot while another person cut the boot down the side, because if he released the pressure and it was a snake, it would most likely bite him. After cutting the boot away they had the lad kick as hard as he could, releasing the boot into the air, and the storyteller shot the snake. Of course, the story would not have been complete as told unless the snake was one of the deadly varieties in Brazil where with one quick bite you are history. Whether fact or fiction I am not sure, but the elderly gent did a marvelous job of telling the tale.

At this gathering, I also met another American doctor and his Hawaiian wife. They had two daughters who were in their late teens and quite beautiful with flowing black hair and tan complexions. George later told Louise, "Maybe Ken would like to wait a few days before going to the Amazon, spend more time in Recife, or maybe spend all of his vacation here."

Moments earlier, Louise had asked me about my family and life in Minnesota. I told her I had a large family. I also showed her a picture of my sweetheart Millie. When George suggested I spend more time in Recife, Louise chided, "I think Ken is well taken care of and happy when it comes to love, George."

Two days later I saw George and Louise for the last time, and it was indeed hard to say good-bye, like leaving family behind. It had been a wonderful several days of insightful conversation, meeting some terrific people and eating American food that made me feel like I was sitting back home at the kitchen table. I could not believe the good fortune of meeting George in Salvador.

After an overnight stop in Forteleza, Bob, Bill, and I flew on to Belém. The plane circled the area for a time, providing us a wonderful perspective of the mouth of the Amazon River and the great island where Belém is located. Our first stop after landing was at the U.S. consulate where we met a man named Paul. Paul was from Iowa, and when he discovered that Bill and I were from Minnesota we became fast friends. Paul had loved going to Minnesota as a boy to fish in many of our ten thousand lakes.

Paul gave us the name of the consul in Manaus. Once we got on the big river there would be few ways of communicating until we reached Manaus fifteen hundred miles away. Paul also introduced us to George Pickerel, an American who had a tourist business in Belém. George was most helpful and personally took us to the office of SNAPP, an Amazon River transport company where we could purchase passage up the river. These companies could be a little shady, so George thought it best to accompany us. Unfortunately, SNAPP was completely booked. George returned alone and got tickets from the captain, but not for the immediate departure we had anticipated and planned for.

We now had five unanticipated days to kill in Belém before leaving for Manaus, days we had hoped to spend traveling up some tributaries from Manaus deeper into the Amazon jungle. It was just as well, however, since Bob became ill and would need time to recuperate before traveling the Amazon by boat. While Bob rested, Bill and I went to the offices of the Pirelli Rubber Company and booked a visit. Initially we had hoped to go to the Goodyear plantation, but there had been a nasty riot there a few days before. Reportedly, the manager had almost been killed. With our open schedule, Bill and I left the next morning to see the ocean and took a boat one hundred miles to Cabo Maquari and the island of Mosqueiro on the Atlantic to go for a swim. The beaches were splendid with great waves, and we wished we could have spent more time there.

Christmas Eve arrived again in the tropics the day after our trip to the ocean. Although over the river and through the woods to Grandmother's house wasn't possible, we did have to cross the immense Amazon to visit the Pirelli rubber plantation. The manager was a Dutchman who had worked for twenty years in the rubber fields of Indonesia before the Dutch were expelled from the country. A domineering chap, he cussed and barked out orders to the workers. I got the sense the laborers were not too fond of him, which gave me insight into possible reasons underlying the Goodyear riot.

Being Catholics, we all attended midnight Mass. On Christmas day we did get a sense of the holiday spirit, meeting a Santa Claus of another sort bearing magical gifts, a modern-day Percy Fawcett hunting for gold in the Amazon. George Victor was an American working a piece of property in an Amazon region the size of the State of Oregon. He wanted us to leave the Peace Corps and come to work for him, offering us fifty percent of all the gold or jewels we mined. He said five other Americans worked for him, but certain details about his operation were rather vague, such as how the actual mining was taking place or who was doing the digging. We suspected he was using indigenous slave labor. At any rate, it was a risky proposition, more appealing to the likes of Dakar Dougy or Plow Thief Dave than us, so we declined his offer.

We finally left Belém the day after Christmas on the *Lobo da Mata*—the wolf of the forest. This was a rather ominous beginning given that the wolf in mythology and fairytales has a reputation varying from ruthlessness to loyalty and kindness. That would indeed be our experience. It rained all day. We soon realized the unfortunate truth of what our friend Paul had told us about the shady practices of some of the boat operators. We were supposed to have a room on the boat, but true to Brazilian form, like the boat operator during Dick and my trip down the Corrente River and the drunken trucker who took me to Lapa to catch a flight to Rio, the operators of the *Wolf* oversold the rooms. We and a few other dumb foreigners ended up stringing hammocks on the back of the boat under a tarp and sleeping in gusts of wind huffing and puffing and blowing rain across the deck. We were quickly finding out what kind of wolf we were dealing with.

Our second day on the Amazon River was hot with little to do but look at the continuous expanse of water and jungle in the distance. Toward evening it rained and blew so hard I thought for sure the boat would sink. The captain must have been concerned too because he decided to get off the river until the storm turbulence subsided. He pulled up into an inlet off the north side of the river for the remainder of the evening.

Like the previous day, little occupied our time the next day on the river other than looking at the endless water and forest canopy in the distance. Occasionally we would see the makings of a village along the banks or a fisherman on the river. We spent another miserable night in our hammocks on the back deck of the boat. The next morning, I awoke feeling ill but had no place to lie down except in my swinging hammock, so I spent most of the day in a chair and ate nothing.

All of this led to a very interesting and embarrassing episode that almost ended my journey on the Amazon, if not my life. I may have contracted what Bob had and was feeling quite sick with incredible stomach cramps. At one point during the night I ran for the restroom as fast as I could and into a stall. The lights on the deck were off, so I had to navigate as best I could on a rainy, windy, moonless night with a small flashlight. When I left the restroom, I met a couple of women on the way in and thought that a bit strange, so I flashed my light up at the sign above the door in the dark and sure enough it said *Senhora*—Women, not *Senhor*—Men. There were no urinals or toilet stools, just holes in the floor, so there was virtually nothing to distinguish the women's bathroom from the men's. And since there was no one in the restroom at the time, I paid it little heed. That is, until the captain and one of his officers confronted me the next morning about the situation, wondering if I might be some sort of pervert. The discussion got rather tense and they threatened to throw me off at the next stop. Since leaving Belém, we three travelers had been harassing the captain quite regularly about the rooms we had paid for but did not get. It was difficult to understand the serious nature of my transgression since I was the only one in the bathroom at the time. Bill and Bob soon joined me in attempting to reason with the officers.

Good fortune sometimes happens in the strangest places. We were traveling with a fun-loving German named Bernard. Our new friend had quit his job in Germany to spend a few years traveling the world. He was now in his fifty-first country and fifth year of travel. Bernard was a large, boisterous chap, broad in the shoulders with deep penetrating eyes, a full red beard.

As the confrontation with the captain escalated, Bernard crawled from his hammock to find out what was going on. Once he got the drift of things, he took over. His voice booming, he told the officials exactly what was on his mind, namely the unacceptable substitution of sleeping in hammocks when a room had been paid for. He blamed the marginal quality of available food as the probable cause of my illness. Bernard's ire rose to the degree that the boat officers must have worried that they might be the ones thrown overboard to feed hungry piranhas, especially with three men lobbying my case. As things progressed though, Bill, Bob, and I took the side of the officers in an attempt to calm down Bernard. If Bernard's paroxysm of rage backfired, any minute we could be hoisted overboard. We eventually got Bernard under control. The captain seemed at least momentarily understanding and apologetic about the whole situation. He even promised to provide us rooms at the next port.

The next part of our journey included an interesting section of the river termed the Narrows, an area between Belém and Santarém where the boat passed closest to the jungle. The current was much faster there and not good habitat for piranhas, anacondas, or alligators; they prefer the still, slow-moving currents. Had I been thrown overboard, this would have been a favorable spot.

On the last day of 1963, we pulled into Santarém at the confluence of the Tapajos River with the Amazon. This town was the site of the old rubber plantation and failed utopia that Henry Ford had built along the Tapajos River and had named Fordlândia. At this point, Bernard decided to leave the *Wolf* and join a trio of men he'd met in a bar who were heading up the wild Tapajos River for a series they were doing about the Amazon for *Life* magazine. They looked like tough characters, well-armed with ammunition belts strung across both shoulders, reminiscent of the militia men at my front door months before. We wondered if the *Life* magazine series was just a ruse, and they were actually hunting gold and diamonds.

We told Bernard we were not too keen on his joining up with these suspicious characters. Maybe it was a bit of selfishness on our part as he'd proven a strong ally in sticky situations. Bernard was obviously quite intelligent, speaking five languages fluently. Thank God one of them was Portuguese when he dealt with the boat captain.

But Bernard could not be swayed. He was concerned that the captain still held a grudge, mainly toward him. He suspected the captain and his cronies still might throw him overboard in the middle of the night, adding that he'd come too far to end up stripped of all his flesh by a pack of wild piranhas. He said, "I have no intention of being the coward that dies a thousand deaths, constantly looking over my shoulder. I'd rather take my chances with my head on some savage's totem pole up the Tapajos River. At least that way I might be admired for my nice red beard and I would count for more than a bag of bones as I leave this world."

Bernard implored us to join him, especially me, if we thought we could not handle the current situation. After all, the captain had his honor at stake. Who would really give two thoughts about a missing American he could brand as a pervert? Bernard was a persuasive fellow. I asked Bill and Bob what they thought. Their main concern was the administration of frontier justice in these towns. They speculated that the Amazon may even come under some weird Brazilian maritime law where the captain was the full deal: prosecutor, judge, and jury, all in one. Bernard's proposition was beginning to sound more and more realistic and I felt nearly at my wit's end. I knew I wasn't a fortune hunter.

Bob and Bill thought it best to continue on the course we had set for Manaus. Being an ex-Marine, Bob had been exposed to a lot of tough characters during his four years of service, and I suspected there was more under that quiet shell than he revealed. In his estimation, the captain would not mess with us. After all, tourism was a big part of his business and he was aware of our connection to the consulate and George Pickerel in Belém, who was sending him a lot of business.

My two friends said they would do all in their power to keep a close eye on me and, if necessary, take turns sleeping to ensure that nothing sinister happened at night. That was good enough for me, so it was on to Manaus. We would part ways with Bernard. After all, he had survived for five years away from home in places and situations most likely worse than this.

The next day, New Year's Day 1964, things began to look up. The captain seemed pleased that the crazy German was not going to continue on the journey and no longer took the attitude of the big bad wolf. We finally said goodbye to the hammocks and got the rooms we'd paid for. The crew became much friendlier after our episode two days earlier. They knew Bernard had left the boat and kept saying to us *muito pedigoso*—very dangerous, while shaking their heads in reference to Bernard's decision to head up the Tapajos River. He would have a hell of a book to write someday, if he survived.

Our friendlier standing with the crew led to a stroke of luck. One of the crew members was an avid sports fan, and in talking with him, Bill and I mentioned that we'd seen Pelé at the national championship in Rio the previous year. As anticipated, this guy was filled with the same sort of awe shown by the people in Correntina. He knew that New Year's Day was a big day for *futebol Americano*—American football, so as a sign of our renewed status, the crew loaned us a radio.

There we were on New Year's Day, riding on a boat along the middle of the Amazon River listening to college football games on the Armed Forces Radio Network. We listened as Navy beat Texas in the Cotton Bowl, 28–6, and later as USC beat Wisconsin in the Rose Bowl, 42–37.

We arrived in Manaus two days later, but not before the captain pulled over to shore and threw four robbers off the boat. Bob's camera was stolen, and it was not found. Realizing the captain was indeed a forceful man caused me a bit of panic. Without the intervention of Bernard, I might have suffered a similar fate a long way from civilization. For the next two days, we toured Manaus. Though we would have enjoyed taking a trip deeper into the jungle along one of the tributaries as originally planned, time limited us. Besides, I'd decided that I'd lived through enough excitement as it was. Maybe Bernard would send me a letter and pictures.

After three weeks on the move, I was anxious to get back to my work and the relative safety of Correntina. I left Bill and Bob in the hotel and headed for the airport to fly from Manaus to Brasilia in the central highlands. Flying in Brazil was starting to fray my nerves. The six-hour flight over nothing but jungle may have been the worst I'd been on. The plane was a dilapidated Curtiss C-46 Commando with faded lettering and scarred tires, sometimes affectionately referred to as the Whale; the Plumber's Nightmare, due to problems with fuel leaks; or the Flying Coffin. Although not used for passenger travel in the United States after World War II because of its high fuel consumption and reputation for maintenance problems, it was widely used in Latin America. Powerful engines made it well suited for mountainous areas where the C46 could climb to great heights and soar over dense jungle terrain.

Since this was a long flight—almost half the length of Brazil—we guessed the Brazilians loaded our plane with all the cargo and passengers it could hold. That theory was validated by the fact that we never ascended more than a few thousand feet above the jungle canopy, flying continuously over dense green jungle until we reached Brasilia. I was riding on faith. It was Sunday, and I hoped that if my diligence in attending mass faithfully in Correntina had any redeeming value, it would pay off now.

This had not been the case for other unfortunate souls who died in an Amazon crash on December 14, 1962. On my flight to Brasilia in January 1964, the earlier jungle crash weighed heavily on my mind. One week before that crash, on December 7, 1962, Millie's dad died of a massive heart attack while at home alone with his daughter— Millie, my high school sweetheart. A few weeks later, early 1963, I happily received a letter from Millie dated Christmas Day 1962, just weeks after her father's passing.

Neither Millie nor my family had received any mail from me during my first three months in Brazil in 1962, so they had no idea of my exact whereabouts. Millie wrote, "I am a bit leery of listening to the news reports because lately every time they tell of some airplane crashing down in your country. Seriously, it frightens me."

She included an article from Reuters News concerning a Brazilian Panair Super Constellation, a much more modern plane than the Whale, which had crashed in the jungle near Manaus. An early search recovered the bodies of twenty-three passengers out of fifty who boarded the flight. Sometime later, a private search party, led by a man whose wife and daughter had been on the flight, found more bodies miles from the crash. The condition of the bodies indicated they had died only recently, most likely of starvation or hostile action. One man was found sitting under a tree, apparently dead from starvation and exhaustion. Some at the time believed others might still have been alive in the jungle.

It was Millie's dad who had delivered a prophetic message when I departed for Brazil about the dangers I would face. That was the day before the Cuban Missile Crisis began. Millie's dad was only fifty-three. His death, the Cuban Missile Crisis and the airplane crash near Manaus was indeed a road paved with trials testing the endurance of our love. My mind full of sobering thoughts, I looked down at the endless green Amazon rainforest canopy.

Fortunately for me, that day I rode with the Lord, as my friend Reverend Reisner was fond of saying. I arrived in Brasilia, never so happy to have my feet on *terra firma*, but the new Capitol in the hinterland was not much to see at this point. Only three years earlier, the government began construction of the new capital city, from scratch, on the site of a cattle ranch in the middle of the country. It had all the trappings of a mirage in the desert with its collection of tall buildings of modern architecture that appeared empty. Most of the government buildings were finished, including those for the major departments like treasury, transportation and defense. Many of them had been hastily built. A couple of the larger buildings had fences around them due to cracks that had developed in the walls. I was told they would have to be razed and rebuilt.

A primary reason for such shoddy construction was simple: the labor force. When unskilled job seekers poured in from the hinterland and got in line for a labor card at the Labor Ministry, they were asked to identify their particular skills. For those who had none, they would repeat what the person in front of them said. If he was a bricklayer, the man behind him became a bricklayer and so forth for plumbers, carpenters, and on down the line of trades. The unskilled did their best to learn by observation, but this was certainly not a recipe for success. Also, many buildings were only partially finished due to insufficient funding.

All there was to see in this isolated mirage in the desert could be seen in a day, so I got on a bus and headed one hundred miles south toward Goiânia, the capital of the State of Goias. We rode through rolling cattle country reminiscent of what I'd seen in Oklahoma. We passed through the modern city of Annápolis where I could maybe do some celebrity star gazing. Word had it that American movie stars owned giant cattle ranches in this area. Two stars mentioned by the bus driver were Mary Martin and Robert Mitchum. Arriving in Goiânia, I discovered it was also a relatively new city built on another cattle ranch, just like Brasilia.

I went to Goiânia to meet José, Antonio, and Adelson of my surrogate Coimbra family who were students there and whom I got to know well when they were in Correntina late the year before while home on holiday. Also, their sister Yvonne and her husband Adherbal, the newlyweds I had signed for, were visiting in Goiânia. I got a tour of the city, recounted good times in Correntina, and watched TV for the first time since I'd left the United States fourteen months earlier.

The next morning, I said good-bye to my friends and left on a puddle-hopping flight to Brasilia, and eventually to Caetité. I needed to refresh my cash supply since inflation continued to spiral upward. There were no flights from Caetité to Lapa, so in the morning I found a car leaving for Lapa and hitched a ride. This mode of travel was always a crapshoot since drivers, the state of repairs with the car and driving abilities were unknowns.

By late afternoon I arrived safely in Lapa, picked up a pile of mail that had accumulated for a month, and spent some time reminiscing with Gaucho Jim who happened to be in Lapa on his way from Barreiras to Rio. Including the time he had spent in Rio Grande do Sul with the 4-H group in early 1962, Gaucho Jim's tour was up and he was heading home to the States.

The commission launch was out of service for repairs, so none of the vehicles available to hitch a ride on could traverse the river. I spent another night in Lapa, and the next day, my luck changed dramatically. The boys in Lapa received a telegram from our good friend Reverend Al Reisner saying he was flying down from his mission at Sítio do Mato. When Al arrived, my good fortune improved even more. Al said he was leaving around noon to fly to Santa Maria and then on to Correntina.

Al took me back home to Correntina. When I arrived, a steady stream of folks showed up to welcome me. You would have thought I was the President or the Pope. I got the feeling that many of them did not believe I would come back to Correntina. Even Padre André seemed to be anxious for my return as he sent over his houseboy to see if I was available for dinner. Because Al was my guest, though, I begged off dinner with Padre until another day. As exhilarating as my month of sightseeing and new experiences had been, coming back to this little town and its people left me in a state of deep happiness. I was home. At least I was home in Brazil, which eased the loneliness I felt for my home in southeast Minnesota. Receiving mail, welcome as it was, left me feeling sometimes more homesick than if I had not received it.

While news from home was a special treat, occasionally the news could also be concerning, like when I learned about how Millie's family suffered over the deaths of her dad and little cousin. I have read that absence makes the heart grow fonder, but as human beings, we also need emotional nurturing. Without the sound of someone's voice, without someone's touch, we are programmed to forget. We cling to memories that too often are not enough.

Because of my travel to the Amazon, well over a month had passed since I read any mail from home. I attempted to send mail during my trip, but I had no idea if any of them made it home. When I retrieved my mail from Correntina, I found a letter from Millie, which caused me to believe most of the mail I'd sent on the Amazon journey did not arrive. Millie's letter echoed concern about our long hiatus from each other, yet optimism.

"It seems as if you will be home in no time at all. Time is more than just whizzing by. Think I am crazy if I say this if you like, but each time I get to thinking of your coming home I am sometimes afraid you won't remember even who I am or for that matter who I ever was. I am getting so anxious for the time however when I can see you once more. Please be taking good care of yourself and be good. Hope you are always in good health and so happy. Bye, Bye, Love Millie. Am always thinking of you."

All told, twenty-one long months would pass between Millie and me, months of nothing but the written words.

19. Johnny Appleseed & Jango

Like Gene Autry singing in the occasional Western movie that came to town, I was back in the saddle again. I felt like Johnny Appleseed on a horse making the rounds of my countryside plantings to see how everything was progressing. I was quite pleased with how many people had followed the directions included in the seed packets. In addition to all of this, Padre was clamoring for me to get back to teaching classes at school. At our first meeting, Padre said he thought I could assume an even heavier schedule of responsibilities and turn over some of my ag business to Dick. He was aware that I had received some basketball and softball equipment from my high school coach and thought I should add the corresponding physical education classes to my daily schedule. I laughed and told him Dick was only interested in engineering. Padre said, "Obviously you have been away too long."

He told me that in my absence, Dick had turned into a regular little Johnny Appleseed himself. Every Saturday he sat dutifully outside the front of our house dispensing seed packets and transplants from my greenhouse. He had laboriously gone through instructions with people on how to plant and care for things. Padre contended that since Dick seemed to be converting to the green thumb, religion would come next. I told Padre that since Dick had a renewed interest, I would welcome his ag contributions, but leave the religious conversion to him.

When Saturday rolled around, Dick and I went out to the soccer field with the new balls, bats, gloves, and a sizeable group of kids. First, we proceeded to lay out a proper diamond for softball. Dr. Raul from the hydro dam came to watch his sons have a go at it. We kept calling the field a diamond, which led to an international geometry controversy as the doctor insisted was a square.

He said, "Although a diamond and a square can both be assumed to be isomorphic, it is difficult for the kids to understand." What was hard to understand was his sophisticated language, but we ended up throwing the ball around the square.

Softball was definitely a sports paradigm shift for the Correntina kids. It was hilarious watching them attempt to catch something as small as a softball with their hands. After all, in soccer using one's hand is absolutely prohibited. Gloves were totally foreign to them, and they inevitably discarded the gloves and attempted to catch with two hands or just stop it with their chest. They would then kick it to the next player. When we hollered to throw the ball to first base, they instead ran over and threw the ball at the base. With or without the gloves, they did not have much success. They ended up with a couple of bloody noses and a few bruises, but insisted they were game to try again the next Saturday.

We were well into the rainy season. A couple months earlier we would have been begging for rain, but now there were days when we wished it would stop. At this time, we had two irrigation engineers visiting out of interest in building an irrigation dam near the confluence of the Corrente and Meio Rivers. Dick and I went with them to a small town called Mocambo, which means shack or hovel, and that was about all we found there. The plan was to visit a farm near the possible dam site to take soil samples to see if the soil conditions deemed the investment worthwhile. Somehow, we forgot about all the rain we'd had the day before and how it typically impacted driving conditions on roads that weren't much more than ox cart paths.

We got stuck in mud no fewer than six times. Near the hamlet of *Mucacos*—monkeys, we got stuck so badly that it took fifteen men two hours to get us through a stretch of road of not more than one-mile long. I knew a man in Mucacos where I had stayed overnight on a few occasions who became a great friend. Folks all around called him *Joãodão*—Big John. Joãodão was indeed a giant and the only one in the region who rivaled Padre in physical stature. I thought maybe Joãodão could pull the Jeep out by himself. Not quite, but he did help us considerably on the last mud hole.

The only other person that I ever met in the region of Joãodão's size was the barefoot soccer player recruited for one game to kick the hell out of me. The story of the soccer match and the beating I took had become legend in the area and Joãodão knew of it. When Joãodão and I became good friends I would tease him and ask him with a wink, "Hey, Big John are you sure you don't have a son I don't know about that you keep in hiding whenever you know I might be in the area? After all, this is Monkeyville and that soccer guy was some kind of ape!" I told Joãodão we could have used him now to help get the Jeep out of the mud as a pay back.

During one visit, Joãodão told me I was only the second *branco*—whitey, that had ever been in Macacos. The first was a German blacksmith who had lived there for a while. I wondered what a blacksmith would be doing in Macacos; very few things were made of iron and it was not a common practice to shoe horses. From Joãodão's description of the man, he had the blond hair and blue eyes typical of many Germans. I later encountered several other men of this exact description in a few other remote hamlets. I surmised they were expatriate Nazis hiding out like the infamous Auschwitz doctor, Josef Mengele. [40]

Because of its size and remoteness, Brazil was a favorite hideout for many fleeing justice or retribution. I recall hearing about former Syrian dictator Abid Bin Hassan Al-Shishakli, who tortured the Druze mountain people during his reign. When he was overthrown in the late 1950s, he fled into hiding in Ceres in the state of Goias, a small town about two hundred miles southwest of Correntina. He lived on a farm across the river from the town itself, and one morning he was found draped over the guardrail of the footbridge leading into Ceres, his throat slit.

We returned to Correntina to find two visitors at our house: Volunteer Pat, the skyscraper builder, and Phil, the new project director for Brazil III. That evening, Pat related an interesting story about a recent visit that Director Leo had made to Santa Maria. Pat and another Volunteer, the Alaskan fisherman named Rick, decided to take their guests duck hunting in the backwaters of the Formoso River. Rick was a seasoned hunter, conducting a brisk business in the Formoso Colony shooting wildcats that harassed the pigs. He even tanned their hides and sold them for a little cash on the side.

Upon arriving for the hunt, they spied some ducks. Alaskan Rick shot one and was going to wade out to retrieve it. Leo questioned this action as he saw some eddies forming around the duck, which he interpreted as a bad sign. As Pat told it, by the time Rick got his boots off to venture out into the pond, they noticed the duck had disappeared altogether and all that was left were feathers twirling on top of the water. Rick immediately decided to put his boots back on.

Shortly after the duck disappeared, a small calf walked into the water and it was not long before it was pulled under. I began to think that what was really getting pulled were not calf legs but ours. The fact that a calf just conveniently showed up seemed a bit of a stretch.

I said to Pat and Phil, "Hey, would you like to hear a story about the guy who shot a flying snake?"

Pat swore up and down that the duck and calf episode was the truth, and we had to assume it was since we doubted Leo would be part of any ruse. Later, Leo did indeed write about the incident and publish it, so it must have been true.

H eavy rains continued through most of January, making mail service terrible. Days would start out bright and sunny and by mid-afternoon the rain came. The most likely source of mail delivery would be Reverend Reisner, but sometimes he flew up just to visit because, like everyone else, he was tired of the rain. In Portuguese there is a phrase, *bate papo*—chewing the fat. *Bate papo* literally means to have your Adam's apple jumping up and down. On several of Reverend Reisner's visits he would spend most of the day watching us work and, as he said, being busy with the art of *bate papo*.

One thing worth *bate papo* happened when picking up the Reverend at the airstrip. We noticed that the front wheel assembly on Reverend Reisner's Cessna was held on with baling wire. We thought the Reverend was living dangerously on the muddy airstrips at this time of year, and we let him know it. But he just quipped, "I ride with the Lord."

One time our former regional leader, Georgia Peach, had flown with the Reverend to Montalvania to visit Plow Thief Dave. It was the rainy season and Reverend Reisner ended up running off the end of the airstrip and getting stuck in the mud. While attempting to extricate the plane from the mud, Georgia Peach saw some tools and baling wire laid by the airplane's engine. Once he saw this, he made up a lame excuse to remain in Montalvania, eventually making his way by bus and truck back to Lapa.

Riding with the Lord or not, we saw the Reverend as our lifeline if anything terrible happened to us, so his safety was also our safety. We took measurements for the missing connecting rod and told him we would fashion something for him and install it on his next visit. I told him we would pray for him in the interim, and for his passenger, the Lord.

About this time, I received a letter from home that told me the long hiatus in my face-to-face relationship with Millie was beginning to wear on her. In my letters, of course, I told tales of the Amazon, Rio de Janeiro and interesting people I met and associated with. I spoke especially often about my Stanford and Berkeley educated townmates with whom I was now playing something as sophisticated as bridge.

I mentioned to her the Mayor's offer of free land to stay in Correntina. I also boasted that prominent Eastern colleges like Yale and Harvard were actively recruiting former Peace Corps Volunteers; what an opportunity that would be for a small-town country boy! Millie later responded, "Are your school plans complete yet? I know you have always wanted to go east and hope so much you can do as you most want to."

My letters had to be troublesome for her. It was while reading that recent letter I recalled Millie telling me in an earlier letter about the drive home from the airport with her dad when I left for Brazil months before. I remembered the subtle message she'd heard from him to temper her expectations because I would be living an exciting life and come home so worldly. He also cautioned her that I might not be interested in a small-town country girl after I returned from the Peace Corps. In another letter, she came right out and said, "From your letters it sounds as if many of the Volunteers are finding souvenirs to take home, namely Brazilians!" Millie added, "However there ... (I won't say it! Ha!)"

More than any other time in the many trying months of solitude, how I wished I could pick up a telephone and talk to her. Despite all her appropriate words and assurance of our enduring relationship, I was left feeling lonely and helpless. Not being able to talk to Millie, I was not much for *bate papo*. I think she wanted to tell me, there is one problem: "What about us?"

It was that time of the year to do little more than *bate papo* for a week as it was once again Carnival in Brazil and no one was doing any real work. During the festivities, a couple of vaqueros most likely had too much to drink. They got into a fight with machetes in the early hours of the morning and cut each other up pretty badly. In fact, one had some of the muscle on his shoulder and upper arm cut away. These locals, knowing there was no surgical doctor in town that would treat them, showed up at our door looking for first aid.

The most severely injured cowboy stood there, leather-skinned, the color of the parched earth in the dog days of winter, a dark stream of blood running down his arm and pooling on our front steps. We had a fairly extensive first aid kit and other medication as well as our trusty Merck Manuals. It was not the first time something like this had occurred. Dick, who was aware I was from the vicinity of Rochester, Minnesota, exclaimed on one occasion, "Who in the hell do they think we are, the Mayo Brothers?"

Sometimes when I went on trips into the countryside, I would take medical supplies to treat minor wounds and infections, especially in children. The two dudes dripping blood on our steps, however, was not a minor situation. We told them we could not fix them up, but we would take them across the square and up the street to Pedro Guerra's pharmacy. Perdo served as the surrogate local doctor for similar emergencies.

As we rolled into early March, the incident with the cowboys was just the tip of the iceberg for excitement. One day a man was gunned down just across the town square from our house. This event gave me a good taste of how frontier justice worked in bandit country. Aligário, the murderer and someone I knew well, was a respected citizen of the town so no one made an immediate move to arrest him. He knew that sooner or later the other man's family would come looking for justice, however, if the law did not come first. There was no local law enforcement per se, so this sort of matter was typically left to the state militia.

Arnaldo, who first described the geography of Correntina to me as "the end of the world," was with the state militia and came by my house sometime later. He'd been working with me to build a basketball court, and it seemed strange that he would be thinking about basketball instead of pursuing the murderer. After all, gunning someone down in the town square was not an everyday occurrence. It was none of my concern, but my curiosity was running high, so I asked him about it.

He told me that before he could do anything he had to get instructions from county attorney Dr. Oswaldo, who was out of town for several days. He'd gone to the telegraph station and sent a telegram to Dr. Oswaldo asking for instructions but had not received a reply. Everyone's hands appeared to be tied while the man lay in the street in the intense heat for an hour or more. No one did anything. Eventually someone found a family member of the victim, and they came and removed him to their house just as the rains began.

The prevailing attitude seemed to be that the murder resulted from a domestic dispute—no money was stolen and no one's horse was missing. Since both the custom and law in Brazil was that the body must be buried within twenty-four hours after death, it stood to reason that the intense rains that were now falling would wash away the crime scene. All evidence of the method of death would head to the grave long before any investigation could take place.

Aligário was no fool and knew that either the dead man's family or the law would eventually come looking for him. Rumor had it that he lit out for the bush immediately after the shooting, then later that evening he snuck back into town to gather some of his things and leave for good. Possible destinations were south to Montalvania, or wherever he might find family protection. [41]

Late that same afternoon, the clinical doctor and a young man I knew from the countryside came to my door. The young man's wife was ready to give birth for the first time, but the baby was in the breech position and the wife could not deliver. The doctor said she needed to be taken to the hospital in Lapa and asked for our assistance. He worried the drive to Lapa would be very difficult in the rainy season, making the trip near to impossible for her. Were we willing to contact the commission in Lapa to summon a plane up for transport by air?

I didn't even stop to consider his request but went immediately to the telegraph office and communicated our need to Lapa. The plane was not available. I then telegraphed Reverend Reisner at his mission. He replied that he could fly up at dawn. Our next concern was getting the woman to the airstrip at the designated time. The husband and I walked some half-dozen miles downriver and arrived at his house near midnight. The husband and I, along with several of the neighbors, fashioned a litter out of a bed with poles tied along the sides and top.

We then draped sheets over this frame, creating a canopy to provide protection for the woman from the morning heat.

The next day a dozen of us took turns, six at a time, carrying the bed with its precious cargo on our shoulders. In the morning heat, we were all drenched in sweat. Several young boys followed us with jugs of water that I did not risk drinking for fear of getting sick. True to his word, the Reverend was at the airstrip by 7:30 a.m. I remember as she lay there in the plane, the young woman's lips were as blue as the water in the Corrente River and she was obviously in great pain.

My mother had told me I was her only child of twelve to be born breech. In contrast to the current circumstances, I was born on a cold day in late March. Deep snow prevented a quick departure for the hospital. It took my father two hours shoveling, then two mighty horses to pull the family car a few feet at a time to get it off the hill where our farm was located. Born premature, I was not expected to live and was baptized in the hospital. But here I was, aiding another young woman in the same situation as my mother so many years before.

Later Reverend Reisner sent a telegram saying the woman had delivered a healthy little boy. I often wondered what the outcome would have been years earlier for this woman—and tens of thousands like her—who lived in such remote places before the advent of the airplane and telegraph. A sad contemplation.

Life's usual routine returned. I make excellent progress on everything I hoped to finish in the two months before leaving Brazil. My twenty-first birthday would fall on Easter Sunday. During the Easter Mass, Padre noted that this was not only one of the two holiest days of the year, but also a great birthday to celebrate as well: that of Senhor Kennege, me. I had not anticipated this but should have, knowing Padre. Embarrassment set in as Padre led everyone in church in a standing ovation. Not only that, he then encouraged everyone to stop by my house later to offer congratulations.

As a special gift, and as affirmation of how far my language skills had progressed, he presented me with a Portuguese bible a few days before Easter. In it he wrote the following: *"Ao carrisimo amigo Kenneth, esta lembrancinha do amigo em Cristo, Padre André F. Berénos, em Correntina, 22-3-1964,"* which translates: "To a very dear friend, Kenneth, this little remembrance of a friend in Christ, Padre André F. Berénos, in

Correntina, March 22, 1964." A very special and memorable birthday indeed.

*T*he national scene was not as copacetic. On March 31, the Brazilian military decided it had had enough of Jango—President João Goulart—and staged a coup. Once again, the country ground to a halt. Everyone was glued to radios following the events as they unraveled. No one knew what would happen with banks and other government services, creating a deep-seated anxiety among the people.

For our remote little village, however, the grip of fear was not as strong. Community activities soon continued, almost normally. For instance, the school held a celebration called *Dia das Professoras*—Teacher's Day—in which all the local dignitaries gave celebratory speeches and many students gave rousing testimonies about various qualities of their esteemed instructors. There were several awards given, and when the time came to present the award for *Professor do Ano*—Teacher of the Year—the recipient was none other than yours truly. During my tenure, I had taught late afternoon and evening classes in English, history, mathematics, agriculture, and of course softball and basketball. The country was falling apart, but I was being honored. Such were the vicissitudes of life.

At this gathering, everyone appeared to be a little tense concerning the status of the country. Dr. Oswaldo spoke about the situation and tried to put everyone at ease. In the process, he gave the first bad news-good news analogy I could ever recall anyone giving since I'd been in Brazil. About the revolution, he said, "The bad news is that we are uncertain what will be the outcome of the coup, but it is highly likely the military will prevail and govern for a time. The good news is, in all the confusion of re-establishing relations with foreign governments, all foreigners in the country, like Senhor Kennege, will have to remain here indefinitely."

While Dr. Oswaldo's words brought loud applause from the students, I could not help but wonder what Millie and my parents back home were thinking when they learned of the Brazilian coup d'état. My time in the Peace Corps was drawing to an end. Millie and my family and friends had emotionally weathered my odyssey: surviving the missile crisis, riots, news of plane crashes, piranhas on the Amazon, and the death of our President, and now this news of a revolution. Revolutions may have seemed like an everyday occurrence in Latin countries, but to Americans, revolution invokes images of chaos and bloodshed. Once again, I suspected they were glued to their television sets in a state of dread.

On April Fool's Day, Presidente João Goulart found out the military was not fooling. In the face of aggressive action to take over the country, Goulart knew his support was eroding rapidly. He decided the best plan would be to flee to Uruguay. None of this affected us Volunteers in any particular way, although the Peace Corps sent telegrams with stand-down orders, or SD. SDs were issued to protect Americans when hostilities suddenly broke out in foreign countries. If we felt we were in danger, we were instructed to find a safe haven and prepare to evacuate the country if necessary. We were further advised to assess our standing with the local administration. The barbershop boys got into the act and told me in jest that they knew of a cave north of town where we could hide. I told them I felt perfectly safe right where I was, and not too excited about a cave where snakes might be cooling their heels out of the heat of Brazil—just like Jango in Uruguay.

Much of the concern for our safety involved Communists in the northeast. Thought to be well-armed, these operatives organized sympathetic Peasant Leagues. If the military forced the Communists to flee the area, American officials worried they might take Peace Corps Volunteers as hostages to protect their escape routes. While my presence in Correntina had taken on an aura of the Pied Piper, I did not think my job was to remove Communist rats from Bahia.

Embassy officials and Peace Corps leaders kept sending messages about a possible evacuation, Mayor Elias França and Dr. Oswaldo made special efforts to personally assure us we had nothing to worry about, that we were safe in Correntina and they would see that we were protected if there were any problems. Recalling how the recent murder case was handled, though, I was concerned as to exactly where this protection would come from.

After a single day of turmoil in some of the larger cities in Brazil, the revolution came to a screeching halt. Brazilians did not yet understand what it all meant, but I had learned from experience in Brazil that just about anything that happened might trigger a celebration. In major cities, the streets suddenly filled with revelers and dancing. No festivities erupted in the streets of Correntina, thank God, but there was a noticeable sense of relief among the residents. Hopefully things would remain peaceful as I headed down the home stretch.

20. Final touches

The change of government was over almost before it started and peace returned to our Brazilian paradise under a military dictatorship. Life in Correntina, meanwhile, marched on as normal as ever. I looked forward to one more celebration at the beginning of the month, the birthday of Padre André. That day started off with fireworks in the streets, ringing of all the bells in town, and music blaring from speakers. A huge group of well-wishers paraded up to his rectory, singing until he came out and acknowledged them. He'd never admit it, but Padre enjoyed it all and loved the attention. In years past, some parishioners had pushed to have a Mass, but he said he would have felt embarrassed saying a Mass for himself. I reminded him that when Dr. José came, he wanted me to take a crack at surgery so maybe I could try doing the Mass. He laughed wholeheartedly at that and said he thought Dick's personality was beginning to rub off on me.

Birthdays seem to inspire reflection on one's life. Such was the case for Padre. After the birthday feast at his place, he asked me to stay for a chat. He talked a lot about his life in Surinam and the wonderful time studying for the priesthood in Rio. He also talked about the challenges of living in Correntina. He confided that Dick's and my presence filled a great void for him, and he sincerely hoped others would follow us when we moved on.

Padre and I were not only collaborators on projects but great friends. Without his wisdom, enthusiasm, knowledge, resourcefulness, and spiritual guidance, my experience in Correntina as a young person filled with doubts and yearnings most likely would have turned out less favorably. He was indeed a great mentor. In our many evenings of conversation, we typically covered a wide range of topics including religion and the confusion surrounding all the saints and holidays. Padre was a most perspicacious individual with avid interests in history, technology, education, and philosophy. Although Christianity was his main bearing, he also liked to study astrology and mythology. He opened my eyes to many new concepts in these disciplines. This was evident in the inclusive attitude he demonstrated toward us both, but especially Dick; Padre was always respectful of Dick's views on religion.

Padre was incredulous to learn we were all born under the astrological sign of Aries, he, Dick and I. Padre said, "While those born under this sign, the sign of fire, are considered courageous, determined and optimistic, they can also be moody, short tempered and aggressive, and do not always work in harmony with others of the same sign."

He went on to say that, "While fire is a destructive element, it is also a necessary element of new birth, as it is fire that burns away old grass and trees so that new seeds can spring forth. It may only be a metaphor, but it is exactly the work you are doing here, replacing old ways with new seeds, gardens, and ideas. It has been amazing to experience the harmony and good will we have with each other in pursuit of mutual success."

After our long evening of conversation Padre said he would leave me with a last piece of wisdom he often thought of when contemplating our coming to Correntina. Years earlier, he had memorized the following verse written in the 1700s by a gentleman named Everett, "Large streams from little fountains flow; tall oaks from little acorns grow."

Padre said, "From where we are sitting you can hear the sounds of the Corrente River. I know you have visited many of the little *capiceidas*—springs—to the west of town where the river starts small before becoming this mighty entity whose waters bring light and magic to this place. Like those little springs, you and Dick have brought much light and magic to our lives in Correntina. I know you come from a land of great oak forests, and I hope your fire continues to burn and create openings for many more unique acorns that lay fallow."

It was almost surreal that Padre would invoke the metaphor of an oak tree. I proceed to tell him that in the front yard of my home grew the second largest oak tree in the state of Minnesota. That tree always fascinated me as a boy and its majesty seemed to have a magical effect. Its stature created a call to adventure in me at the same time I felt a serene sense of protection from the perils of life. In 1962, one month before I departed for the Peace Corps, a tornado struck our farm. Of a dozen or so buildings only the house and a barn next to it remained standing.

I explained to Padre that the tornado struck on the night of my brother's high school graduation party. There were more than fifty people in my parents' house. A large metal beef barn, more than a hundred feet in length, was transported intact through the air by the tornado. When this large structure hit the power lines, the night sky lit up for a moment, almost as if an atomic bomb had been detonated. At that very moment, sitting on the back porch, I witnessed the huge oak upside down, its massive limbs inverted, pointing toward the ground like a giant mushroom. The great tree bent but did not break, most likely forcing the tornado over the home and saving everyone inside. My journey to Brazil might have ended in that instant were it not for the mighty oak. Padre said, "Praise the Lord, that must be a sacred tree. I hope to someday come stand under it and absorb its energy."

With that final piece of wisdom and Padre's blessing, I made my way home across the Corrente River. I stopped for a bit to listen to the beautiful sound of the river singing its harmonious melody as it passed over the rocks on the way to the falls. I reflected on Padre's words and on how fortunate I had been to come to this place. It made for a lonely, pensive feeling. Tears welled in my eyes as I thought of how I would soon be leaving Padre behind along with all the joyous celebrations and wonderful evenings we had shared together.

It was not only Padre I would soon be leaving, but also the various projects we had initiated; and there was serious work to be done to ensure their success. The vegetable programs I managed throughout the county were coming along exceptionally well and remained my principal focus. With all the rains, I had been preaching for some time that unless we could control the *bichos*—bugs and insects—much of the program's success would be negated. By now my relationship with the county commissioners had evolved to a level beyond my expectations. I told the mayor and commissioners that I was accumulating a good supply of insecticides and managed to get a half-dozen sprayers. But I was one person and could not operate six sprayers by myself to service so many gardens.

During Saturdays at the market and on my travels in the countryside, I assured folks we would be spraying their plantings at some point. Many thought I would do the spraying since they considered it to be a sophisticated process using a complicated machine. I had once explained to the locals that we milked three dozen dairy cows twice a day on our family farm. They said that would take all day. When I told them it took only a couple of hours and described how our milking machines worked, they found it unbelievable. In their minds, what cow would ever allow that to happen?

The moment of triumph in my relationship with local authorities arrived when they approved funding to hire six new county workers and horse-powered transportation to establish a countywide spraying service. In the weeks ahead, I would spend several hours training these young men. The mayor officially launched the program on a Saturday at the market, where the men paraded around and gave demonstrations. The only thing missing was the local brass band. I even offered to get my trumpet to bring the crowd to attention with the mellifluous sounds of *Pomp and Circumstance* as part of the ceremony.

The sprayer service was called the *esquadra do bombeiros*—the bomber squad. In Portuguese, *bomba* is the word for both bomb and pump. The sprayers needed to be pumped to work, thus they became the original bombers in Correntina. As the bombers headed out, the mayor and commissioners adjourned to the nearby bar to receive congratulations and drink a few toasts to their success. I passed on the bar festivities as I wanted this to be the mayor's moment in the sun.

One day, Reverend Reisner telegraphed to let us know that he was flying in to pick up a sick woman to transport to the hospital in Lapa. I welcomed the excuse to see him and bid a final adieu. Dick and I helped settle the woman into the plane, feeling badly for her but also sad for ourselves. It was the last we'd see of Reverend Reisner because he would be heading back soon to his church in California. Like Padre André he had truly been a godsend to us and a very special friend. At times, we really needed to have another American to visit with who looked at things like we did. It was probably good he needed to attend to the urgent situation at hand as it forced him to leave and not linger to *bate papo*.

In addition to the spraying program, another project we had long labored at since first arriving in Correntina finally saw progress: the infamous road grader. Like us, Dr. Raul considered it a travesty that this wonderful machine was sitting idle simply due to lack of parts, so he prioritized obtaining what was needed from the commission to make it operational. Perhaps part of his motivation was the fact that his two sons liked basketball. Without the grader to level the ground for a court, however, no one would play basketball. I had already built and installed the finished standards and rims in an area by the school. Now we just needed a court.

We finally got the grader working and featured it in a grand parade through town on a market day. Along with the hydro dam, airplanes, and Jeeps, this was the fourth wonder of the modern world to grace Correntina. I indeed felt like the Pied Piper again as there must have been a hundred kids following as we drove the grader through town. We approached the rickety bridge over the Corrente River and crossed our fingers as this would undoubtedly be the heaviest load ever to navigate the old bridge. The bridge held and off we went. By late afternoon we finished leveling an area for the basketball court. Since we had installed the baskets some weeks earlier, full court play was ready to begin. Dick thought the work of the grader was such a monumental event that he brought the county commissioners, all decked out in their finest, to watch the proceedings. Our intention was to demonstrate the future capabilities of this wonderful asset: improving roads, leveling areas for irrigation plantings, and much more.

For a long time, we'd been chatting with the mayor about the grader's far-reaching potential, and he had asked us to draw up some plans for *casas popular*—public housing. Noting our production of roofing and door jamb materials at the saw mill, the local administration was in the preliminary stages of setting aside a parcel of land for such a project. They planned to raze some of the stick-and-mud houses in the poor areas of town, many of these built on the hillside or in low areas that would flood when heavy rains came. Seeing the grader perform heightened their excitement for this project.

But the mayor was not all business, evidenced soon after the grader episode by a contest I dubbed "the corn caper." As previously mentioned, the mayor and I had each planted a hectare plot of corn on opposite sides of the main road everyone used to get to market on Saturdays. For the sake of comparison, I'd planted hybrid corn and he'd planted traditional corn. It was a Saturday and market day and the corn ready for picking; time for the big corn payoff, the day we would see whose plot yielded the most corn.

All during the growing season, the mayor held court in the bar near the market where he would tease me and make my corn the brunt of jokes. The locals generally joined ranks with him and laughed about how small and puny my corn looked. Traditional corn was tall and sometimes produced as many as four to five ears per stalk, whereas mine was short and generally had two to three ears per stalk. The mayor had found it all so engaging that somewhere in the course of the growing time he wagered a bet that whoever had the least amount of corn when we harvested it would have to buy free drinks for anyone who walked into the bar on the day of reckoning—which meant everyone from the countryside.

By this time, I'd mastered the art of negotiation, having survived the state militia episode, nearly being fed to the piranhas on the Amazon, and other perils. I was, therefore, savvy enough to get the mayor to agree that the results would be based not on who had the most sacks of corn as he had suggested, but rather on whose corn weighed the most based on similar amounts. After all, the more body the corn had the more it would provide for feed and fattening animals. This made good sense to everyone who was in the bar at the time of the wager. The mayor, being a good sport, agreed.

Well, there they were, all the sacks of corn piled up by the scale at the market and hordes of people awaiting the results. There was little reason not to laugh at the gringo since it appeared the mayor had twice as many sacks of corn to be weighed. His amount went to the scale first. Then I put the same exact amount of my corn on the scale. A hushed silence fell on the crowd as all eyes locked on to the measurement. The final results appeared. My corn weighed three times as much as the mayor's corn. As the adage goes, he who laughs last laughs loudest. Now it was my turn for a moment in the sun.

I suspected that Elias had anticipated these results and gone along with the caper to impress upon the local farmers the value of using better seeds. I also suspected ulterior motives were involved on his part. He already exercised a monopsony when it came to certain commodities such as gasoline. Owning the only truck in town, he stood to corner the market for transporting surplus hybrid seed commodities to larger markets. Overall, the corn caper provided the most fun I'd had in many months. It also revealed which side of the fence, or in this instance the road, the mayor was on. He was both smart and shrewd. When we first arrived in Correntina, I was unsure if he supported our presence in his town. To see that he had come this far in a year and a half was a very rewarding experience.

Another big project that involved the mayor and commissioners needed to be completed before I left town: the library. Over the course of many months I'd received books from USAID and Brazilian sources. After we moved into town, I built and installed shelves in the front room of my house and filled them with books, where student assistants catalogued them. As a final step, we developed a system that allowed our patrons to check out books. This rudimentary library became very popular. With my impending departure, I had been discussing my concerns about the uncertain future of the library with the mayor. Good news arrived one day when I returned from a trip to Santa Maria and the colony. I found a letter at my house from the mayor and commissioners announcing the establishment of the first-ever public library in Correntina staffed by a paid county librarian. Added to the bomb squad, this increased the county worker staff by seven, nearly doubling the original number. I was in seventh heaven!

My greenhouse represented one more loose end to tie up. I needed to replant many of the beds so there would be a good supply of transplants in the future. Texas Ken from Santa Maria had agreed to come to Correntina to look after things. To ensure the plants' success, Padre showed up with a bottle of holy water to sprinkle on the beds to bless them. Dick appeared within minutes. As soon as Padre finished, neither of them could hold their laughter. It was apparent the two had been in cahoots, and Padre admitted that Dick had told him that he thought this should be done before my leaving.

As we turned the corner into our last month in Correntina, the Peace Corps wanted to summarize our work. Two researchers who'd been tracking our project from its inception arrived from the University of Texas. They had just come from Montalvania after visiting Plow Thief Dave. Despite nearly being rejected from the program at first, he had become their poster child for the Peace Corps. They wasted no time waxing on about his endeavors, much of which

I found to be naive. For example, in their final report about Dave's hybrid corn project they wrote, "The corn was at that time twice the Volunteer's height, with full big ears." [142] Since Dave stood at six feet tall, this corn would have measured twelve feet in height. Friends, that is standing in tall corn. The corn the researchers raved about may have been a local variety. It was certainly not the hybrid variety Dave had planted, similar to the seeds I used in the corn caper.

The researchers went on to comment about Dave's vegetable garden. "There were vegetables of all kinds, tomatoes, radishes, onions, garlic, and okra. The people of the area had never seen a carrot, or a tomato or a radish." [143] This was a dubious statement. Locals may not have seen a radish, but I can assure you they saw tomatoes and carrots. While the quality was not outstanding, this produce was available in the small towns I traveled through north of Montalvania, just as it was in nearly every other rural market I'd seen in Brazil.

The visit went downhill from there. The research team spent only a few hours in our fair town, much of it consumed in a long discussion with Dr. Raul at the hydro dam. Although Raul proved helpful to us on a few occasions during his short tenure in Correntina, he sometimes struck me as a bit of a sycophant. He possessed sufficient hubris to try to persuade others that he and the commission, not the locals, were the pillars of our success. Dr. Raul proceeded to fill the researchers' heads with misguided opinions about the faults of the local political structure and personalities, even though his experience was limited.

Consequently, the researchers filtered certain elements of their final report through his lens. For instance, they wrote that the present mayor had driven away the only doctor in the town—the mayor's political rival—as well as the pharmacist and only nurse and midwife. According to Dr. Raul, these people were now living eight hundred miles away in Salvador, in fear for their lives, leaving the town without any medical care. This was both a malicious characterization and a total fabrication of the truth. The pharmacist, the nurse-midwife, (Pedro Guerra and his daughter Narinha) still resided in Correntina, not in Salvador on the coast, fearing for their lives. Pedro Guerra, not some doctor who fled the town, had been the previous mayor, and his relationship with the current mayor was excellent in all political matters. If they wrote this sort of fairy tale about affairs in Correntina, what was one to believe about the other findings in their report? \44

The researchers did get one part right, however, when they wrote that they had expressed to Dr. Raul their "concern not only for the Brazilians, but also for the Volunteers who might become ill at any time and had no means of obtaining immediate medical attention." \45

Word of this apparently got back to Peace Corps administration in Rio because within two weeks a group of four heavyweights paid us a visit: Leo, Lou Miller from the U.S. Embassy, the new Peace Corps doctor, and a commission official, Dr. Cunha. In embarrassed disbelief, they realized it had been six months since anyone from the Peace Corps administration in Rio had visited Correntina, including the Peace Corps doctor. No Volunteer was to go more than three months without a medical visit or checkup. Infectious diseases, such as Chagas, were a main concern. It did seem shocking that it wasn't until two weeks before the end of our project that someone finally understood the dearth of medical care we had endured for almost two years.

Leo, Lou, and the doctor left the next morning on the beautiful Aero Commander, its engines screaming at full rpm as I watched it clear the cotton gin one last time. Dr. Cunha, a former priest, decided to stay another day in Correntina and attend church. During Mass, Padre announced to the congregation that it was "the last waltz in Dixie" for me. He gave a long speech about all the things we had done and how faithful I had been in coming to Mass. At his invitation, I stepped up to the pulpit to say a few words. I thanked everyone for all the friendship and support we had received over the many months, and then I expressed special appreciation for how Padre had been such a dear friend, confidant, and spiritual guide to me, and how that had made my time so meaningful and enjoyable. Padre then led the congregation in applause that lasted at least five minutes. It was more emotion than I could handle. It must have been tough for them to see a gringo with tears in his eyes.

The Peace Corps visit triggered a round of farewell dinner celebrations. Miguel and Dona Maria Coimbra, my dear family friends, hosted the first one. They had provided me with a home away from home during my many months in Correntina, and I relished the wonderful evenings spent with them reminiscing about our times together. Their children were my closest friends, and it was at their farm that I first undertook agricultural pursuits. Miguel presented me with a ring that had belonged to his grandfather, the man who had first brought the Coimbra family to Correntina decades before. Despite my objections, he insisted I keep it.

Next, we were invited to attend a special meeting of the county commissioners. There I received an official document from the mayor acknowledging both my donation of books to the new public library and the council's gratitude for many other services provided. This was extremely gratifying to me since it represented the solid relationship we had forged and come to enjoy.

With only days remaining before we left, final business details and packing consumed our time. Items we no longer needed we took to Santa Maria. While there, we visited with many old friends, including Wilson, who made a trip over from the colony. By late afternoon, we were back in Correntina.

We'd had no visits in some time. Likewise, a couple of months had passed since we'd received any mail. Leo went into Lapa and collected mail that had piled up at the post office. I received three letters from Millie, the last of roughly fifty letters I'd received from her.

"These must be your last days in Correntina," she wrote. "It's rather sad I imagine. I have the spring fever again something awful just like last year. You cannot imagine how anxious I am to see you and hear of all your encounters. Get so excited just thinking of it. I am looking forward to seeing you. Hope all goes well on your return trip. I will be so anxious to see you Ken, bye and love Millie."

Her letters that had sustained me emotionally during my long odyssey had become more infrequent. Although her sentiments warmed my heart, I felt a growing sense of foreboding that left me to wonder, were written words alone enough to appease the devil of time? How many seasons of spring fever would pass before the pain of separation and loneliness would be satisfied or forever go unfulfilled?

My last market day arrived. Word of my departure had spread via Padre and others throughout the county, resulting in a huge crowd that gathered that Saturday to say final goodbyes. Tears were shed all the way around, and it was hard to get away from some folks.

Fortunately, I had a good excuse not to linger too long. New springs finally had arrived for our Jeep, and we spent much of the day installing them. They were thinner and made of tougher material. In fact, they had one more spring leaf in them than the old springs, so we would be riding to Rio in style. When we took the old ones off for the last time, how well we remembered the many times we had welded the old springs back together.

That evening Dr. Raul hosted a grand reception for Dick and me with all of the city dignitaries present. The speeches were so numerous and the praises so touching that I noticed they elicited tears even from Dick, the ultimate stoic. If one of our missions in Brazil had been to change the Brazilians' image of Americans, I believe we surely had achieved that.

Our last day in Correntina finally arrived. That morning I went to the school one more time to take a photo of the students, to wish them well in their future endeavors, and to invite them to come visit me in America. During the remainder of the morning I visited many other dear friends such as the Guerras and Dona Vivi at the boarding house.

At noon, we attended another grand dinner, this one at the home of Padre André, very appropriate since that was where we had first dined when we arrived in Correntina. Most of the city dignitaries were there, and there were lots of speeches, toasts, and praises once again. It was most difficult saying goodbye to Padre. From his very first encounter with us, he had realized we would be assets to the community, and he did all he could and more to help us achieve our goals.

During our final moments with Padre, he and Dick had the most fitting of endings to an inimitable relationship that had involved so much banter about religion and many other subjects. As they shook hands and embraced for the last time, Dick, albeit still clinging fervently to his agnostic leanings, told Padre, "Well Padre, I guess this is the last time we'll most likely see each other until we meet in heaven. That is, if you get there!"

The paroxysms of laughter Dick's comment ignited seemed to last forever. Padre laughed so hard I was afraid he would have a heart attack. What a fitting finale for their relationship.

We made our way slowly back across the old bridge that I had traversed hundreds of times to teach, and work on the garden project at the school, go to the saw mill, get a horse from Padre's pasture, or just to spend an evening at Padre's home conversing on every imaginable topic. It was on that bridge where I had first learned of the death of President Kennedy. The image of that place will remain imbedded in my memory until my last days.

We returned to our house and bid farewell to our faithful maid, Jacinta, and took one last look at the place that we had called home for so long. At four o'clock we drove around the town square and up Rua Góes Calmon, which leads to the road to Santa Maria. As we emerged from the west end of this small street into the town center, hundreds of townspeople and every school-aged child in the town lined the streets, clapping their hands.

The band played *The Star-Spangled Banner* to the best of their ability, and many of the men from the countryside sat perched on their horses waiting to escort us out of town. The crowd pressed in around our Jeep with many wishing us well, and many others wanting to shake our hands and begging us to please stay. Fortunately for me, Dick was driving and he slowly kept edging up the street as best he could. We finally made it to the top of the long street and started our journey to Santa Maria, the miles passing on in silence as each of us wiped away a stream of tears.

As two young Americans, I don't know if we truly understood the magnitude of the relationship we had cultivated with this remote little village in the central highlands of Brazil, but I do know that it sure felt like something special. If emotions were any indication, I believe the bond of respect we strove to forge as Peace Corps Volunteers between our nations and peoples had been fully realized right there in Correntina.

21. Sunday morning

*I*t was a beautiful Sunday morning when I first arrived in the little village of Correntina, and a Sunday morning when I finally left Brazil. The Lord's Day seemed to be mileposts in my Peace Corps journey. I had left for training in Oklahoma on a Sunday in midsummer of 1962. Three months later, I left for Brazil on a Sunday.

On Sunday, July 12, 1964, the familiar odors of windswept fields, fragrant mowed clover, awoke me just as the sun rose over indigo hills and lush green valleys of southwest Wisconsin. Soon, the Greyhound bus crossed the mighty Mississippi River into Minnesota.

A few more miles north and I was back in Kellogg, the small river town where my family attended church. Waiting for me at the old general store were my dad, several of my brothers, my young sister and my dear grandparents. It had been 620 days since I'd last spoken in person with or seen anyone of my family.

This was an emotional moment—including strong embraces from everyone—unlike any I had ever experienced with my stoic farm family. My mother, shy by nature, was conspicuously absent in Kellogg. My dad explained she was afraid she would not be able to handle her emotions, which might have possibly been the first such public display for her in front of the family.

On the way out of town, I asked my dad to stop at the church. As a young boy, I'd rarely missed Sunday Mass. The building was similar in size, color, and stature to the one in Correntina, and I took a moment to reminisce about the totality of my adventure. All of it seemed surreal, but I thanked the Lord that I was back safely to a place I loved. In the afternoon, there was a big family picnic at the farm in the front yard under the mighty oak tree that may well have inspired and protected me on my journey. Lots of friends and neighbors stopped by to welcome me home, and yes, there, beside the great oak tree, stood Millie with her beautiful, radiant smile. Millie had played such a big part in sustaining me during the months I was away. But while the homecoming gave me unbelievable joy, a part of me still lingered in Brazil.

I thought back to just days earlier and how, after leaving Correntina, Dick and I made our last trip to Lapa, where the muscle men ferried us across the Formoso once more, ours the only vehicle on board. They offered to ferry us free of charge due to our generous tipping in the past, but we insisted on paying and gave them double this time. They were elated. The commission barge met us at the São Francisco River as ordered by the district chief, and on we traveled to Lapa for some final adieus. I made a last stop at the grotto to offer a prayer of gratitude for all the good I had experienced on this very unique journey.

From there we followed the course to Rio de Janeiro we'd taken in early 1963 with our newly acquired Jeep. The final two weeks in Rio were filled with exit interviews conducted by the State Department, medical examinations, and dental work to ensure we were fit enough to return home. We enjoyed social time with fellow Volunteers, most of whom we had not seen since leaving Três Marias twenty months before, and we spent considerable time recounting old times and hearing about many uncommon experiences and stories.

We spent our final night in Brazil at a church on Copacabana Beach attending the wedding of two fellow Volunteers, Rochester Jim, who'd been stationed in Barreiras, and Chattanooga Susan, who'd been stationed in Lapa before moving on to Rio. Jim and Susan had decided they wanted to get married in the presence of their friends with whom they had lived such an unusual experience. It was a beautiful marriage in a paradise setting. Afterward, we all attended a wonderful reception at the home of our leader, Leo and his wife. It would be the last major gathering in Brazil for most of us, a fitting end to the great friendships we had developed throughout trying yet eventful times as part of our incredible sojourn. The festivities lasted until the wee hours of the morning. No one really wanted to leave.

Dick and I travelled through several Latin American countries after leaving Rio. We thought the hazards of our long journey were behind us, but we experienced an earthquake in the Andes Mountains of Peru on an evening when there was also an eclipse of the moon. This plus another near-calamity while flying foretold that our adventure was not yet complete. We eventually arrived in New York City, never happier to be back on *terra firma*, on the Fourth of July. A magnificent holiday parade made our homecoming all the more memorable. It was also in New York that I had last heard the voices of my dad and mom twenty-one months earlier; and in New York I called to let them know I was safely back in the U.S.

The 1964 World's Fair was being held in New York, and since each of us had a profound interest in science and innovation, we couldn't miss a chance to attend. The World's Fair was billed as the innovation spectacular of the century and all the latest advances were on display: colored televisions, jet packs, spacecraft, picture phones, computers, and more. Culture shock slapped us in the face. Viewing it all, we couldn't help but think back to Correntina and how people had been so mystified by electricity, automobiles, milking machines, and other technology. We laughed as we imagined what their reactions would have been to all of this.

From New York we went to Washington, D.C. to pay homage to our great inspirational leaders. We had the privilege of meeting with Senator Hubert Humphrey from my home state, the originator of the name and concept of the Peace Corps. [46] Then we visited the gravesite of President Kennedy in Arlington National Cemetery. Standing in front of his marker brought back a flood of memories of our time in Brazil, especially the ineffable tragedy of his assassination. Although we felt a sense of sadness, we also felt a sense of pride about the roles we had played in completing the mission for our country that Kennedy had challenged every American with at his inauguration; and the promise we had made to ourselves and kept. The Peace Corps was becoming a lasting institution. Already it was touted as one of the hallmarks of Kennedy's brief administration.

I thought back to my visits with Padre André and our many discussions about philosophy, especially the last intimate visit I had with him just before leaving Correntina. In that conversation, Padre said that he believed certain people served as guides on the journey through life. He pointed out to me the recurring motif of kings in mythology and fairy tales. Padre said that the ancient Roman and Greek philosophers believed we each have within us a daemon or angel, the seed of individual good fortune, a mentor in effect who will provide a hint as to where one's destiny lies. Padre believed that every extraordinary life starts with a vision, an ideal. The daemon is like the acorns put forth by an oak tree, each one unique unto itself. The mythological kings were rare individuals whose lives connected us to a higher purpose, and whose deaths plunged us into darkness, fear, and uncertainty.

As I stood there reflecting at President Kennedy's grave, I realized that he was truly a personal mentor for me, like Abraham Lincoln, an example of such a king. Both were leaders whose aura permeated the ground upon which I stood, their deaths at the hands of assassins; a catastrophe for generations. With Kennedy's life gone, much of the optimistic spirit of the New Frontier seemed to have left with him.

A young American who had rarely traveled out of the Minnesota county in which I was raised, my odyssey to the remote central highlands of Brazil proved to be all I could have hoped for. Indeed, just as its slogan promised, Peace Corps was the toughest job I would ever love. In one of her letters, Millie teasingly noted that JFK stood for a "Job for Kenny."

I was at a crossroads in my life when I pined to join the Peace Corps in the spring of 1962. Indeed, it was a job I would never forget. Much of the chaos surrounding the Brazil II project did not directly affect my efforts in Correntina the same way it did many other Volunteers who left the project. Of the ninety Volunteers who came to Brazil in October 1962, only fifty-four completed service in the São Francisco Valley. Me and my colleague Dick, although located possibly in the project's most isolated location, were two of only twenty-eight Volunteers who remained for the duration in the towns to which they were originally assigned. Many Volunteers relocated due to personal incompatibilities. Upon arriving in Correntina, I discovered there were no agricultural facilities and I questioned why the Peace Corps had decided to place me there. In hindsight, I cannot imagine how I was so fortunate to have had two people like Padre André and my colleague Dick to work with. Their maturity, dogged determination to succeed, jovial personalities and leadership called to mind the mighty oak tree so important to sustaining my youthful existence.

In the Brazilian backlands, the sacred Umbú tree remains green during the long dry season by storing up to 3,000 gallons of water in its roots, thus providing feed for animals and man. Speaking of the

Umbú tree, Euclides Cunha in *Os Sertões* said: "It sustains itself in the seasons of misery on the copious reserves of vital energy which it has stored up in its roots in more propitious times. This energy it shares with man. It feeds him and assuages his thirst." [47]

The lessons and mentors of my youth, like the mighty oak trees at home, were eclipsed in many ways by the actions of the many masters I met on my journey. Like the Brazilian Umbú tree, these encounters surely sustained me in times I might have felt misery. For me, any success that we achieved in Correntina also echoed the words of my fellow hometown pioneer Volunteer, Walt Mischke, "We were on a mission to succeed no matter the impediments … rusty old nails that weren't going to be pulled out." [48]

Walt, who served in Venezuela, was a rural farm boy, and Catholic like me. If we had been taught anything in our youth, it was that any job was a promise-kept to our parents, teachers, community elders and our faith, and that we would fulfill our mission no matter the circumstances.

For the survivors of the Brazil II project to have overcome all that had been thrown at them, and still to accomplish something meaningful, was a tremendous testimony to all the Volunteers who learned to compete, in the words of Warren Wiggins, associate director of the Peace Corps in 1964, "on real man-to-man terms with mankind's oldest enemies: confusion, ignorance and despair." [49]

The extraordinary nature and accomplishments achieved by the Brazil II project are possibly best summarized in the words of the project director, Leo Fanning: "The Peace Corps recruited its most technically diverse group at that time. There were, however, several problems: initially poor leadership, the Peace Corps was new and they were necessarily probing and experimenting; the group was probably too large since two years later there were only 54 of them remaining; and there was also initially poor direction and support. I felt sorry for them, they were such an excellent group; highly motivated, well trained and desirous of providing useful services. Fortunately, the experiences of this group contributed most significantly to the good development of other groups in and out of Brazil." [50]

Early on, the Peace Corps was labeled by many—including certain prominent national figures—as an expensive joke and a haven for draft dodgers. In 1961, columnist Robert Ruark dubbed the Peace Corps a "Crewcut Campaign," "Kiddy Korps," and a "Brownie troop of do-gooders." But by the middle of 1963, he changed his tune and wrote, "All I've heard is praise for the Peace Corps' solid helpful work." [51] By the end of my two years of service, the negativity had all but ceased. The Peace Corps became a highly respected institution that numerous other developed countries emulated. Indeed, it had come a long way in a short time.

On the occasion of the fiftieth anniversary of the Peace Corps, the prominent author and historian, Doris Kearns Goodwin, cast an appropriate perspective when she stated that the Corps had "produced an enduring American legacy of service in the cause of peace, a timeless symbol of some of America's most honorable ideals and aspirations." [52]

O ver the centuries much has been written about the hero's journey, starting with the ancient Greek tales recorded in Homer's *Odyssey*. While this may have been the first account of the process of young men coming to manhood, it is actually a story concept that transcends all cultures going back to the very beginning of communal societies. [53] In the end, I believe that my Peace Corps adventure fit the essence of a hero's odyssey. When I first joined, my future felt vague, yet I knew intuitively that I needed to seek out the answers to life. The Corps seemed like a good way to find them, the right journey for me to take.

On his journey, the hero meets characters of influence along the path through adventure. In my adventure, men like John Kennedy, Sargent Shriver and Hubert Humphrey symbolized the sacred kings of the hero's journey. They set the direction I was to pursue. Padre André, Reverend Reisner, George Leiby, and Director Leo served as wise men that helped me stay a true course while wild men or tricksters, namely Plow Thief Dave and Wild Bill, assisted in energizing the journey. Of course, every tale of a hero's journey also contains a mythological woman, presented sometimes in fairy tales as a woman with golden hair. In my case, Millie, a girl with golden hair, possessed savvy, charm and allure that in large measure provided me, the hero, the incentive to achieve my goal and return from the odyssey. Finally, the warriors, Dick, my Correntina colleague; Bernard the German on the Amazon; Marine Bob, and other Volunteers, provided me strength, a purpose to the journey, and the wherewithal to confront and handle difficulties. [54]

In October 1962, my Peace Corps journey carried me into the unknown on a flight to Brazil. I truly had no idea what experiences waited ahead, including the Cuban Missile Crisis that nearly crippled the world. Lived to its fullest, the hero's journey results in the ascent or flight of an individual from unconsciousness to illumination and to a newfound freedom of understanding. The flying white dove on the Peace Corps emblem fittingly symbolizes this ascent. My work and adventures as a Brazil II Volunteer expanded both my world-consciousness and my self-consciousness, leading to a deeper understanding of life. Brazil became my portal of transformation. I crossed a great divide and came back with a new perspective on life.

When I returned to my childhood home, it wasn't entirely the idyllic place I had left, yet the idyllic sense of it had served me well when I was away. Still a small Minnesota town, Plainview was slow to change, its values remaining much as I had remembered them. The reassuring familiarity of my family and community so dear to me in my youth, and the farm, surrounded by golden fields and forests, remained a treasure at the end of the rainbow.

When I left for Brazil, I was fortunate to transform, to grow and mature in a place so very similar to my home. I suspect that one day, upon returning to its moonlit rivers and rolling hills, Brazil too will have lost some of the idyllic impressions so vivid in my memory. But the quality and value of life that permeated my consciousness when I departed remains to this day. The wonderful sense of Brazil and its people will always be a part of my soul.

Postscript

The two years I spent with Peace Corps in Brazil involved in entrepreneurial endeavors had a profound and lasting effect on my life. Over the next fifty years, I had numerous private and public opportunities in the United States and in Brazil, as well as in several other foreign countries, that flowed directly from my Peace Corps experience. Peace Corps tremendously broadened my understanding of the world, its people and cultures, in a way that many of my generation never experienced.

Millie Binder

My beloved high school sweetheart was a tremendous force in sustaining me during my Peace Corps adventure. In August of 1965, a little more than a year after I returned from Brazil, we were married. Millie became an accomplished business and social entrepreneur. She would go on to raise three sons, one of them adopted from Cambodia. While Millie never had the opportunity to fulfill her dreams of Hollywood, one of her sons, J.B., would play Billy Wedman in the 1994 movie *Little Big League*—produced by Castle Rock Entertainment, a division of Time Warner. Her son Elliott, author of the novel *Whispering Pines* (Wise Ink Publishing, 2015), was an Indie Book Awards finalist.

Millie visited Correntina for the first time in 2002. During her visit, people in the streets constantly came up to touch her; no shop owner let her pay for anything. If any of the barbershop boys had still been around, they would surely have appreciated her poise and beauty. By this time in her career, one of the nation's largest modeling agencies had also retained her as a model. One Sunday evening attending mass in Padre's new cathedral, more than a hundred people from all around the area came just to touch her. Millie, you see, had lovely silver hair, an anomaly among Brazilians. She possessed an ageless profile quite similar to her 1963 photo. After church, we asked Padre what the touching was all about, and he simply said, "With the silver hair and exquisite profile they believe she is an angel with a connection to the other world."

The farm boy who answered JFK's call to adventure in 1962 has entered into the backlands once more. Written words proved strong enough to appease the devil of youth. My love affair with Millie only grew stronger after our long separation in the 1960s. After five years of courtship, fifty-two years of marriage, and an incredible journey as sweethearts and partners, my beloved soulmate passed away in April 2017 following a seven-year battle with breast cancer.

Millie kept a journal during much of her life. In her last entry she wrote: "I was born in the beautiful heartland of America and enjoyed every privilege a girl could really want. Greatest among them was the love of a profoundly decent and exceptional family ... there were far more blessings in my life than I ever deserved, and so I cannot pinpoint one or two moments of happiness amongst the many wonderful years of my life. My greatest joy however has come from several simple moments since my marriage to my high school sweetheart Ken, then the arrival of our sons. To my husband who provided a life of adventure, travel and more joy that I could ever imagine, and to my sons who taught me more than I taught them ... you have been both the rock and joy of my life. I have absolutely no regrets. Life with you has been the absolute best and I thank you for your love and support all these years."

On occasion I return to the old swimming hole in the hilly Driftless Area, where in the evening twilight long ago I first saw the little girl in the red swimming suit. I like to listen to the melody of the cascading Whitewater River. The music of moving water brings to mind the Corrente in Brazil, which still haunts my memory. I hope that the happiness and euphoria of those times can be lived once again. But just as in the backlands of my youth, my life now demands that I take new risks and move forward the way America's first Peace Corps volunteers did, the young men and women who believed that they had the character, skills, and fortitude necessary to complete their mission in a place far from home, far from the great forests, far from the mighty rivers, far from the ones who loved them and who in return they loved most.

Now again, as I did on my odyssey, I rely on the three pillars to sustain me—the first, my strong religious faith and practice; the second, my family, friends and close colleagues, and my ability to integrate into my community just as I did in my youth. The third great pillar of course, remains my commitment to the love of my life and her commitment to me. In so many ways I too am once again far from home, far from the great hardwood trees, far from the mighty rivers, far from the one who loved me most and who in return I loved most.

Sadly, death has also been the fate of many of my Peace Corps and Brazilian friends from the backlands. Allow me to conclude this memoir with an update on former friends and colleagues.

Correntina Colleagues

I have mentioned many Brazilian colleagues and friends who were instrumental in my development in Brazil and instrumental likewise in the many things we were able to achieve. Many of these were adults at that time and have passed, either by now or by the time I had returned to Correntina for the first time in 2002.

Among the adult colleagues, the most significant of course was Padre André. Padre would continue in Correntina for the remainder of his life, completing many of the projects we initiated, including the maternity hospital, which was one of his leading focuses. This hospital is now owned and managed by the State of Bahia and is named the Saint Alfonso Maternity Hospital. On the sight of the sawmill Padre built stands a magnificent Cathedral that is now a regional center of worship.

In 2005, on the fiftieth anniversary of his ordination, Padre, who by then had been promoted to Monsignor, was recognized and honored by the Brazilian National Congress for his many years of service to Correntina, the State of Bahia and the Country of Brazil. At that time, the town square with the infamous statue of St. André, known formerly as the Praça da Matriz, had its name officially changed to the Praça Padre André Frans Bérénos.

Padre André passed on September 1, 2006. If I am to believe local lore, the town was shut down for a week for his funeral celebration.

Given the celebration of holidays during my stay in Correntina I believe it to be true. He is buried in a beautiful vault in the Cathedral in Correntina.

Of the other significant leaders in the town, Elias França, who was the mayor much maligned by Dr. Azevedo of the hydro dam and by the University of Texas in their report on Correntina, sold all of his Correntina businesses in the 1990s and moved to the neighboring State of Goias, where all of his children lived. His son Adherbal, who married Yvonne Coimbra and who was of tremendous assistance with so many things in Correntina, also lives in Goiânia, and both he and Yvonne are civil attorneys. Elias has since passed.

The other major civic leader and great friend, former Mayor Pedro Guerra, the pharmacist who Dr. Raul indicated had been forced to move away by Mayor Elisa França, which was also falsely reported in the Texas study, passed in 2010 at the age of 102. His wife had passed two years earlier at 96 years of age. Obviously Correntina was a little piece of Paradise where longevity of this sort was not uncommon. I last saw Pedro in 2008 and had one more spirited game of checkers and backgammon with him and as usual lost.

As I mentioned, I became almost like a son and brother to the Coimbra family that lived in Correntina; they were in so many ways my surrogate family. To this day, on the anniversary of all Coimbra family celebrations, they include my name as part of their family. The father Miguel passed twenty some years ago and Dona Maria the matriarch of the family passed in 2015 in Goiânia at the age of ninety-eight. The Coimbra parents also moved to Goiânia many years ago to be close to their family, as all the children lived there, although the family kept a home and their farm in Correntina.

The Coimbras were strong proponents of education, thus after their children completed middle school in Correntina, they were all sent some 450 miles away to Goiania to continue their educations. This paid handsome dividends, as all their children have had very productive professional lives. Their oldest daughter is a retired nun. José the oldest son is a leading endocrinologist working at both a private and state clinic in Goiânia. Daughter Oilde is the County Recorder in Correntina where she lives with her husband, the tailor "Keno of Correntina." Their son Marcelo and daughter Dora are both prominent attorneys in the town. Daughter Yvonne who married Adherbal França, the Mayor's son, is a civil attorney in Goiânia. Son

Adelson—the upside-down guitar man—became a dentist. He drowned in a car accident in Mato Grosso in the 1990s. His Brother Antonio survived. Antonio is also an attorney and served as the chief law prosecutor in the large city of Annápolis, as well as other cities in the State of Goiás.

All of these family members were great friends when they returned to Correntina on school holiday from Goiânia; three younger sons were students of mine in Correntina. Of these: João Bosco is a Surgeon and owns and runs a hospital in central Goiás; Pedro, a former Math student of mine, is a retired mathematics professor from the Federal and Catholic Universities in Goiânia. Years ago, Pedro purchased the Coimbra farm in Correntina and built a beautiful new home on the property is now retired there. The youngest son, Paulo, lives in Goiânia and works for the city. He is the only family member to visit us in Minnesota, traveling to the U.S. in 2014 for a government convention.

Many of the other locals and farmers I worked with, like Joãodão, Quinto and others, have all passed, as have various personnel we worked with at the hydro dam. Marinhão, the Carlos Jobim of Correntina, our guitar teacher, retired in 2012, his fingers being much too stiff from years of hard labor in the fields to stroke the strings anymore.

Former Brazil Volunteers

Only twice during the fifty years since our service in Brazil has the Brazil II group gotten together for reunions, once at twenty-five years and again in 2015 on the golden anniversary of our completion of service. Having only two reunions in fifty years is a bit unusual among Peace Corps groups, as some meet at least every five years and some even more often. I believe part of the reason, in large measure, was the size of the Brazil II group and the lack of an opportunity to get to know each other in a deeper fashion. Also, the significant attrition and movement of many Volunteers to other posts, as well as other difficulties the group suffered along the way, added to the diminishing of relationships.

Several in the group returned to Brazil and made it their permanent home. John Cadman, Princeton, geologist and nemesis of Plow Thief Dave, earned a PhD in geology and has lived in Brazil for thirty years, consulting on the building of several large hydro dams in the country, particularly in the Amazon region. John worked as lead designer on the third largest hydro installation in the world, the Belo Monte dam on the Tapajos River.

Steve Alexander lives in Santarém, which I visited on my trip down the Amazon; he runs an eco-tourism enterprise there.

My old buddy Dave Knoll, the Plow Thief, eventually made Brazil his permanent home and developed a large farming operation in the State of Rio Grande do Norte.

At our fiftieth reunion in 2014, out of approximately ninety Volunteers who went to Brazil, the whereabouts of forty-two of the original Volunteers was known. Twenty-two members of the project had passed away and the whereabouts of twenty-six remained unknown. Approximately one-third of all the Brazil II Volunteers who completed their service in Brazil in the São Francisco Valley from 1962-1964 returned to work permanently or on some part-time capacity in Brazil.

A significant number of the Brazil II group, at one time or another in their careers, lived and worked in other foreign countries: Portugal, Spain, Ireland, El Salvador, Thailand, Malaysia, Ukraine, China, Korea, Saudi Arabia, Japan, Turkey, Uganda, Laos, South Vietnam, many other European countries and other countries. Of course, given the young age of several of the male members of the group and the on-going Vietnam War, several were drafted into the military or served in the National Guard or other branches of the military including Jimmy Peace, Gary Chafee and Dwight Shetler, all of whom served in Vietnam.

Dick Wittman

After serving in the Peace Corps, Dick returned to San Diego and got a job with Univac, one of the major computer companies in the 1960s and 1970s. In 1966 Dick, like me, married his childhood sweetheart. Dick's wife Roberta had dual U.S.-Canadian citizenship. They moved to Vancouver, British Columbia, in 1966 so Dick could go back to working in an area he loved, namely hydro development.

From 1966 to 1972, Dick worked for British Columbia Hydro and Power Authority developing computerized control systems for all the hydro generating facilities in the province. After completing the project, he took a leave of absence, and with his wife and daughter, he returned to Brazil where he worked until 1974. His many projects included developing computer control systems for hydro facilities with IECO, CEMIG and FURNAS, as well as installations in the São Francisco Valley.

In 1975 Dick returned to Vancouver to work with B.C. Hydro. There he continued to develop state of the art computerized control systems for the large São Simão and Revelstroke plants in British Columbia. One had three units each twenty-five times the output capacity of the little facility in Correntina and the other composed of four units each with a mammoth sixty times the output of the Correntina plant. Dick continued to work on these types of systems in British Columbia and also has spent time in Malaysia doing hydro development.

In 2011, Dick retired from B.C. Hydro in Vancouver and lives there with his wife Roberta. His son Robert, an artist, lives in Vancouver. Dick's daughter is an international animal's rights attorney.

Gail Novak

In the spring of 1963, Gail, (Silvia) the third person of the original Correntina triumvirate, moved to Rio de Janeiro to work on a health project there and marry Dr. Ken Cairns, our Peace Corps Doctor. At the end of 1963, they returned to Rochester, New York, where Ken completed his medical studies, and their son Casey was born. From 1965 until 1969 they lived in Portland, Oregon and returned in 1969 to New York and settled in Southampton in 1972. Ken had a practice there for many years taking time off periodically to work in clinics in Africa and Central America.

After returning to New York in the late 1960s, Gail was involved in family planning. She later returned to school at Columbia University and earned her Master's in Public Health. Gail continued to work in international health projects at Columbia for several years and then joined the Epidemiology Office of the New York City Health Department to work with the growing HIV epidemic in New York.

Years later after retiring from the New York City Health Department Gail moved to Pittsburgh. Gail and Ken had divorced by this time. Gail later joined the staff as an Assistant Professor in the

Center of Public Health Practice in the Graduate School of Public Health. Gail passed away in June of 2010 at the age of 69.

Dr. Ken Cairns later remarried and moved to northeast Montana. In Montana, he runs a health clinic that is located on a major Native American reservation.

Dave Knoll

After Brazil Dave returned to Cornell and completed his BS in Agronomy in 1966. After graduating, Dave entered the International Development Program at the University of California at Davis. While there he got involved in a project to study the effect of different fertilizers on soils in Brazil.

Dave decided to make Brazil his home in 1967 when he took a job with Utah State University to run the agricultural section of the University's Industrial Assistance Program (RITA) in the Açu Valley in the State of Rio Grande do Norte.

Dave remembered that I was the tomato expert from Correntina with my garden plantation and was convinced he could get me a position on the project. After I graduated from college in 1967, Dave asked me to join the project as it economist. With a young family, I declined the offer. It would have been an interesting venture.

This was the last I heard of my old friend. I did receive word from former Brazil II PCV Steven Alexander, who later moved to Santarém in the Amazon, that Dave became very successful with ag projects in the Açu Valley. Steve indicated that Dave became a major exporter of food products, especially melons, to the U.S. and Europe. Dave married a Brazilian dentist and is presumed retired in Forteleza, Brazil

Acknowledgments

I n 2011, the Kennedy Administration and Peace Corps reached the age of fifty. This anniversary renewed interest and focus on this dynamic era and an organization that many, fifty years before, thought was a starry-eyed dream of a young, new President. My experience with the Peace Corps in 1962–1964, like that of many others from the first days of the organization, had become somewhat of a distant memory by 2011.

After forty years as a business and social entrepreneur, I was beginning to wind down my career and put many of the things that constituted that career and life in order. In so doing, I found a wealth of documentation I had kept from my Peace Corps experience. This included a diary, letters written to family and friends, journals and articles written for media, and many photos. The question was, would this still have some validity and interest for today's reader?

Mary Karr in her authoritative work, *The Art of Memoir*, states relative to the timing of writing a memoir: "If the events you're writing about are less than seven or eight years past, you might find it harder than you think, distance frees us from our former ego vanities, to see deeper into events. Also, if you're young you might wanna wait." [55]

I was but nineteen years of age in 1962, indeed young, as was the Peace Corps. So with sufficient distance, and who I am now with a bit of who I was then, I proceeded to compile my materials into a comprehensive historical document, resulting in this memoir.

Some of the information, episodes, events, and stories recorded in my source documents are anecdotal, related to me directly or indirectly by others during my time in Brazil or since. One of the precepts of writing a Peace Corps memoir is that the author researches his or her experiences from the input and validation of fellow Volunteers and in-country hosts. Unfortunately, after fifty years, many have passed, and the whereabouts of many others are unknown. To the best of my ability, I have validated all material involving other individuals with available information or with existing individuals who were directly or indirectly aware of the particular events presented in this work.

Special thanks goes out to my fellow Volunteers and administrators, the people of Correntina, Bahia Brazil and all the Brazilian friends and associates for the hospitality and love they demonstrated to me and their contribution to this memoir. A special thanks to my Peace Corps colleague in Correntina, Dick Wittman, who lived this adventure with me and whose collaboration was essential.

Special thanks to my son, author Elliott Foster, for his review and guidance through the editing and publishing phases. Likewise, the manuscript may never have come to fruition without the encouragement of Ann Regan of the Minnesota Historical Society, and my initial editor, Rondi Feyereisen.

I was indeed fortunate to discover Tom Driscoll, Managing editor of Shipwreckt Books Publishing Company. Tom helped me develop and enrich the original manuscript, and he patiently ushered it into print. A former Peace Corps Volunteer, USAID development and design officer, publisher of other international works of fiction and non-fiction, and a writer, Tom brought his unique perspective to the subject matter and how to best frame it for the audience of a Peace Corps memoir. For his sustained interest, I am tremendously grateful.

Endnotes

1 Herb Vanderwood and Paul Wegner, Brazil Evaluation Report (Peace Corps: Washington DC, April/May 1963), 50-51.

2 Joseph Campbell, The Hero with a Thousand Faces (Princeton: Princeton University Press, 1968), 49–58.

3 Peace Corps Training Program. The University of Oklahoma, Brazil II Project–São Francisco River Valley Development. Norman: Peace Corps, July 23–October 13, 1962, pg. 2

4 Ibid.

5 Elizabeth Cobbs Hoffman, All You Need is Love: The Peace Corps and the Spirit of the 1960s (Cambridge: Harvard University Press, 1998), 21-22.

6 For an outstanding discussion of the basis of Latin American poverty from the perspective of a Peace Corps Volunteer see: Mortiz Thomsen, Living Poor: A Peace Corps Chronicle, (Seattle, University of Washington Press, 1969) pgs. 260-261

7 Peter Gribbin, "Brazil and CIA," Counterspy, April/May 1979, 4–20. Last modified March 3, 2001, http://www.pir.org/brazil.html

8 Brazil II Project, 23

9 Hearing on S. 2000 before the Senate Comm. On Foreign Relations, 87th Cong. 60 (1961).

10 Lambros Comitas, Consultant, "Evaluation of Brazil II project, University of Oklahoma." Memorandum for the Office of Planning and Evaluation, Aug 30, 1962, 11-12.

11 William Doyle, An American Insurrection: The Battle of Oxford, Mississippi, 1962 (New York: Doubleday, 2001), pg.280

12 Jeff Greenfield, Then Everything Changed (New York: G.P. Putnam Sons, 2011).

13 Taylor Papers, Cuban Crisis: Operational Aspects. National Defense University, December 26, 1962

14 Oliver Stone and Peter Kuznick, The Untold History of the United States (Gallery Books, New York, 2012, 305.

15 Noam Chomsky, "Cuban missile crisis: how the U.S. played Russian roulette with nuclear war," The Guardian, October 15, 2012, http://www.theguardian.com/commentisfree/2012/oct/15/cuban-missile-crisis-russian-roulette.

16 Michael Dobbs, One Minute to Midnight (New York: Alfred A. Knopf, 2008).

17 On October 27, 1962, Rudolf Anderson Jr. streaked through the stratosphere, 14 miles above a planet tied up in knots. Shortly after Anderson entered Cuban air space, his unarmed, high-altitude U-2 spy plane appeared as a blip on Soviet radar. As the Soviet military tracked the intruding aircraft, their concern mounted that the pilot was photographing secret locations of tactical nuclear weapons positioned near America's Guantanamo Bay Naval Base. Two surface-to-air missiles rocketed into the sky near the eastern port city of Banes. One exploded near the U-2. Shrapnel pierced the cockpit along with Anderson's pressurized flight suit and helmet, likely killing him instantly. The U-2 plunged 72,000 feet to the tropical island below. Target number 33 was destroyed. (www.History.com)

18 Brazil II Project, 2.

19 Euclides da Cunha, Rebellion in the Backlands (Os Sertões), trans. Samuel Putnam (Chicago: University of Chicago Press, 1944), 176.

20 Note: Starting in the 1980's the Cerrado, including this area, experience an agricultural revolution and would become the great bread basket of Brazil catapulting into world leadership is agricultural commodities.

21 Hoffman, All You Need Is Love, 124.

22 Andrew Kopkind, "Peace Corps' Daring New Look," (The New Republic, February 5, 1966). Appeared as reprint in Peace Corps Seminar Discussion Manual, vol. X, The Peace Corps: Where Has It Been and Where Is It Going? Ed. David Christensen, Consult. Robert Goldwin, Aspen, American Enterprise Institute under contract with the Peace Corps, 1966, 21.

23 Da Cunha, Rebellion, 175.

24 Ibid. 176.

25 Norman Cousins, "Confrontation," Saturday Review, March 21, 1961. Appeared as reprint in Peace Corps Seminar Discussion Manual, vol. II, Cultural Confrontation Terrifying and Illuminating. Ed. David Christensen, Consult. Robert Goldwin, Aspen, American

Enterprise Institute under contract with the Peace Corps, 1966, 11–13.

26 Sinopse Estatístca do Município de Correntina (Estado da Bahia, Rio de Janeiro: Instituto Brasileiro de Georgrafia e Estatística, 1948).

27 Ibid.

28 Ibid.

29 This was referred to as one of the "Peace Corps Traps." For an excellent discussion of this principle see: Moritz Thomsen, Living Poor: A Peace Corps Chronicle, (Seattle, University of Washington Press, 1969), pgs. 281-282

30 Letter Walt Mischke to Author

31 Tom Carter, If You Think It will be Picturesque Forget it, From Peace Corps Files, reprint Peace Corps Seminar Discussion Manual, Vol II, CULTURAL CONFRONTATION TERRIFYING AND ILLUMINATING. Ed. David Christensen, Consult. Robert Goldwin, Aspen, American Enterprise Institute under contract with the Peace Corps. 1966, 41

32 The emu is the second largest living bird by height after its ratite relative the ostrich. They are found in the Cerrado region in Brazil and when necessary can run up to 30 miles per hour.

33 Mark Twain, A Connecticut Yankee in King Arthur's Court, 1895, p.53

34 Letter, Walter Murray to author, 1964

35 Ibid

36 Xique Xique, also Chique, Chique means Ouch Ouch. This is the local vernacular for the Cactus peruvianus, a form of cactus teeming with thorns.

37 Da Cunha, Rebellion, 182

38 Ibid, 424, 475

39 Proclamation No. 3560, 5 U.S.C. 87b, (November 5, 1963).

40 Josef Mengele, the Nazi doctor known as the "Angel of Death," was living obscurely in a town near São Paulo in Brazil at this very moment. He drowned swimming off the coast in 1979, and was buried under an assumed name and positively identified in 1985.

41 Note: Some forty years later in 2002, just weeks before I arrived once more in Correntina, seven men robbed the Bank of Brazil in town. The State Militia hunted them down in the caatinga (bush) and killed all of them; obviously they became much more efficient over time.

42 Wayne Holtzman, The Peace Corps in Brazil: An Evaluation of the São Francisco Valley Project (Austin, International Office: University of Texas, 1966).p 55

43 Ibid, The Peace Corps in Brazil, p.55

44 Ibid, The Peace Corps in Brazil, p. 59-60

45 Ibid, The Peace Corps in Brazil, p. 59

46 "Hubert H. Humphrey: An Inventory of his Speeches,) text files at Minnesota Historical Society, Manuscript Collection. June, 16, 2016.

47 Da Cunha, Rebellion, pg. 37

48 Walter Mischke to author, 1963.

49 Warren Wiggins, The Limits of Leadership. Appeared as reprint in Peace Corps Seminar Discussion Manual, vol. III, Freedom, Round or Square? Consult. Robert Goldwin, Aspen, American Enterprise Institute under contract with the Peace Corps, 1966, 7.

50 Leo Fanning, "A Collection of Brazilian Experiences," self-published. June 1970

51 Peace Corps, 2nd Annual Report, 54.

52 Doris Kearns Goodwin, "Recognizing the Lasting Significance of the Peace Corps' Creation in 1961", from "Co-Sponsor, H.R. 854, Statements Endorsing the Peace Corps Commemorative," accessed June 11, 2016,

53 Campbell, The Hero with a Thousand Faces. p.245-246

54 Robert Bly, Iron John: A Book about Men (New York: Vintage Books, 1992).

55 Karr, Mary, The Art of Memoir, (New York, Harper Collins, 2015)

Bibliography

Bly, Robert. Iron John. A Book about Men, New York, Vintage Books, 1992

Campbell, Joseph. The Hero with a Thousand Faces. Princeton: Princeton University Press, 1968

Carter, Tom, If You Think It will be Picturesque Forget it, From Peace Corps Files, reprint Peace Corps Seminar Discussion Manual, Vol II, Cultural Confrontation Terrifying and Illuminating, Ed. David Christensen, Consult. Robert Goldwin, Aspen, American Enterprise Institute under contract with the Peace Corps. 1966

Chomsky, Norman "Cuban missile crisis: how the U.S. played Russian roulette with nuclear war", The Guardian, Monday 15 October 2012, http://www.theguardian.com/commentisfree/2012/oct/15/cuban-missile-crisis-russian-roulette

Comitas Lambros, Consultant "Evaluation of Brazil II project, University of Oklahoma." Memorandum for the Office of Planning and Evaluation, Aug 30, 1962

Cousins, Norman, Confrontation, Seminar Discussion Manual, Vol II, Cultural Confrontation Terrifying And Illuminating, Ed. David Christensen, Consult. Robert Goldwin, Aspen, American Enterprise Institute under contract with the Peace Corps. 1966

Cunha, Euclides da, Rebellion in the Backlands (Os Sertões), trans. Samuel Putnam, Chicago, University of Chicago Press, 1944

Dobbs, Michael, One Minute to Midnight, New York, Alfred A. Knopf, 2008

Doyle, William, An American Insurrection, The Battle of Oxford, Mississippi, New York, Doubleday, 1962

Fanning, Leo, "A Collection of Brazilian Experiences," self-published. June 1970

Greenfield, Jeff. Then Everything Change, New York, G.P. Putman Son's, 2011

Gribbin, Peter. Brazil and CIA, Counterspy, April-May 1979, 4-20, last modified March 3, 2001, http://www.pir.org/brazil.html

Goodwin, Doris Kearns. Recognizing the Lasting Significance of eh Peace Corps' Creation in 1961Co-Sponsor, H.R. 854, Statements Endorsing the Peace Corps Commemorative

Hoffman, Elizabeth Cobbs. All You Need is Love, The Peace Corps and the Spirit of the 1960s, Cambridge, Harvard University Press, 1998

Holtzman, Wayne. et al, The Peace Corps in Brazil, An Evaluation of the São Francisco Valley Project, Austin, International Office, University of Texas, 1966

Humphrey, Hubert H. An Inventory of his Speeches, Text files at Minnesota Historical Society, Manuscript Collection.

Karr, Mary, The Art of Memoir, (New York, Harper Collins, 2015)

Kennedy, John F. Proclamation 3560 Thanksgiving Day 1963, November 5, 1963

Kopkind, Andrew. Peace Corps' Daring New Look, (copyright by The New Republic, issue of February 5, 1966), From Peace Corps

Files, reprint Peace Corps Seminar Discussion Manual, Vol. X, The Peace Corps: Where Has It Been and Where Is It Going? Ed. David Christensen, Consult. Robert Goldwin, Aspen, American Enterprise Institute under contract with the Peace Corps. 1966

Mischke, Walter, Letter, Calle 2 No. 3-62, La Grita, Tashira, Venezuela, March 9, 1963

Murray, Walter, Letter, 1032 Portland Ave., St. Paul, MN, 1964

Peace Corps, 2nd Annual Report, Peace Corps, Washington DC, June 30, 1963, accessed June 11, 2016, http://files.peacecorps.gov/manuals/cbj/annualreport_1963.pd,

Peace Corps: Hearing on S. 2000 before the Senate Comm. On Foreign Relations, 87th Cong., 1st Sess. 60 (1961)

Sinopse Estatístca do Município de Correntina, Estado da Bahia, Rio de Janeiro, InstitutoBrasileiro de Georgrafia e Estatística, 1948

Stone, Oliver and Peter Kuznick. The Untold History of the United States, Gallery Books, New York, 2012,

Taylor Papers, Cuban Crisis, Operational Aspects, December 26, 1962; National Defense University

Thomsen, Mortiz, Living Poor: A Peace Corps Chronicle, University of Washington Press, 1969

Vanderwood, Herb and Paul Wegner, Brazil Evaluation Report, Peace Corps, Washington DC, April/May 1963.

Wiggins, Warren. The Limits of Leadership, reprint Peace Corps Seminar Discussion Manual, Vol III. Freedom Round or Freedom Square? Ed. David Christensen, Consult. Robert Goldwin, Aspen, American Enterprise Institute under contract with the Peace Corps. 1966

About the author

I n addition to ***Into the Backlands,*** Ken Fliés is the co-author of the memoir *Retrieving Isaac & Jason*, published by Hiawatha Press in 2012; and he collaborated on the novel *Whispering Pines: Tales from a Northwood's Cabin.* He has also authored numerous essays and articles on rural America and the American Civil War and, is a past recipient of The Editor Choice Award of the National Library of Poetry.

Ken's endeavors in the Peace Corps and growing up on a rural Minnesota dairy farm lead to a career as an accomplished entrepreneur, involved in the startup and development of more than a dozen companies nationally and internationally including a market research and agricultural development company in Brazil. In addition to being a pioneer in the Peace Corps and business, Fliés was one of the founders of the Rural America Writers' Center and Rural America Arts Partnership; and founded and assisted in developing what is now the Great River Ridge State Recreation Trail. Ken Fliés was recognized by Minnesota Governors Tim Pawlenty and Mark Dayton, first in 2002 as an outstanding rural entrepreneur and in 2012 for his more than fifty years of entrepreneurial contributions to the State of Minnesota.

Ken and his wife Millie raised three sons, all of whom work for international corporations.

Lost Lake Folk Art
SHIPWRECKT BOOKS PUBLISHING COMPANY

IN®
DIE

Minnesota

Made in the USA
Lexington, KY
01 September 2018